1001 MORE HUMOROUS ILLUSTRATIONS FOR PUBLIC SPEAKING

If you would like information on *Parables, Etc.* or *The Pastor's Story File*, please write to Michael Hodgin at the Saratoga Press, P.O. Box 8, Platteville, CO 80651, or call 1-970-785-2990.

1001 ~~MORE~~ HuMOROUS ILLuSTRATiONS
FOR PUBLIC SPEAKING

MICHAEL HODGIN

ZondervanPublishingHouse
Grand Rapids, Michigan

A Division of HarperCollins*Publishers*

1001 More Humorous Illustrations for Public Speaking
Copyright © 1998 by Michael Hodgin

Requests for information should be addressed to:

ZondervanPublishingHouse
Grand Rapids, Michigan 49530

Library of Congress Cataloging-in-Publication Data

  1001 more humorous illustrations for public speaking : fresh, timely, and
compelling illustrations for preacher, teachers, and speakers / [collected by]
Michael Hodgin.
    p.   cm.
  Includes indexes.
  ISBN: 0-310-21713-X
  1. Public speaking. 2. American wit and humor. I. Hodgin, Michael, 1953– .
PN4121.A16   1998
808.5'1—dc21   97-17503
                                                                      CIP

Interior design by Sue Vandenberg Koppenol

Printed in the United States of America

98 99 00 01 02 03 04 05 /❖ DC/ 10 9 8 7 6 5 4 3

This book is dedicated to those who made it possible.

Seventeen years ago Jim Hewett was inspired by an idea to publish resource letters of jokes, anecdotes, poems, and stories for public speaking. The genius that made Jim's resource letters unique was that he gathered most of his illustrations from the subscribers themselves. I dedicate this book t o Jim Hewett.

The resource letters Parables, Etc. *and* The Pastor's Story File *became a forum in which communicators such as teachers, speakers, and pastors could share, one with the other, the illustrations that had worked for them. I dedicate this book to those who over the years have shared the best of their illustrations so that others could excel in bringing their messages to life.*

And finally, I dedicate this book to those who have subscribed to Parables, Etc. *and* The Pastor's Story File *over the years. Their continuing subscriptions have provided the platform for us to gather more than 14,000 illustrations for public speaking. It is through their support that we are able to offer the very best of what we have to those who use this book.*

Contents

Preface

Four years ago Zondervan published our first book of humorous anecdotes. We called it *1001 Humorous Illustrations*.... There were several reasons to do so. First, there were 1001 of them. Second, they were funny. Third, they had the power to illustrate.

We wanted that book to provide humorous illustrations-jokes, quotes, stories, and poems-that were relevant and ready to use. Thousands of copies later, we are overwhelmed by the responses from readers. We receive comments from pastors, teachers, and other communicators that this book is their favorite resource on humor. The only complaint we ever receive is that there are only 1001 illustrations. So we are addressing this complaint by publishing a second book. Put the books together, and you have 2002 humorous illustrations!

1001 More Humorous Illustrations for Public Speaking is a collection of the newest of our 14,000 illustrations, all arranged topically and fully indexed. Robert Strand of *The Preacher* magazine says that our illustrations are "his number one recommended source of current and usable material ... fresh stuff!" We like what Robert says. We want to infuse your messages with the word pictures that wake up your listeners, that get them to listen, and that burn your message into their memories for years to come.

Permissions

The compiler acknowledges his indebtedness to the many publishers and writers whose illustrations appear here through right of public domain or the principles of fair use. He further expresses his gratitude for express permission to use the following illustrations:

#25 No Peer Pressure: *Rotarian Magazine,* Evanston, IL

#550 Devil in the Family: H. A. Ironside, *Joshua, Nehemiah, Ezra and Esther,* published by Loizeaux Bros. Inc., Neptune, NJ

#573 Four Kinds of Bones: *Rotarian Magazine,* Evanston, IL

#651 Wrong Name on the Ball: *Rotarian Magazine,* Evanston, IL

#855 She's Out of Sight: "The Way I Heer'd It," *Ozarks Mountaineer,* May–June 1985

1

The Lady Said "Pew"

A cowboy went to church for the first time in his life. He enthusiastically told a friend about his church experience. He recalled, "I rode up on my horse and tied up my horse by a tree in the corral."

The friend said, "You don't mean 'corral'; you mean 'parking lot.'"

"I don't know, maybe that is what they called it," he said. "Then I went in through the main gate."

"You don't mean the main gate; you mean the front door of the church."

"Well, anyway, a couple of fellows took me down the long chute."

"You don't mean the long chute; you mean the center aisle."

"I guess that is what they call it. Then they put me in one of those little box stalls!"

"You don't mean a box stall; you mean a pew!"

"Oh yes! Now I remember!" said the cowboy. "That's what that lady said when I sat down beside her!"

Dates & Places Used:

2

Duck Turkey

The man on the scaffold was painting the building when he dropped his paintbrush. As he leaned over the rail to watch his brush fall, he yelled, "Quack, quack, gobble, gobble."

Below a man walking under the scaffold was hit by the brush.

"Why didn't you warn me?" the man yelled up at the painter.

"I did," the painter replied. "I yelled 'Quack, quack, gobble, gobble.'"

"What does that mean?" the man hollered angrily.

"Duck, turkey!"

Dates & Places Used:

3

Make Your Own Butter

An effective speaker gets milk from many cows, but makes his own butter.

Dates & Places Used:

4

An Even Account

The senator was quite full of himself. At every occasion he took the opportunity to remind everyone how important he was. On one such speaking opportunity he extolled, "All that I now am I owe to my fine parents."

An anonymous voice from the back of the room spoke the sentiment of the crowd: "Then why don't you give them twenty cents and pay off your debt?"

Dates & Places Used:

5

Learning to Duck

A Sunday school teacher told the class the story of David and Goliath. He embellished the story with great detail. He animated with gestures and movements, concluding with all the details of how little David killed Goliath with a rock from his sling.

At the end of the story he asked the class what lesson they had learned. One of the little boys popped up and said: "Duck!"

Dates & Places Used:

6

Actions Better

Well done is better than well said.

Dates & Places Used:

7

No Place for Worry

The source of this illustration is unknown, but the philosophy of this soldier applies to many of us:

One of two things is certain: either you're mobilized, or you're not mobilized.

If you're not mobilized, there is no need to worry; if you are mobilized, one of two things is certain: either you're behind the lines, or you're at the front.

If you're behind the lines, there is no need to worry; if you are at the front, one of two things is certain: either you're resting in a safe place, or you're exposed to danger.

If you're resting in a safe place, there is no need to worry; if you're exposed to danger, one of two things is certain: either you're wounded, or you're not wounded.

If you're not wounded, there is no need to worry; if you are wounded, one of two things is certain: either you're wounded seriously, or you're wounded slightly.

If you're wounded slightly, there is no need to worry; if you're wounded seriously, one of two things is certain: either you recover, or you die.

If you recover, there is no need to worry; if you die, you *can't* worry.

Dates & Places Used:

8

TOPIC: Actions

What's Happening?

People can be divided into three groups:
Those who make things happen
Those who watch things happen
Those who wonder what happened
Dates & Places Used:

9

TOPIC: Advertising

Limited Stocking Up

From an ad for color film in the *Akron Beacon Journal*: "Stock up and save. Limit ONE."
Dates & Places Used:

10

TOPIC: Advertising

Priced to Not Sell

The man pulled into a service station in the deep south, walked to a soda machine, and stared at the sign, which said $2.00.

"Two dollars for a soda," he said. "That's incredible."

"Wall, it ain't really two dollars. The machine's broke. I put up an outa-order sign, but people kept puttin' their money in anyways, and I had ta git it out again, so's I put that sign up and ain't had no trouble since," the friendly serviceman said.

We keep putting our money, time, and efforts into worldly things, instead of investing in God's love, and find we lose our money. When the price of living without God gets too high, we will quit trying to buy the goods.
Dates & Places Used:

11

TOPIC: Advertising

Let Them Know

Doing business without advertising is like winking at a girl in the dark. You know what you're doing, but nobody else does.
Dates & Places Used:

12

TOPIC: Advice

Umpires and Catchers

Veteran American League baseball umpire Bill Guthrie was working behind the plate one afternoon, and the catcher for the visiting team was repeatedly protesting his calls. Guthrie endured this for a number of innings, and then called a halt.

"Son," he said softly, "you've been a big help to me in calling balls and strikes today, and I appreciate it. But I think I have got the hang of it now, so I'm going to ask you to go to the clubhouse and show whoever's there how to take a shower."
Dates & Places Used:

13

TOPIC: Age

Pushing Eighty

When the doctor asked what I did for exercise, I said pushing eighty is exercise enough!
Dates & Places Used:

TOPIC: Age

Did She Start at One?

Some children who were touring a retirement home were asked by a resident if they had any questions.

"Yes," one girl said. "How old are you?"

"I'm ninety-eight," she replied proudly.

Clearly impressed, the child's eyes grew wide with wonder. "Did you start at one?"

Dates & Places Used:

TOPIC: Age

Age Changes Things

Who changed everything when I wasn't looking? I've noticed lately that everything is farther away than it used to be. It's even twice as far to the corner now, and they've added a hill!

I've given up running for the bus; it leaves much earlier than it used to. And it seems to me that they are making the stairs steeper than in the old days, and have you noticed the smaller print the newspapers are now using? And there's no sense in asking anyone to read aloud anymore, as everyone speaks so softly that I can hardly hear them.

The material in clothes is so skimpy now, especially around the waist and hips, and the way they size the clothes is much smaller than it used to be. Why, I have to buy clothes two sizes larger than what I wear just so they will fit me right!

Even people are changing. They are so much younger than they used to be when I was their age. On the other hand, people my own age are much older than I am. I ran into an old classmate of mine the other day, and she had aged so much that she didn't recognize me! I got to thinking about my poor dear friend while I was combing my hair this morning, and in doing so, I glanced at my own reflection in the mirror ... Really now! They don't even make good mirrors anymore.

So tell me now ... Who CHANGED things?

Dates & Places Used:

16

Rich, Old, and Fat

By the time a man can afford to buy one of those exotic little sports cars, he's too fat to get into it.

Dates & Places Used:

17

Low-Maintenance Kisses

A woman who was approaching her four-score and ten years was always blessed with little gifts from her friends and relatives for her birthday and Christmas, usually in the form of knickknacks for the house.

Finally when she reached the age of ninety, the aging woman was asked by a friend what she wanted this year.

"Give me a kiss," she replied, "so I won't have to dust it."

Dates & Places Used:

18

Forget the Eye Exam

It had been many years since my last eye exam, and my wife was pestering me to make an appointment. The more she nagged, the more I procrastinated. Finally, she made an appointment for me.

The day before I was to see the doctor, I was in an affectionate mood. After kissing and hugging her, I told her she really looked good to me.

"That does it," she said. "I'm canceling your appointment."

Dates & Places Used:

19

TOPIC: Age

Theft-Proof Music

I knew I was getting old when a thief broke in to my car and stole my tape deck but left my tapes behind.
Dates & Places Used:

20

TOPIC: Age

Two Things at Once

Old age is when a person notices that his shoelace is untied and asks himself: "Is there anything else I can do down there when I lean over to tie my shoelace?"
Dates & Places Used:

21

TOPIC: Age

Only Survivor

The little boy asked his grandfather if he had been in the ark with Noah. The grandfather chuckled a little and told his grandson that he was not on the ark.

The confused grandson asked, "Then why didn't you drown, Grandpa?"
Dates & Places Used:

22

TOPIC: Age

It's How You See It!

"I don't want my face washed!" cried Jane.

"Oh, come now," Grandmother coaxed, "I've washed my face three times a day since I was a little girl like you."

Jane (looking at her grandmother's wrinkles) answered, "Yes, and just look how it has shrunk."
Dates & Places Used:

23

TOPIC: Age

Old Fortunes

Old folks are worth a fortune, with silver in their hair, gold in their teeth, stones in their kidneys, lead in their feet, and gas in their stomachs.
Dates & Places Used:

24

TOPIC: Age

My Get Up and Go Has Got Up and Went

How do I know that my youth's all spent?
Well, my get up and go has got up and went.
But in spite of it all, I am able to grin
When I recall where my get up has been.
Old age is golden, so I've heard it said,
But sometimes I wonder, when I get into bed.
My ears in a drawer and teeth in a cup,
My eyes on the table until I wake up.
The sleep dims my eyes, I say to myself—
"Is there anything else I should lay on the shelf?"
And I am happy to say as I close my door,
My friends are the same, perhaps even more.
When I was young, my slippers were red,
I could kick up my heels right over my head,
When I grew older my slippers were blue,
But still I could dance the whole night through.
Now I am old, my slippers are black.
I walk to the store and puff my way back;
The reason I know my youth is all spent,

My get up and go has got up and went.
But I really don't mind, when I think with a grin
Of all the grand places my get up has been.
Since I have retired from life's competition,
I busy myself with complete repetition.
I get up each morning, dust off my wits,
Pick up my paper, and read the "Obits,"
If my name is missing, I know I'm not dead.
So I eat a good breakfast, and go back to bed.

Dates & Places Used:

25

TOPIC: Age

No Peer Pressure

A lady celebrating her 102nd birthday was asked what she enjoyed most about her advanced age.

"The lack of peer pressure," she replied.

Dates & Places Used:

26

TOPIC: Age

Not Much at Age Twenty

Anybody who can still do at sixty what he was doing at twenty wasn't doing much at twenty.

Dates & Places Used:

27

TOPIC: Age

Ageless Honesty

Man is the only creature who spends two-thirds of his lifetime saving up for old age, and the last third denying that it has arrived.

Dates & Places Used:

28

TOPIC: Agreement

Too Late for Agreement

Sign on a pastor's desk: "It's too late to agree with me—I've already changed my mind."

Dates & Places Used:

29

TOPIC: Alcohol

Something Worth Taking Home

A group of ministers and a salesmen organization were holding conventions in the same hotel. The catering department had to work at top speed serving dinners to both. The salesmen were having "Spiked Watermelon" for dessert. But the harassed chef discovered this alcoholic tidbit was being served to the ministers by mistake. "Quick," he commanded a waiter. "If they haven't eaten the watermelon, bring it back and we'll give it to the salesmen."

The waiter returned in a minute and reported it was too late; the ministers were eating the liquor-spiced dessert.

"Well," demanded the excited chef, "what did they say? How did they like it?"

"I don't know how they liked it," replied the waiter, "but they were dividing up the seeds and putting them in their pockets."

Dates & Places Used:

30

TOPIC: Alcohol

Wishy-Washy on Whiskey

Barry Lorch in his *San Diego Union* column told of a debate on the floor of the United States Senate about 130 years ago. The issue was whether alcohol should be sold in the territories seeking statehood. One notoriously anti-alcohol senator, who according to one description was so dry he was a known fire hazard, challenged one of his colleagues to state his position on alcohol. Supposedly his colleague stood up and said this:

"You asked me how I feel about whiskey. Well, here's how I stand on the question. If, when you say whiskey, you mean that Devil's brew, the poison spirit, the bloody monster that defiles innocence, dethrones reason, destroys the home, creates misery and poverty, yes, literally takes bread from the mouths of little children; if you mean the evil drink that topples the Christian man from the pinnacle of righteousness and gracious living and causes him to descend to the pit of degradation, despair, shame, and helplessness, then I am certainly against it with all my heart.

"But if, when you say whiskey, you mean the oil of conversation, the philosophic wine, the ale consumed when good fellows get together, that puts a song in their hearts and laughter on their lips, the warm glow of contentment in their eyes; if you mean Christmas cheer; if you mean the stimulating drink that puts the spring in an old man's footsteps on a frosty morning; if you mean the drink whose sale puts, I'm told, millions of dollars into our treasury which are used to provide tender care for our little crippled children, or blind or deaf or dumb, our pitifully aged, and our infirm, to build highways and hospitals and schools, then I am certainly in favor of it. This is my stand, and I will not compromise."

Dates & Places Used:

---

31   TOPIC: Allowances

The Differences in Allowances

Allowances have always been around, but there is a difference. Allowances used to be based on a percentage. Dads would let their children keep a small percentage of what the children earned.

Dates & Places Used:

32

TOPIC: Angels

The Speed of an Angel

My wife picked up a little craft item in the shape of an angel at a garage sale. In the hand of the angel was a note that said, "Don't drive any faster than your guardian angel can fly!" We may never be able to tempt God beyond the point that he is able to protect us, but we may certainly tempt him beyond that which he is willing to protect us.

Dates & Places Used:

33

TOPIC: Anger

Blessed Flexibility

Blessed are the flexible, for they shall not be bent out of shape.

Dates & Places Used:

34

TOPIC: Anniversary

Remember Carefully

I have never forgotten a wedding anniversary. I have an easy one to remember: August 14. This date is exactly six months from Valentine's Day. Remembering is not everything, however. I used to add the comment that this day was the farthest day from Valentine's Day. I now boast that my wife and I celebrate Valentine's Day twice a year. My wife likes my new outlook on these dates! Remembering is one thing; positive presentation is another!

Dates & Places Used:

35

All the Answers

The person who has all the answers either is getting easy questions or is giving wrong answers.

Dates & Places Used:

36

Fear or Advice

A good scare is worth far more to a man than all the advice in the world.

Dates & Places Used:

37

Baby Price Tag

A father brought his little daughter to the hospital to see her newborn baby brother for the first time. She looked at the baby through the window in the nursery. Attached to the baby's hand was the usual identification label. The girl turned to her father and asked, "Daddy, when are they going to take off the price tag?"

The price tag never comes off. Children cost their parents an awful lot from the time they are born, all the way through life. And I am not just talking about money either. I am talking about sleepless nights and days full of love and service and worry and concern.

Dates & Places Used:

38

TOPIC: Appearances

Get a Watch

A man, taking his grandfather clock to be repaired, rounded a corner and ran right into another man, sending him sprawling. After receiving profuse apologies, the man on the ground got up, dusted himself off, and snarled, "Why don't you wear a watch like everybody else?"

Dates & Places Used:

39

TOPIC: Appearances

Chasing Trains

A railway stationmaster watched a man run after a train as the train left the station. The man finally turned around and walked back to the station. The stationmaster asked the man, "Did you miss your train?"

With sweat streaming down his face onto his sopping wet clothes, the man looked up from the handkerchief in his face: "No, I just didn't like the looks of it, so I decided I would chase it away from the train station."

Dates & Places Used:

40

TOPIC: Appearances

Whose Problem Is It?

A man went to visit his friend. As he stepped inside his friend's house, a large, dirty dog walked in with him. The house was beautiful with white carpet and couch and was elegantly decorated. The dog proceeded to mess on an expensive oriental rug and jump up on the couch with his muddy paws. In the process, he also overturned and broke a rare vase—all within five minutes. Exasperated, the homeowner said, "You are going to have to do something about your dog!"

"My dog!" the man exclaimed. "I thought it was your dog!"

We sometimes forget whose dog or problem it is.

Dates & Places Used:

41

Lost Dog

Every Sunday afternoon, the family went for a drive out in the country after lunch and a nap. On one such country drive, they were about six miles onto a gravel road. There was nothing for miles around except for a small hill with a little dirt road ascending the top of the hill. As they drove by this desolate dirt road, they passed a dog that seemed lost and disoriented. But the dog seemed friendly. The family discussed their options and concluded that they could not just leave the lost dog. They backed up to the dirt road and compassionately allowed the dog into the car. The dog hopped into the back seat and curled up on the kids' laps. The family fell in love with their new friend.

After a couple of days, the family figured they had better make sure someone was not looking for this lost dog. They put a small ad in the local paper that described the dog. The first day the ad was printed, a man called about the dog. The man identified the dog and said he would come get it.

When the man arrived, he and his dog had a joyous reunion. He paid the family a reward for the dog–plus the expenses for the newspaper ad. The family was so attached to the dog they followed the man and his dog to his pickup that was parked in their driveway. The man opened the pickup door and the dog hopped into the passenger seat. The man turned to the family before getting into the truck and said, "I sure am sorry about the trouble my dog caused you. I've never had a bit of trouble with him before. He usually stays close to the house. And I live about six-and-a-half miles from the highway on a dirt road a half mile from the gravel road. He's never strayed much past that gravel road as far as I know."

Dates & Places Used:

42

Old Is New

Tag sewn into clothing: This garment is sewn and scientifically laundered to give the look of being old and worn. Flaws and imperfections are part of the total desired look.

What you see isn't always what you get.

Dates & Places Used:

TOPIC: Appearances

Humphrey's Double

There is a story told by Representative David Obey of Wisconsin about Hubert Humphrey and Federal Judge Miles Lord. These two dignitaries were on a fishing trip in northern Minnesota. While in a sporting goods store, Judge Lord noticed a tour bus from California that was broken down outside the store. Feeling a bit mischievous, he went out and introduced himself as the mayor of the town. He told them he was sorry about their plight; if there was anything he could do for them, just come by his office. Then he set his trap for Senator Humphrey. He told them that there was an old-timer in town who looked, talked, and acted like Senator Hubert Humphrey. This poor fellow even thought he *was* Senator Humphrey. Judge Lord told the people on the bus that this man would probably pay them a visit and masquerade as the senator. He asked the tourists to be kind to this confused man and humor him. He warned them not to give him money, but assured them that he was harmless.

Lord then returned to the store and told Humphrey that there was a busload of tourists who wanted to meet him. Hubert Humphrey loved people and immediately entered the bus to meet his admirers. Upon his return, Judge Lord asked him how it went. He told the judge that he shook hands with everyone on the bus. With a puzzled look on his face he told Lord that he just did not understand those California people. Every time he shook one of their hands, that person would turn to the other and they would all giggle.

Dates & Places Used:

TOPIC: Appearances

Blooming Chickens

Little Mary was visiting on her grandparents' farm. Investigating the chicken lot, she came upon a peacock. She ran quickly to the house, shouting, "Granny, come quick! One of your chickens is in bloom!"

Dates & Places Used:

45

Involuntary Disobedience

The attendant at a movie theater was walking up and down the aisle between showings of the movie. While doing so, he noticed that in the back of the theater there was a man lying across three seats. The attendant told the man that he would need to sit up in one chair. The only answer that came from the man was a muffled groan; the man did not even turn around and look at the attendant.

The attendant went to get the manager. The manager approached the man who was still lying across the three seats in the back of the theater. "Sir, you cannot lie down in this theater; you must sit up or I will have to insist that you leave!"

The man responded to the manager the same way he had responded to the attendant. The manager warned the man once more, but the reaction was the same.

The frustrated manager returned to his office and called the police. A police officer arrived and spoke to the man who was lying across three seats in the back of the theater: "I understand there is a little problem here; I'm afraid I'm going to have to ask you to leave this theater. So, what do you have to say for yourself now?"

With great hesitation, the man slowly turned toward the police officer and groaned out an answer, "You don't seem to understand at all; we have a big problem here: I fell from the balcony and can't get up!"

Dates & Places Used:

46

Words or Paragraphs

The problem with communication in marriage is that every time the husband has words with his wife, she has paragraphs with him!

Dates & Places Used:

47

Last Words

St. Thomas More, on the way to his execution, came to the scaffold and turned to the executioner and said, "Would you mind helping me up? I can get down by myself."
Dates & Places Used:

48

The Position of the Drawback

The little boy's first grade teacher asked him, "What position does your older brother play on the football team?"

The boy thought for a moment and proudly answered, "I'm not real sure what it's called, but I think he's a drawback."

Perhaps too many of us are willing to settle for that position in our jobs, in our churches, in our families, in our relationships. It's not enough to just be on the team; we need to also find a position of valuable service.
Dates & Places Used:

49

In Time of Need

If you help a friend in need, he is sure to remember you–the next time he's in need.
Dates & Places Used:

50

TOPIC: Assistance

The Starfish

As the old man walked the beach at dawn, he noticed a young man ahead of him picking up starfish and flinging them into the sea. Finally catching up with the youth, he asked him why he was doing this.

The boy answered, "The stranded starfish will die if left until the morning sun."

"But the beach goes on for miles ... and there are millions of starfish," countered the old man. "How can your effort make any difference?"

The young man looked at the starfish in his hand and then threw it to the safety of the waves. "It makes a difference to this one," he said.

Dates & Places Used:

51

TOPIC: Assistance

The Place to Find a Helping Hand

The best place to find a helping hand may very well be at the end of one's wrist. But there are times when it's necessary to help someone find that hand by holding it for a while.

Dates & Places Used:

52

TOPIC: Assumptions

Grace Assumed

There was a pretzel stand in front of an office building in New York. One day a businessman came out of the building, plunked down a quarter, and then went on his way without taking a pretzel. This happened every day for three weeks. Finally, the

30

old lady running the stand spoke up: "Sir, excuse me. May I have a word with you?"

The fellow said: "I know what you are going to say. You're going to ask me why I give you a quarter every day and don't take a pretzel."

And the woman said, "Not at all. I just want to tell you that the price is now thirty-five cents."

Dates & Places Used:

53

TOPIC: Atheists

Atheist Funerals

Question: "What does one say at an atheist funeral?"
Answer: "Good luck! All dressed up and no place to go!"

Dates & Places Used:

54

TOPIC: Atheists

Atheistic Prayer

They now have Dial-A-Prayer for atheists. When you call—no one answers.

Dates & Places Used:

55

TOPIC: Attitudes

Close-Minded Concrete

Some minds are like concrete—all mixed up and permanently set.

Dates & Places Used:

56

Seventeen-Camel Inequality

An Islamic man died and left his seventeen camels to be divided among his three sons. One was to get one-ninth; one was to get one-half; and the other was to get one-third of the camels. But seventeen camels aren't divisible by three or even two. The sons argued long and loud about how to divide the camels.

Finally in desperation they agreed to ask a certain wise man what to do. He was seated in front of his tent with his own camel staked out back. After hearing the case, this wise man took his own camel and added it to the other seventeen camels.

This confused the young men until he gave one-ninth of the eighteen–or two camels–to the first young man.

Then he gave one-half–or nine camels–to the second young man.

And finally, he gave one-third–or six camels–to the third young man.

Besides that, he still had his own camel left.

The brothers were so engrossed in their controversy that they failed to realize that their point of reference was too small. The sum total of their fraction was one-eighteenth too small. The wise man saw this controversy from a more enlightened view. His momentary sacrifice of his own camel provided a solution for the brothers at no cost to himself.

We need to remember that sometimes there are solutions to our problems that we just can't see. That's why we need others. That's why we need the church. That's why we need to pray. When we allow others and especially God to enter in with a differing viewpoint, it may be the very viewpoint that extricates us from our problems and conflicts.

Dates & Places Used:

57

Close Your Eyes to the Truth

An old story tells of a desert nomad who awakened in the middle of the night. He lit a candle and began eating dates from a bowl beside his bed.

He took a bite from one and saw a worm in it; so he threw it out of the tent. He picked up a second date, took a bite out of it, and found another worm. He threw that date out of the tent too. Then he picked up a third date, took a bite out of it, and found another worm. He threw that one away also.

He was very hungry, and reasoning that he wouldn't have any dates left to eat if he continued, he blew out the candle and very quickly ate the rest of the dates.

Many of us are like that. We prefer darkness and denial to the light of reality.

Dates & Places Used:

58

TOPIC: Attitudes

Seriously or Over

A history teacher would regularly tell his class: "You can take this class one of two ways—SERIOUSLY or OVER."

We had better take life seriously. We don't get to take it over.

Dates & Places Used:

59

TOPIC: Attitudes

Police Priorities

After being pulled over for speeding, the speeder confronted the officer and said: "Why don't you people get organized? First you take away my driver's license and the next day you ask to see it."

Dates & Places Used:

60

TOPIC: Authority

Horse Mechanic

A man was taking a drive in the country when his car suddenly stopped running. He had coasted to the side of the road and lifted the hood when an old horse came trotting by. The horse never slowed down. He just looked at the man and said, "Better check the gasoline!"

The man was shocked. He ran to the nearest farmhouse and frantically knocked on the door. When an old farmer opened the door, the man told the farmer what had happened.

"Was this a horse with a floppy ear?" asked the farmer.

"Yes, yes!" the man exclaimed.

"Oh, well," the farmer drawled, "don't believe everything he says; he doesn't know the first thing about cars."

Dates & Places Used:

TOPIC: Authority

61

Head of the Household

A couple was being questioned about the way they had completed their tax form. They were asked why they had failed to answer who was the head of the household. Their answer was simple: "We have been arguing over the answer to that question for seventeen years. As soon as we agree, we'll answer the question!"

Dates & Places Used:

TOPIC: Authority

62

Ask Your Father

The young daughter's mother was gone for the evening, so the daughter was sitting in her mother's chair and "playing mother" for her father and her brother.

Her father watched this maternal performance with amusement, but her brother was annoyed. Her brother decided to challenge her authority by asking her a domestic question: "So, if you are Mother, how do you make beef stroganoff?"

The girl answered, "I am much too busy to answer your questions right now, young man. Ask your father."

Dates & Places Used:

63

TOPIC: Balance

Fat, Faint, or Fit

If you take in and don't give out, you become FAT.
If you give out and don't take in, you become FAINT.
If you give out and take in, you become FIT.
Dates & Places Used:

64

TOPIC: Baptism

In the Hole You Go!

Maybe you've heard the story about the two little girls who went to a Baptist church with their grandmother and witnessed their first baptism by immersion.

When they got home, they excitedly told Mom all about it. "It was neat, Mom. Grandma's church has a swimming pool in it, right behind the choir. The preacher got in there with some other guy. He grabbed this guy by the nose, pushed him under the water, and yelled, 'In the name of the Father, and the Son, in the hole you go!'"
Dates & Places Used:

65

TOPIC: Baptism

Baptizing Puppies

Veterinarians have various ways to identify brand-new litters of puppies from each other. Some look exactly alike, you know. One such veterinarian used a method of wetting the head of each puppy as the shots and examination were completed. As the veterinarian reached for the final puppy, the stunned owner finally mused, "I didn't realize the puppies had to be baptized!"
Dates & Places Used:

66

TOPIC: Baptism

Baptize Them All

William P. Barker tells of a machinist at Ford Motor Company in Detroit who became a Christian and was baptized. He became a devout follower of Christ and desired to right his many wrongs. He had been stealing parts and tools from Ford for many years. The morning after his conversion, he acted out his public confession of Christ by taking all of the stolen tools and parts back to his employer. He explained his situation and recent conversion to his foreman and asked for forgiveness.

This response by an employee was without precedent. Mr. Ford, who was visiting a European plant, was cabled concerning all the details of this matter with a request for his response. Mr. Ford immediately returned a cable with his decision: "Dam up the Detroit River, and baptize the entire city."

Baptism is a public proclamation; our lives should be the same.

Dates & Places Used:

67

TOPIC: Baths

Weight Loss a Bath Away

Childhood is now looked back to with nostalgia because it was the one wonderful time when all you needed to do to lose weight was to take a bath.

Dates & Places Used:

68

TOPIC: Beauty

Look More Often

A husband and wife are walking along the sidewalk. The wife asks her husband if he still finds her attractive after all these years.

36

The husband stops and faces his wife. He tells her that the more he looks at her the prettier she gets.

His appreciative wife is taken aback by such a display of emotion and thanks him for his enduring love.

As the couple continue to walk along the sidewalk, the man begins to think to himself . . . "I guess I ought to look at her more often!"

Dates & Places Used:

69 TOPIC: Beauty
We Need Our Skin

Beauty is only skin-deep . . . but it is skin-deep:

My wife was grading a science test at home that she had given to her elementary school class and was reading some of the results to me. The subject was "The Human Body," and the first question was: "Name one of the major functions of your skin."

One child wrote: "To keep people who look at you from throwing up."

Dates & Places Used:

70 TOPIC: Beliefs
Wrong Floor

A woman visited a psychiatrist and said, "You've got to come help my husband. He has delusions and thinks he's an elevator."

"Bring him in to see me," replied the psychiatrist, "and I'll try to straighten him out."

"Oh, I can't do that," answered the wife. "He's an express elevator, and he doesn't stop on your floor."

What you think can make a profound impact on your life.

Dates & Places Used:

71

The Real Bible

I went to visit a family. Before leaving I asked if they would like for me to read from the Bible. The lady of the house said to one of the boys, "Go bring the Big Book we read out of so much!"

The boy brought the Sears Roebuck catalog.

Dates & Places Used:

72

Belief in the Word

Someone once asked Jay Kesler, former president of Youth for Christ International, if he believed that God could make a fish big enough to swallow a man. As a college president and above average in intelligence, in a world in which we have learned to split the atom and go to the moon and send spaceships to Neptune, did Kesler really think that God can make a fish big enough to swallow a man? I mean *really?*

Dr. Kesler's reply is one of simple trust in a great God. He answered, "Let me tell you, I not only believe that he can make such a fish, but the God who made the sun and the moon and the stars, if he wanted to, could air-condition and carpet the fish!"

Dates & Places Used:

73

Deluvian Statistics

The company library of the Atlantic Mutual Insurance Company in New York City has one of the most complete sets of records of marine disasters outside of England. The works are so complete that they have become truly legendary. Someone once asked the insurance company if they had a record of Noah's Ark. In due time, the inquirer received the following reply:

PRODUCTION: Built 2,448 B.C. of Gopher wood.
SIZE: Length, 300 cubits; width, 50 cubits; height, 30 cubits.
STORAGE: Three decks. Cattle carrier.
OWNER: Noah and Sons.
LOCATION: Last reported stranded on Mount Ararat.
Dates & Places Used:

74

TOPIC: Bible

The Hidden Books of the Bible

In the paragraph below you will find fifteen books of the Bible. As you find them, underline them:

I once made some remarks about hidden books in the Bible. It was a lulu: kept some people looking so hard for facts, and to others it was a revelation. Some were in a jam, especially since the books were not capitalized. But the truth finally struck home to numbers of readers. To others, it was a real job. We want it to be a most fascinating few minutes for you. Yes, there will be some really easy ones to spot; others might require judges to determine. We will quickly admit it usually takes a minister to find one, and there will be loud lamentations when you see how easy it is. A little lady says that if she brews tea she can concentrate better.

We have reprinted below the same paragraph as before, except that the fifteen books of the Bible are now underlined for those of you who want to check your results or gave up.

I once made some re<u>marks</u> about hidden books in the Bible. It was a lu<u>lu: kep</u>t some people loo<u>king s</u>o hard for <u>facts</u>, and to others it was a <u>revelation</u>. Some were in a <u>jam, es</u>pecially since the books were not capitalized. But the <u>truth</u> finally struck home to <u>numbers</u> of readers. To others, it was a real <u>job</u>. We want it to be <u>a most</u> fascinating few minutes for you. <u>Yes, there</u> will be some really easy ones to spot; others might require <u>judges</u> to determine. We will quickly admi<u>t it us</u>ually takes a minister to find one, and there will be loud <u>lamentations</u> when you see how easy it is. A little lady says that if <u>she brews</u> tea she can concentrate better.

Dates & Places Used:

75

Does Mom Really Know?

A little boy asked his mother, "Marriage makes you have babies, doesn't it, Mom?"

The mother reluctantly answered her son, "Well, not exactly. Just because you are married does not mean that you get pregnant."

The boy continued his inquiry: "Then how do you get pregnant?"

His mother, not at all enthusiastic about continuing this discussion, answered, "It's kind of hard to explain."

The boy paused and thought for a moment. He then walked closer to his mother, looked directly into her face, and carefully said, "You don't really know how it works, do you, Mom?"

Dates & Places Used:

76

TOPIC: Birth

Birth of Anticipation

Before the arrival of their son, a husband and wife attended birthing classes at the hospital. One day they toured the maternity ward. The instructor told all about what would take place while they were in the hospital. In passing, the instructor said that on the last evening of their stay they would be treated to a complimentary dinner for two and mentioned the menu selections. As they continued the tour, the woman was thinking about all the exiting things that would take place when the baby arrived. She turned and whispered to her husband, "Honey, I'm getting so excited."

"Me, too," he replied. "I'm going to order the lobster."

Dates & Places Used:

77

TOPIC: Blame

Blame It on Santa

The parents of a five-year-old boy were so excited about a very special gift they had purchased for their son. They had

40

saved up their money and bought him a combination compact disc-cassette tape player. They were sure their son had no idea what was in this package under the Christmas tree. He had asked for this, but had also told his parents that he knew they could not afford to get it and that was all right.

Two days before Christmas, they realized that they did not have any CDs for the player. It would not be right to get a present for their son that he would not be able to enjoy. So they took the package from under the tree and took one final shopping excursion to find some CDs their boy would like and that would fit in the player.

The son noticed that the package was missing and asked his parents about its absence. His resourceful father came up with the perfect alibi. "You see, son, Santa wanted to look at your present and bring you the perfect presents to go with what we were getting you. After he looked at it, he wrapped it up again in different wrapping paper and just gave it back to your mother and me while we were out shopping."

The boy appeared to listen with wonder and delight as his father spun this outrageous tale. The relieved father boasted to his wife what a wonderful cover-up he had accomplished with the boy. Later that night the father and mother were walking past the room of the boy. They noticed that the boy was kneeling beside his bed, praying to God. They were both touched by the sight and peeked through the crack in the door and listened to their son's prayer.

As the parents listened, the boy prayed: "God, you know I already prayed to you once tonight, but I just have to say one more thing to you without Dad and Mom here. I don't know why Dad blamed Santa for swiping my CD player, but I just want to thank you for getting Dad to bring it back."

Dates & Places Used:

TOPIC: Blessings

Heaven Comes Down

When you think of the blessings of God, remember one child's description of an elevator: "I got into this little room, and the upstairs came down."

So it seems when we serve Christ. We get in him, and heaven comes down and glory fills our souls!
Dates & Places Used:

79 TOPIC: Bloopers

One-Liner Wisdom

"Did you ever stop to think, and forget to start again?"

"There are three kinds of people: those who can count and those who can't."

"Don't use a big word where diminutive verbiage will suffice."

"Check carefully to see if you any words out."

"I used up all my sick days, so I'm calling in dead."

"Help Wanted: Telepath. You know where to apply."

"Department of Redundancy Department"

"Don't be so open-minded that your brains fall out."

Dates & Places Used:

80 TOPIC: Bloopers

One of Mom's Boyfriends

Four-year-old Marie watched as her older sister Michelle and her mother looked through a family picture album. In the album were old pictures of Mom's family, friends, school friends, boyfriends, and such. Later that day, a man came to the house to service the vacuum cleaner. Little Marie greeted him at the door and asked, "Are you one of my mom's boyfriends?"

Dates & Places Used:

81 TOPIC: Bloopers

Political Puzzles

C. Richard Stone of Normal, Illinois, sends some quotes from what he calls "razor-sharp political minds."

I believe that this country's policies should be heavily biased in favor of nondiscrimination. *Bill Clinton*

If we don't make some changes, the status quo will remain the same. *Clinton staff member*

We're going to have the best educated American people in the world. *Dan Quayle*

I support efforts to limit the terms of members of the Congress, especially members of the House and members of the Senate. *Dan Quayle*

Things are more like they are now than they have ever been. *Former President Gerald Ford*

I didn't say that I didn't say it. I said that I didn't say that I said it. I want to make that very clear. *Former Michigan Governor George Romney*

Who cares about posterity. What's posterity done for us?

I don't want to beat a dead horse to death.

This mortality rate is killing us.

I am not sure I understand the question, but I agree with you.
                    From unnamed Louisiana lawmakers

Those who throw rocks in glass houses had better look at yourself. *Senator Dennis DeConcini*

Those who survived the San Francisco earthquake said, "Thank God I'm still alive." But, of course, those who died, their lives will never be the same again. *Senator Barbara Boxer*

Dates & Places Used:

82 ▸ TOPIC: Bloopers

Rosebuds for You

During the dedication of babies ceremony in his church, a young southern pastor would always refer to the baby girls as "Rosebuds." No wonder that it brought smiles to his congregation when they heard him say, as he lifted the child up in his arms: "This BUD is for you ..."

Dates & Places Used:

TOPIC: Bloopers

A Willing Accomplice

Mickey Mantle had a friend who would let him hunt on his ranch. One day they went to the ranch to hunt along with teammate Billy Martin. Billy stayed in the car while Mickey checked with his friend.

Mickey was given permission to hunt, but the rancher asked him for a favor. His old mule was going blind and had become crippled, but the rancher just didn't have the heart to put him out of his misery—so he asked Mickey if he would shoot the old mule as a favor.

When Mickey came back to the car, he decided to play a trick on Billy and pretended to be angry. "What's wrong?" asked Billy.

"My friend told me NO HUNTING!!!" Mickey pounded his fist on the dashboard feigning anger and said, "Why, that guy got me so mad I'm going into the barn and shoot one of his mules." With that, Mickey jumped out of the car and headed for the barn. In quick order he took care of the mule and started back to the car to tell his friend it was just a joke. At that moment Mickey heard two shots fired and found Billy Martin standing over two dead cows. "What are you doing?" asked Mickey.

Martin answered, "Why, I saw how mad you were, so I wanted to let the rancher know he couldn't fool with me either."

Dates & Places Used:

TOPIC: Bloopers

Looking for Trouble

The new minister had just moved into town. It was late at night when his wife remembered that their dog, very aptly named "Trouble," had not been taken out yet. Since it was late and most of the neighbors were asleep, she just slipped on her robe, put the dog on a leash, and stepped out the back door.

Unfortunately the leash slipped out of her hand and the dog took off to explore the new territory. She ran around the house hoping to see which direction he had gone. Just then a police car was passing by and stopped to see if she needed help.

"No, thank you," she said, "I'm just out here looking for Trouble."

Dates & Places Used:

85

TOPIC: Bloopers

Fat Man Floating Deep and Wide

It was at the closing program of Vacation Bible School. All the children had been brought up front to sing some of the songs they had learned during the week.

As fate would have it, the loudest four-year-old girl was positioned the closest to the microphone. She belted out song after song to the pleasure and slight amusement of the gathered adults until she came to the song, "Deep and Wide." On that song, her motions were correct, her tone was sincere, but the entire congregation roared with laughter as they listened to her new lyrics to this old song:

Deep and wide, deep and wide,
There's a fat man floating deep and wide.

Dates & Places Used:

86

TOPIC: Boredom

Class Dismissed

The teacher was the only one left in the entire classroom who was even listening, let alone excited, about what he was saying in his extended lecture. The entire class was bored and just waiting for class to end. The teacher made what he considered an intriguing observation, paused for full impact, and then said, "What more can I say?"

An anonymous voice of reason from the back of the room suggested with renewed enthusiasm: "How about 'CLASS DISMISSED'?"

Dates & Places Used:

87

TOPIC: Boss

Accomplishment's Path

One of the strongest motivations is the sound of the boss's footsteps.

Dates & Places Used:

88

TOPIC: Bragging

Eggs in the Wind

One day two farmers were bragging about the strongest wind they'd ever seen. "In California," said one, "I've seen the fiercest wind in my life. You know those giant redwood trees? Well, the wind once got so strong that it bent them right over."

"That's nothing," said the other. "Back on my farm in Iowa, we had wind one day that blew a hundred miles per hour. It was so bad, one of my hens had her back turned to the wind and she laid the same egg six times."

Dates & Places Used:

89

TOPIC: Catholics

Keep the Towels

Said a priest to his bishop: "I won a his-and-her set of towels in a raffle. What shall I do?"

The bishop, who had been wondering whether the priest had missed his calling, *encouraged* him to keep the towels, saying, "The way things are going for you, you may need them."

Dates & Places Used:

90

TOPIC: Catholics

Catholic Cop

An Irish cop stopped a speeding car. The driver was a priest. Putting away his citation book, the cop said, "Father, I just stopped you to tell you there's a Protestant cop at the next light!"

Dates & Places Used:

91

TOPIC: Caution

Time to Watch Your Step

By the time some men learn to watch their step, they are too old to go anywhere.

Dates & Places Used:

92

TOPIC: Caution

Fair Warning

I was taking my mother for a drive, and she'd scold me whenever I went over the speed limit. Unfortunately I dismissed her advice, and a state trooper pulled me over and issued a ticket. As my mother and I continued on our way, I complained that he should have let me off with a warning.

"Joan," she said, "I gave you the warning. He gave you the ticket."

Dates & Places Used:

93

TOPIC: Challenges

Most Challenging Message

In a recent cartoon, a tourist is standing next to a Native American Indian who is sending smoke signals. The Indian answers the tourist's question: "The most challenging message I have ever sent?

"It's raining like crazy here!'"

Dates & Places Used:

94

TOPIC: Change

Fixing the Pieces of the Heart

God can fix a broken heart,
but only if we give him all the pieces.

Dates & Places Used:

95

Sooner Said Than Done

It's amazing how much we are creatures of habit and resistant to change. A radio announcer on KLOS in Los Angeles, about thirty minutes after a major earthquake, made these conflicting statements: "The telephone company is urging people to please not use the telephone unless it is absolutely necessary in order to keep the lines open for emergency personnel. We'll be right back after this break to give away a pair of Phil Collins concert tickets to caller number 95."

Dates & Places Used:

96

TOPIC: Change

A Welcome Change

Have you noticed that the only people who truly welcome change are wet babies?

Dates & Places Used:

97

TOPIC: Change

May Take Longer

Alfred Adler, a famous psychologist, once put an ad in the paper for his Fourteen-Day Cure Plan. He claimed that he could cure anyone of any mental or emotional difficulty in just fourteen days if they would do just what he told them to.

One day a woman who was extremely lonely came to see Adler. He told her he could cure her of her loneliness in just fourteen days if she would follow his advice. She was not very enthusiastic, but she still asked, "What do you want me to do?"

Adler replied, "If you will do something for someone else every day for fourteen days, at the end of that time, your loneliness will be gone."

She objected profusely, "Why should I do anything for some-one else? No one ever does anything for me."

Adler supposedly responded jokingly, "Well, maybe it will take you twenty-one days."

Dates & Places Used:

98

TOPIC: Change

Swimming Against the Stream

Many years ago I saw a magnificent tapestry in a home for recovering alcoholics in Germany. It was a picture of a stream with a shoal of fish heading one way and a solitary fish swim-ming in the opposite direction. Underneath were the words: "Any dead fish can float downstream—it takes a live one to swim against it."

Dates & Places Used:

99

TOPIC: Change

He Leaks

In the mountains of Tennessee they have a type of religion in which people get saved in the spring, grow cold in the summer, backslide in the autumn, and fall away completely in the winter; then they get saved all over in the spring revival.

A story goes that the revival had gone on about ten days, and people knew it was nearing its climax. A certain man came into the meeting and sat in the back row. The next night he moved halfway toward the front. The third night he was sitting in the front row. The fourth night he broke out in prayer, "Lord, fill me!"

Over to one side there was a woman who knew the man well. She cautioned the Lord, "Careful, Lord! He leaks!"

Dates & Places Used:

100

TOPIC: Character

Abiding Grace

Legend has it that Jonathan Edwards, third president of Princeton and one of America's great preachers, had a daughter with an uncontrollable temper. As often happens, this fault was not known to many people outside the family. A young man fell in love with this daughter and asked to marry her.

"You can't have her" was the abrupt answer of Jonathan Edwards.

"But I love her," the young man replied.

"You can't have her," repeated Edwards.

"But she loves me," replied the young man.

Again Edwards said, "You can't have her."

"Why?" asked the young man.

"Because she is not worthy of you."

"But," he asked, "she is a Christian, isn't she?"

"Yes, she is a Christian. But the grace of God can live with some people with whom no one else could ever live!"

Dates & Places Used:

101

TOPIC: Character

The Steps of Compromise

The collapse of character falls back down the steps of compromise.

Dates & Places Used:

102

TOPIC: Character

Let Others Discover

It is far more impressive when others discover your good qualities without your help.

Dates & Places Used:

103

A Grouchy Cheer

A grouch is a person who spreads good cheer wherever he doesn't go.

Dates & Places Used:

104

Bundled Up for the Bathroom

Show me a child who has just been dressed in multiple layers of warm clothing, driven to an isolated hill at the edge of town, and fitted into a pair of skis ... and I'll show you a child who has to go to the bathroom!

Dates & Places Used:

105

God Already Blessed Mom

My brother and sister-in-law have gotten used to people exclaiming over the fact that they are the parents of eight children, now grown.

But recently a young woman, the mother of one very active year-old son, on meeting my sister-in-law for the first time and hearing about the eight children, exclaimed, "Eight children! Oh, Mary, God bless you!"

Mary replied, "He has."

Dates & Places Used:

106

Place or Temperature

Our church is located in the town of San Luis Obispo, California–about 200 miles north of Los Angeles. Two younger brothers were overheard talking about the temperature one day.

The older brother said: "It sure is hot today, don't you think so?"

The younger brother said: "Yeah! I wish it was only one degree outside; then it would be cooler."

The older brother said: "One degree? Fahrenheit or Centigrade?"

The younger brother looked a bit puzzled and then said: "No, I mean right here in San Luis Obispo."

Dates & Places Used:

107

Coping with Customs

The wife of an army colonel had made an all-night flight to meet her husband at his latest military assignment in Germany. She arrived weary at Rhein-Main Air Base in Germany with her nine children, all under age eleven.

Collecting their many suitcases, the ten of them entered the cramped customs area. A young customs official watched them in disbelief. "Ma'am," he said, "do all these children and all this luggage belong to you?"

"Yes, sir," she said with a sigh. "They're all mine."

The customs agent began his interrogation: "Ma'am, do you have any weapons, contraband, or illegal drugs in your possessions?"

"Sir," she calmly answered, "if I'd had any of those items, I would have used them by now!"

She was allowed to pass without having to open a single suitcase.

Dates & Places Used:

108

Teenage Terrorism

Here's a great way for you kids to turn the tables on your frustrated parents the next time you get in trouble. Just ask your parents this question: "If you're trying so hard to raise me correctly, then why am I in so much trouble?" Remember, transferred guilt is always the best policy.

Dates & Places Used:

109

TOPIC: Children

Switch for the Home

The modern home has all the conveniences and latest technologies.

There is a switch for this and a switch for that.

There is now one last frontier for the home:

There is still a need for a switch that works for the children.

Dates & Places Used:

110

TOPIC: Children

No Focus

A typical father is reading the paper and sharing that which he reads with his teenage son. He is telling his son about the lack of attention and low educational achievements of children today. They are lazy, have little concentration, and barely any listening skills at all. The father asks his son for his reaction to this study ...

The son halfheartedly lifts his head, "What was that again, Dad?"

Dates & Places Used:

111

A Maalox Moment

Good old Mr. Wilson is sitting in his chair reading the newspaper. Mrs. Wilson is looking out the window as Dennis the Menace walks past the house. You can almost hear the sigh of relief from Mr. Wilson. He says to his wife, "There goes a Maalox moment waiting to happen."

Dates & Places Used:

112

Clean Houses and Children

When you have children, cleaning a house is like shoveling snow while it's still snowing.

Dates & Places Used:

113

UPS Will Get You!

When the father of a little girl in our congregation had taken all he could and would finally get fed up and holler at his daughter, he would yell, "If you don't settle down, I'm going to call UPS and have them come get you." It was sort of Dad's final warning signal said thoroughly in jest. And it was only hollered in that moment of total frustration that all parents face from time to time.

One day their daughter had been a particular pill. There wasn't any kind of trouble the daughter hadn't gotten into that day. Dad was about ready to tear his hair out. Then three things happened. The daughter crossed the line. Dad hollered, "If you don't settle down, I'm going to call UPS and have them come get you." And the doorbell rang.

All attention was drawn to the door as Dad opened it. The minute the door opened, the daughter took one look, screamed, and went running down the hall. Dad nearly fainted. Standing there with a look of total bewilderment was a UPS man with a package in his hands. That was the last time Dad used that phrase.

Dates & Places Used:

114

TOPIC: Children

Don't Blame Me

A mother was taking a nap while her eight-year-old son was playing in the living room. While the boy was playing, a van crashed through the picture window. The boy was surprised, but unhurt. The mother raced into the living room and screamed out the name of her son.

Now the boy was afraid. "But Mom—honest, I didn't do it!"

Dates & Places Used:

115

TOPIC: Children

Set Limits on Children

Mom and Dad are sitting and talking. Mom is reading the newspaper and she says, "According to this, parents should set limits where children are concerned."

Dad replies, "I agree, and my limit is two."

Dates & Places Used:

116

TOPIC: Children

One Loud Baby Brother

Mom Ryatt is talking to a little neighbor boy. "Hi, Timmy. How is your baby brother?

Timmy responds, "Okay, I guess. But he sure is loud when he's crying! Mommy said she got him from heaven. I guess that's why God gave him away!"

Dates & Places Used:

117 TOPIC: Children

Ineffective Deception

A little boy is sitting on the school bus talking to a friend and says, "At breakfast my stomach hurt, I was dizzy, and my throat was sore. But my mom didn't buy it."

Dates & Places Used:

118 TOPIC: Children

A Lowercase d

At the beginning of a speech therapy lesson with a first grade group, tone of the little girls was staring intently at the teacher's quite pregnant body. After some consideration, the child blurted out, "You look just like a lowercase d."

Dates & Places Used:

119 TOPIC: Children

Can't Read Yet

A young mother was writing a letter as her preschool son sat at the table and watched her. He finally asked his mother if he could write a letter as well. The mother affectionately handed her little boy a pencil and paper. As she finished her letter, she watched her son scribble and mark on his paper with all the precision his little fingers could deliver.

Mom leaned over and curiously looked at his letter. "And what have you written, young man?"

The little boy looked up at his mother, looked back down at his paper, then looked at his mother again. "I don't know, Mommy, I haven't learned to read yet!"

Dates & Places Used:

120 TOPIC: Children

More Than Movement

An eight-year-old little girl was trying to teach her younger brother how to ride a bicycle. After several fruitless attempts, the little brother finally steadied himself. As he wobbled from side to side, he excitedly shouted, "I'm moving, I'm moving!"

His older sister, in a cold voice that evoked disdain and a much keener wisdom, replied. "Yeah, you're moving all right, but you aren't going anywhere!"

This illustrates what many Christian lives and families are like. They move aimlessly about but never go anywhere for or with Jesus.

Dates & Places Used:

121 TOPIC: Children

Catch of the Day

A sad-looking little boy had been waiting quite some time for his order of *the catch of the day* to be filled.

Finally, the waiter showed up and said, "Your *catch of the day* order will be ready in just a few minutes now."

The little boy brightened up a bit and asked, "Tell me, what kind of bait are you using?"

Dates & Places Used:

122

Tills and Afters Are Tough

A young child is explaining to her family how well she is doing as she learns to tell time: "I know my 'o'clocks' now, but I'm still having trouble with my 'tills' and my 'afters.'"

Dates & Places Used:

123

No Money for Collect Calls

A couple decided to take a much-needed vacation and leave their young children behind with a trusted baby-sitter. The first night away from home they called home to see how the children were getting along with their baby-sitter. Their daughter answered the phone. Since the parents had called collect, the operator asked the girl if she would pay for the call. The girl who had never received a collect call before apologized and told the operator that she wanted to talk to her parents but was unable to pay for the call—she did not have any money. Contrary to the girl's initial response, the call did go through.

The resources and solutions to meet our needs are not always obvious. But it serves us well to remember that when God seeks to communicate with his children, the call will go through.

Dates & Places Used:

124

Choirs Beyond Comprehension

Rev. Allan Stuart, pastor of North Bay Community Church in Clearwater, Florida, was approached by a parishioner who announced that he had visited a charismatic church. "The choir sang in tongues," he said. "It was beautiful."

"Nothing remarkable about that," Stuart replied. "We can't understand what our choir is saying either."
Dates & Places Used:

TOPIC: Chores

Your Wife Can't Find You

Leisure time is when your wife can't find you.
Dates & Places Used:

TOPIC: Chores

Thinking Out Loud

The best way for a woman to have a few minutes to herself at the close of the day is to start doing the dishes.
Dates & Places Used:

TOPIC: Chores

Beats Dishes

1st Bride: "I have my husband eating out of my hand."
2nd Bride: "Beats washing dishes, doesn't it?"
Dates & Places Used:

TOPIC: Christians

Lifestyle Evangelism

Live so that when you tell someone you are a Christian, it confirms their suspicions instead of surprises them.
Dates & Places Used:

TOPIC: Christmas

Case of the Missing Jesus

"Daddy, guess what's missing!" seven-year-old Johnny yelled. The place rang with excitement as the family put up the life-sized manger scene on the lawn.

"What?" his father asked, as he fastened Joseph to a pole for support.

"The baby Jesus," Johnny replied, twisting his face into a frown. "Daddy, if we can't find Jesus, there's no need for us to put up the manger scene at all."

If we cannot include Jesus in our Christmas, then there is no reason to celebrate Christmas at all.

Dates & Places Used:

TOPIC: Christmas

Presents or Presence?

A military expert was asked to deliver a speech in St. Louis, Missouri. It was during World War II, and he had a difficult time getting a seat on the plane. However, he secured it and departed from his hometown, Boston. En route he was "bumped" in Washington, D.C., by an army general who had top priority. Disgruntled and frustrated, the lecturer sat and cooled his heels while his plane left for Missouri.

His disappointment was nothing, however, compared to the general's disgust when he arrived in St. Louis only to discover that the speaker had to cancel out. The general's dismay was complete when he realized that the speaker was the man whose plane seat he had preempted in Washington!

The story points up an interesting question for the Advent season: Are our presents to one another crowding out his presence in our midst? What has top priority to us this Christmas? Before it is too late, let's give him first place in our hearts.

Dates & Places Used:

131

Car Seat for Jesus

A little girl was helping her mother unpack the nativity set and set it up. As she unpacked each of the pieces she said, "Here's Mary and Joseph." When she got the figurine of Jesus in the manger she said, "And here's the baby Jesus in his car seat."
Dates & Places Used:

132

Urchin Mary

A little girl was involved in her church's Christmas program. This year they were going to be telling the Christmas story in their own words. Everyone had practiced and thought it was delightful. This little girl kept referring to the Virgin Mary as the Urchin Mary. And if you stop and think about it, she was probably right. Although she didn't realize it when they left Nazareth, she and Joseph soon would be homeless. Mary was an urchin, young and homeless and on the run.
Dates & Places Used:

133

Santa Disproved

If God wanted us to believe in Santa Claus, he would not have waited about giving Dad the shape of Santa until the children were old enough to know better.
Dates & Places Used:

134

TOPIC: Christmas

Christmas Trimmings

Christmas is a time
When the tree gets trimmed
And so does the budget.
Dates & Places Used:

135

TOPIC: Christmas

No Peace and Quiet at the Mall

Skyler: "What was it you wanted for Christmas, Uncle Cosmos?"

Cosmos: "I told you, Skyler, just a little peace and quiet."

Skyler: "I know, but I just came from the mall. I think they're all out of that."

Dates & Places Used:

136

TOPIC: Christmas

In Ex Selfish Deo

One Christmas a four-year-old boy was singing "Angels We Have Heard on High" with great fervor, but the chorus came out differently: "Gloria, in ex selfish deo."

Dates & Places Used:

137

TOPIC: Christmas

Christmas Before Santa

A little boy returned from Sunday school with a new perspective on the Christmas story. He had learned all about the wise men from the East who brought gifts to the baby Jesus. He was so excited he just had to tell his neighborhood friends. This is how he told it:

"I learned in Sunday school today all about the very first Christmas. Ya see, there wasn't a Santa way back then, so these three skinny guys on camels had to deliver all the toys!

"And Rudolph the Reindeer with his nose so bright wasn't there yet, so they had to have this big spotlight in the sky to find their way around."

Dates & Places Used:

138

TOPIC: Christmas

A Giving Opportunity

A mother was sick and tired of hearing her children always telling her what they wanted Santa to bring them. On one such occasion she reminded them of the real meaning of Christmas—Christmas is a time of giving and not receiving.

The children could tell that Mom really believed what sounded like absolute nonsense to them. They secretly met and tried to figure out what was going through their mother's head. They finally came to a conclusion as to what must be done.

They went to their mother in a very concerned manner. The oldest child acted as the spokesperson: "Mom, we've been thinking about what you told us about how important it is to give at Christmas; with all of our talk about Santa, you must have felt left out. We don't want you to feel this way, Mom. So I'll tell you what we have decided to do. Santa doesn't have to get us all the presents; if you want to get us some, too, we're going to let you!"

Dates & Places Used:

139

TOPIC: Christmas

A Box of Love

While helping her mother prepare for Christmas, a little girl asked about the meaning of this holiday. The mother told her that Christmas was the time of the year we celebrate the birthday of Jesus, God's Son. The little girl asked her mother why Jesus didn't get the presents if it was his birthday. The mother explained the tradition of gift exchange as a way of showing love for one another and the matter was dropped at that.

The evening before Christmas the little girl brought a gift-wrapped package from her room and placed it under the tree. "What's in the box?" her mother asked.

"A gift for Jesus. I am leaving it under the tree so he can open it tonight while I am asleep."

The mother did not want her daughter to be disappointed, so during the night she opened the package. But there was nothing in it. The next morning her daughter raced into the living room to see if her package had been opened. It had! She shouted to her mother, "Jesus opened his present last night!"

The mystified mother walked over to her daughter and asked what she had given Jesus.

The little girl explained, "I figure that Jesus has about everything he needs, and I can't give him much cuz I'm just a little girl. But there is one thing I can give him. So I decided to give him a BOX OF LOVE."

The little girl is right; all Christmas really is is a big box of love.

Dates & Places Used:

140 **TOPIC: Christmas**

In Need of Another Christmas

Nancy Dugan was nearly four as Christmas drew near. The parents and four older children all had tried to prepare Nancy for Christmas by talking with her about the real meaning of Christmas and why the family celebrated it.

Nancy had a wonderful Christmas with a lot of presents and toys. A few days later, Nancy was talking with her older sister about what a great Christmas she had, and said: "I sure hope Joseph and Mary have another baby."

Dates & Places Used:

141

Mother Mary Held Hostage

Once there was a little boy who was really mean. No matter what his parents tried, he continued to be self-centered, selfish, and—well—mean. Christmas was coming soon, so the little boy, in his usual selfish way, made his "Dear Santa" letter—twelve pages of gadgets and toys!

When his parents saw the monstrous letter, they were outraged. Father picked up the little boy and carried him to the living room, setting him firmly on the floor in front of the family's nativity scene. "I want you to sit right here and look at this scene until you remember what Christmas is all about. Then you must write a letter to Jesus."

So the little boy sits there a while and then returns to his bedroom. Finding paper and pencil, he begins to write: "Dear Jesus, if you will bring me all the presents I want, I will be good for a whole year." Then he thinks for a moment and tears up the paper. He writes again: "Dear Jesus, if you will bring me all the presents I want, I will be good for a whole week," but once again he tears up the paper.

The little boy quietly leaves his room and returns to the living room, looking intently at the nativity scene. He gently reaches down and picks up the figure of Mary. Returning to his room, he places the figure in a shoe box and sets the box in the back of his closet. Then he writes another letter: "Dear Jesus, if you ever want to see your mother again . . ."

—Who knows where it began!

Dates & Places Used:

142

Christmas Activity Scene

This past Christmas, one little girl told me that her sister kept asking her parents when they were going to set up the activity scene.

Dates & Places Used:

143

TOPIC: Christmas

Mary's Little Lamb

Another little girl was taking all the figures out of the box and listing them off, "Here's Mary and Joseph and the baby Jesus and the wise men and Mary's little lamb."

Dates & Places Used:

144

TOPIC: Church

Church Membership

A wise old pastor told how some people get mad at the church and decide they will hurt the church by leaving. He explained that they were wrong in thinking that their leaving would hurt the church. The tree is never hurt when an old dried-up apple falls to the ground.

Dates & Places Used:

145

TOPIC: Church

Accelerated Doctorate

The church is the only hospital where you can go in sick and come out the doctor.

Dates & Places Used:

146

TOPIC: Church

Church in Silk Pajamas

When Eddy Arcaro retired as one of the nation's most successful jockeys back in 1962, a reporter asked him if he still got up early to walk his mounts around the track when dew was still on the ground. Arcaro confessed frankly, "It becomes difficult to get up early once a guy starts wearing silk pajamas."

The Christian church seems to be in the silk pajama stage. It gets harder and harder to rise early.

Dates & Places Used:

147 TOPIC: Church

Churches with Plus Signs

You can be sure that America is no longer a Christian nation when the children ask their parents why all those churches have plus signs on top of them ... and their parents don't know!

Dates & Places Used:

148 TOPIC: Church

Soul Healing

The engraving above the library of the former monastery of Saint Gall reads: "Enter Here the Pharmacy of the Soul."

Dates & Places Used:

149 TOPIC: Church

Qualified Preacher

To be a preacher today you have to make more speeches than a lawyer, more house calls than a doctor, fix more things than a plumber, and know how to run an adult nursery.

Dates & Places Used:

150

TOPIC: Church

Absentees Love Church

If absence makes the heart grow fonder, a lot of folks must love our church.

Dates & Places Used:

151

TOPIC: Church Attendance

Time for Church

Sign seen on a church bulletin board:
"Don't wait for the hearse to bring you to church."

Dates & Places Used:

152

TOPIC: Church Attendance

Bad Day for Church

Four associates were playing a round of golf on Sunday morning. None of their scores was good. On top of this embarrassment, it began to rain. The men returned to the clubhouse only to learn that the electrical power line had been hit by lightning, so the restaurant was closed. As the men prepared to rush for their cars, one of them remarked: "We could have just as well gone to church this morning."

Another of the men disagreed: "Oh, I couldn't have gone to church, anyway. My wife is sick in bed this morning."

Dates & Places Used:

153

TOPIC: Clothes

Bible Clothes

A little boy found an old family Bible and began to look through it. As he was turning the pages, a pressed tree leaf fell out. "Hey, this must be where Adam and Eve left their clothes!"

Dates & Places Used:

154

TOPIC: College

College Bred

"College bred" describes a four-year loaf made out of the old man's dough.
Dates & Places Used:

155

TOPIC: College

Same Old Story

An alumnus returned to his old college dorm and wanted to see the room in which he once lived. The new occupant let him in, and the alumnus looked around. "Same old room. Same old furniture. Same old view from the window. Same old closet."

He opened the closet door. There stood a girl, looking scared. "That is my sister," said the present occupant of the room.

"Yes," replied the visitor. "Same old story."
Dates & Places Used:

156

TOPIC: Commitment

A Good Investment

The bonds of commitment are a good investment as long as interest is paid.
Dates & Places Used:

157

TOPIC: Committees

Committees

While observing yet another huddle at another football game, writer George Will had this observation about the game:

It combines the two worst things about American life.
It is violence punctuated by committee meetings.
Dates & Places Used:

158

TOPIC: Committees

Committees and Nothing

A committee is a group of people who can do nothing individually and decide collectively that nothing can be done.
Dates & Places Used:

159

TOPIC: Committees

Kennedy's Committees

A committee is twelve men doing the work of one.

Dates & Places Used:

160

TOPIC: Communication

Know Your Audience

A man walked into the drugstore and asked the pharmacist if he had a cure for hiccups. The pharmacist walked around the corner and approached the man. He reached out and slapped the man in the back. The pharmacist then hopefully asked the man, "Do you have the hiccups now?"

As the man composed himself after such a sudden blow, he answered the pharmacist, "No, I do not! But I'll just bet you that my wife out in the car still does."
Dates & Places Used:

161

TOPIC: Communication

Dry Rot and Worms

An English vicar, concerned with his congregation's aging and decaying building, made an announcement just before taking up the morning offering. He said, "The proceeds from the offering this morning will go toward the alleviation of the dry rot in the pulpit and the extermination of the worms in the pews."

Dates & Places Used:

162

TOPIC: Communication

Socrates on Oration

Once a young man came to the great philosopher Socrates to be instructed in oratory. The moment the young man arrived, he began to speak, and there was an incessant stream for some time.

When Socrates could get in a word, he said, "Young man, I will have to charge you a double fee."

"A double fee, why is that?"

The old sage replied, "I will have to teach you two sciences: first, how to hold your tongue, and then how to use it."

Dates & Places Used:

163

TOPIC: Communication

Ring the Bell Yourself

A man was driving past a country estate and saw a sign on a gatepost: "Please ring bell for caretaker."

So the man rang the bell, and an ancient fellow appeared. "Are you the caretaker?" asked the man.

"Yes, I am—may I help you?" responded the old man.

"Oh, no," replied the man. "I was just wondering why you can't ring the bell yourself."

Dates & Places Used:

TOPIC: Communication

A Gun by Any Other Name

During the first week of basic training with the U.S. Army, our drill sergeant was explaining the course of events we would experience during the next two months. One young private asked a question from the back of the formation: "Sergeant, when do we get our guns?"

The drill sergeant quickly corrected the private, "Private, we don't have 'guns' in the army. We use the M-16, A-1 Military Assault Rifle. If I catch any one of you calling the M-16 a 'gun,' I'll have you drop and give me fifty pushups. Now then, private, repeat your question."

The private nodded, then said, "Sergeant, when do we get our guns?"

Sometimes we should remember that our best preaching still falls on deaf ears!

Dates & Places Used:

TOPIC: Communication

Getting the Message

A preacher said to a farmer, "Do you belong to the Christian family?"

"No," said he, "they live two farms down."

"No, no! I mean are you lost?"

"No, I've been here thirty years."

"I mean are you ready for Judgment Day?"

"When is it?"

"It could be today or tomorrow."

"Well, when you find out for sure when it is, you let me know. My wife will probably want to go both days!"

Dates & Places Used:

166

Wrong Token of Gratitude

This bulletin misprint emphasized the need to know the difference between momentum and memento:

"Our minister is leaving the church this Sunday. Will you please send in a small donation? The congregation wants to give him a little momentum."

Dates & Places Used:

167

Tolerance over Communication

A couple was asked, "What is the secret for staying married for such a long time?"

"That's simple," one of them answered. "One of us talks, and the other one doesn't listen!"

Dates & Places Used:

168

Letters Better Than Money

I ran short of money while visiting my brother, so I borrowed fifty dollars from him. After my return home, I wrote him a short letter every few weeks, enclosing a five-dollar check in each one. He called me up and told me how much he enjoyed the letters regarding the money I owed; I had never written regularly before.

Finally I sent off a letter and the last five-dollar check. In my mailbox the next week I found an envelope from my brother. Inside was another fifty dollars.

Dates & Places Used:

169

TOPIC: Communication

Keeping Posted

I heard of one young man who was determined to win the affection of a girl who refused to even see him. He decided that the way to her heart was through the mail, so he began writing her a love letter every day. When she did not respond, he increased his output to three notes every twenty-four hours. In all, he wrote her more than 700 letters—and she married the postal carrier.

Dates & Places Used:

170

TOPIC: Communication

Selling Out Spelling

A teenage tourist approached a businessman in a busy section of Denver, Colorado. He asked the man if he could help him find a certain location. He continued, "I think it starts with an 'S.'"

The businessman thought for a moment and asked, "The Civic Center?"

The teenager exclaimed, "That's it!"

Proper spelling or not—communication was complete.

Dates & Places Used:

171

TOPIC: Communication

Imposed Proposals

"Special note to Teri: If you don't have a ring yet, it wasn't YOUR Bob proposing marriage on that billboard."

Bob Bornack's proposal on a sign did the trick with his Teri—Teri Ungar—but left more than ten other Teris wondering whether it was their Bob who popped the question.

"I talked to one Teri who called in a total panic because she's dating two Bobs," Mike Richards, who works for the billboard

74

company, said Wednesday. "She didn't know which one might be proposing, and she had to know whom to answer."

The sign in this Chicago suburb reads, "Teri, Please Marry Me! Love, Bob."

Bornack drove Ungar past the sign Saturday, then pulled a ring from his pocket. The couple plan a spring wedding.
Dates & Places Used:

172

TOPIC: Communication

Know It to Learn It

A man stopped his car and asked for directions at a rural convenience store:

"Keep going down this road until you get to the old Jones homeplace, then turn left. Stay on that road, and just before you cross Brown's Creek there will be a road that goes off to the right . . ."

"Wait! Jones homeplace? What's that look like?"

"Well, you can't see it from the road. It's about a half mile past where the big oak used to be."

"What big oak?"

After several tries, the local gave up and said, "Mister, you've got to know something before I can tell you something."
Dates & Places Used:

173

TOPIC: Communication

Walk, Don't Run

My three-year-old son loved the outdoors so much he often would not take the time to get dressed before entering it. In the city that can cause quite a bit of embarrassment. One morning his mother caught him playing outside with only his underpants on. She called to him through the living-room window, "What are you doing running around outside in your underwear?"

Innocently he responded, "I'm not, Mom. I'm walking."
Dates & Places Used:

TOPIC: Communication

174

TOPIC: Communication

Wrong Prescription

An explosion occurred in the back room of the drugstore. The pharmacist emerged with black smoke marks on his face and his jacket in tatters.

Staggering up to the woman customer, he said, "Would you mind having your doctor write out the prescription again, and this time tell him to print it!"

Dates & Places Used:

175

TOPIC: Communication

Gender Bender

The following was a reply to a church advertisement: "I am responding to your ad for an organist and choirmaster, either a lady or a gentleman. I have been both for many years."

Dates & Places Used:

176

TOPIC: Communication

Military Talk

Our language is one of our greatest barriers to understanding and peaceful coexistence. David Evans postulates the military would take the following statement and revise it out of existence:

1st Draft: A word to the wise is sufficient.

2nd Draft: A word to the wise may be sufficient.

3rd Draft: It is believed that a word to the wise may be sufficient.

4th Draft: It is believed by some that a word to the wise may be sufficient under some conditions.

5th Draft: Indications are that it is believed by some that a word to the wise may be sufficient under some conditions, although this may possibly vary under differing circumstances. This conclusion may not be supportable under detailed analysis and should be used only in a general sense with a full realization of the underlying assumptions.

To which we must include the addenda:

Army View: The above statement may have restricted use in joint papers but is believed that it fails to properly consider assigned roles and missions or the impact of such a conclusion when applied to the peculiar conditions of ground warfare.

Air Force View: The above statement may be generally acceptable but fails to properly recognize the predominant role of air power in a five-minute war characterized by a high requirement for flexibility, mobility, firepower, and shock action on a potentially global scale.

Navy/Marine Corps View: The naval services accept this view with the reservation that the Navy and Marine Corps' capability for immediate effective action in strikes from the sea may preclude the possibility of a war of such duration.

Of course, we don't do that in religion, do we?

Dates & Places Used:

177 TOPIC: Communion

No Eat, No Pay

There was a little boy with a quarter to give during a Sunday offering. This Sunday, however, happened to be Communion Sunday and as the elements were being passed, the boy's parents told him not to take any. "You're not old enough," they explained.

Later when the offering plate came by, however, the boy's parents urged him to put in his quarter. Loudly he proclaimed, "If I can't eat, I won't pay!"

Dates & Places Used:

178 TOPIC: Comparisons

Eggs the Size of Footballs

Coming upon a white leather football the farmer's son had brought into the yard, the rooster called his hens around him. "Now, ladies, I don't want to appear ungrateful, but I do want you to see what's being done in other yards."

Dates & Places Used:

179

TOPIC: Comparisons

Unhealthy Comparisons

Comparisons are unhealthy because we compare our insides with their outsides.

Dates & Places Used:

180

TOPIC: Comparisons

Compared to His Brother

Two brothers were the most wicked scoundrels in this small rural village. Upon the death of one of the brothers, the surviving brother engaged a preacher. He wanted the preacher to say his brother was a saint. After much discussion, the preacher agreed and at the end of the funeral made this statement:

"This man, lying here, was a scoundrel, but compared to his brother he was a saint."

Dates & Places Used:

181

TOPIC: Compassion

Wrong One Wronged

While traveling on a train, a wealthy Jewish merchant treated a poor old man with rudeness and disdain.

When they arrived at their common destination, the merchant found the station thronged with pious Jews waiting in ecstatic joy to greet one of the holiest rabbis in all of Europe. The merchant surmised to his chagrin that the poor old man riding in his compartment was this saintly rabbi.

Embarrassed at his disgraceful behavior and distraught that he missed a golden opportunity to speak in privacy with a wise and holy man, the merchant pushed his way through the crowd to find the old man. When he reached the rabbi, he begged his forgiveness and requested his blessing.

The old rabbi looked at him and replied, "I cannot forgive you. To receive forgiveness you must go out and beg it from every poor old man in the world."

Dates & Places Used:

182 TOPIC: Compassion

They Are Not Listening

An old Portuguese story depicts a young Christian lad who is forced to beg on the streets of his village. One day the beggar boy is scorned and teased by a wealthy atheist's son. "If God really loves you, why doesn't he take better care of you? Why doesn't he tell someone to send you a pair of shoes?"

Sadly the lad replies, "I think God does tell people, but they aren't listening."

Dates & Places Used:

183 TOPIC: Competition

Bad Bids

A man bought a parrot at an auction after some heavy bidding. "I hope this bird talks," he told the auctioneer.

"Talk?" the auctioneer replied. "Who do you think has been bidding against you for the past ten minutes?"

Dates & Places Used:

184 TOPIC: Completion

Cut It Half in Two

Several years ago there was a woman who moved from northern Michigan to Arkansas. During the move, she was helping to supervise some of the construction on their new home.

When construction was nearly complete, one of the carpenters was helping to do the final cleanup of the work site. There was a twelve-foot 2-by-4 left over that would be hard to store at that length, so he asked her, "Would you like for me to cut that 2-by-4 half in two?"

Without much pause she responded, "No, just go ahead and cut it all the way."

Dates & Places Used:

185

TOPIC: Compromise

Whose Money?

The preacher was taking a special offering. Suddenly the town saloon owner jumped up and said, "I'll give five thousand dollars for the building fund!"

The preacher was in a catch-22 and responded, "Thank you, but as badly as we need the money, I just can't accept such money."

Then from the back of the church came this loud voice, "Take it, Reverend–that's our money, anyhow."

Dates & Places Used:

186

TOPIC: Compromise

Golf Settlement

Man hit with a golf ball: "I'll sue you for five thousand dollars!"
Other golfer: "I said 'fore'!"
Injured man: "I'll take it!"

Dates & Places Used:

187

TOPIC: Compromise

Cannibal Compromise

Compromising with this Congress is like paying the cannibals to eat you last.

Dates & Places Used:

TOPIC: Compromise

Compromise with a Bear

A Russian parable tells of a hunter who raised his rifle, or so the story goes, and took careful aim at a large black bear. When he was about to pull the trigger, the bear spoke in a soft, soothing voice, "Isn't it better to talk than to shoot? What do you want? Let us try to negotiate this matter."

Lowering his rifle, the hunter replied, "I want a fur coat."

"Good," said the bear, "that is a negotiable question. I only want a full stomach, so let us negotiate a compromise."

They sat down to negotiate, and after a time, the bear walked away alone. The negotiations had been successful. The bear had a full stomach, and the hunter had his fur coat.

Compromise can be such a dirty word. Oh, I know that it has some merit, but to be honest, I don't like it. I much prefer black or white. Gray is simply a recipe for "chicken" soup.

Dates & Places Used:

189

TOPIC: Computers

Wrong Mouse

The director of an office didn't know anything about computers. When a worker casually mentioned that there was a need to switch ports for the mouse, she screamed, "Mice! We have mice in the office?"

Dates & Places Used:

190

TOPIC: Computers

Computer Intelligence

Computers are not intelligent. They only think they are.

Dates & Places Used:

191

TOPIC: Computers

Computer God

A theologian asked the most powerful supercomputer, "Is there a God?" The computer said it lacked the processing power to know. It asked to be connected to all the other supercomputers in the world.

Still, it was not enough power. So the computer was hooked up to all the mainframes in the world, and then all the minicomputers, and then all the personal computers. And eventually it was connected to all the computers in cars, microwaves, VCRs, digital watches, and so on. The theologian asked for the final time, "Is there a God?"

And the computer replied: "There is now!"

Dates & Places Used:

192

TOPIC: Confession

Nuns' Confessions

A Roman Catholic priest described the hearing of the confessions of nuns as "like being stoned to death with popcorn."

Dates & Places Used:

193

TOPIC: Confidence

Blind Confidence

Confidence is simply the inner feeling you have before you really understand the problem.

Dates & Places Used:

194

TOPIC: Confidence

A Self-Assured Texan

A Texas oilman died and went to heaven. After a few days, his bragging was getting on St. Peter's nerves. No matter what part of paradise he was shown, the oilman claimed it failed to measure up to Texas. Finally St. Peter took him to the edge of heaven so he could look straight down into hell. "Have you got anything like that in Texas?" he asked.

"No," the oilman replied. "But I know some ol' boys down in Houston who can put it out."

Dates & Places Used:

195 TOPIC: Conscience

Conscience Stops Enjoyment

Your conscience may not keep you from doing wrong, but it sure keeps you from enjoying it.

Dates & Places Used:

196 TOPIC: Conscience

Fair Warning for Hunters

I was reading that on opening day of hunting season in one state, game wardens put up a sign on a certain highway that read as follows: "Check Station 1,000 yards ahead." At 500 yards, there was a convenient side road.

Lawful hunters went straight ahead. Over-limit and doubtful hunters ducked down the side road. The check station? It was 500 yards down the side road.

An uneasy conscience can get you into trouble!

Dates & Places Used:

197 TOPIC: Conscience

Conscience or Consciousness

Consciousness is when I am aware of something;
Conscience is when I wish I wasn't.

Dates & Places Used:

198

Careless Credit Card

Cindy Penka of Hauppauge, New Yor, had her credit card stolen. She called her husband Thomas who was ten miles away at work to tell him about her loss. The Associated Press reported that while they were talking, the two credit card thieves walked into Thomas Penka's electronics store to use their newly acquired credit card.

The clerk recognized the name on the credit card and motioned to Thomas while he was on the phone with his wife. Thomas called the police who came and arrested the men with charges of grand larceny, attempted grand larceny, and forgery.

Sometimes it takes a long time for your sins to find you out, sometimes it does not take long at all.

Dates & Places Used:

199

Justice Bribed *or* Unwise Choice

A man on trial for murder bribed a member of the jury to hold out for a lesser verdict of manslaughter. After debating several days, the jury finally brought in the verdict, "Guilty of manslaughter."

Sometime later the murderer asked the man if it had been hard to influence the others. "Yes," said the man, "I had a lot of trouble. All of them wanted to vote not guilty."

Dates & Places Used:

200

Can of Worms

Don't open up a can of worms without knowing how to get the worms back inside.

Dates & Places Used:

201

TOPIC: Consistency

A Tougher Sermon

If you think practicing what you preach is hard, try preaching what you practice.

Dates & Places Used:

202

TOPIC: Conversation

Weather Communication

Don't knock the weather. If it didn't change once in a while, nine out of ten people couldn't start a conversation.

Dates & Places Used:

203

TOPIC: Convictions

Standing Up on the Inside

A father took his boy into a toy shop. The boy got away from his dad and found a statue of a man made of balloons. The boy looked at it for a minute, and then he drew back his fist and hit the balloon man just as hard as he could. The man fell over and then popped right back up.

The confused boy backed off and looked at him again and then backed up and hit him again as hard as he could. Again the man fell over, and again he popped right back up.

The boy's father walked around the corner and saw his son hit that balloon man. The father asked his son, "Why do you think he comes back up when you hit him and knock him down?"

The boy thought for a minute and said, "I don't know; I guess it's because he's standing up on the inside."

Dates & Places Used:

204

TOPIC: Cooking

Burnt Offerings

"My wife treats me like a god; she keeps giving me burnt offerings."
Dates & Places Used:

205

TOPIC: Cooking

Defrosting 101

My wife went to cooking school; she majored in defrosting. She has the best meals you ever thaw.
Dates & Places Used:

206

TOPIC: Cooking

Just Like Mom Made It

The young bride just could not live up to the standards set by her husband's mother. She tried her best to cook like his mother, and he would continually coach her with suggestions. Her constant failures brought her great discouragement. One morning she was so depressed she just stayed in bed. Her depression lasted throughout the day.

She finally dragged herself from bed, draped some clothes over herself and went to the kitchen. She reached into the cupboard and pulled out a can of stew. She dumped it into the pot and warmed it in time for her husband to have his supper. In utter defeat she dished the stew from the pan to her husband's bowl. Her husband took one bite and praised her, "Finally!!! This is it!!! It is just like my mother used to make it!!!"
Dates & Places Used:

207

TOPIC: Cooperation

Movers and Shakers

Jumbo the elephant and Flick the flea were longtime friends. They often walked and chatted together. One day they were walking along a backcountry road when they came to a flimsy wooden bridge swaying and creaking under the weight of the elephant. When they got across, the flea asked his big friend, "Did you notice how we shook that bridge?"

Dates & Places Used:

208

TOPIC: Cooperation

Getting Along

The only way to get along with some people,
is to get along without them.

Dates & Places Used:

209

TOPIC: Corruption

Thousand-Dollar Cigar

The contractor walked confidently into the office of the state highway commissioner. With one word from the commissioner, the multimillion-dolar contract was his. He shook the commissioner's hand and placed a thousand-dollar bill on his desk.

"Would you like to celebrate with a cigar?" the commissioner asked.

"I would love to!" the contractor answered as he took the cigar, sniffed it, and stuck it into his mouth.

The commissioner took a lighter from his desk, ignited the thousand-dollar bill, and then extended the burning bill to light the contractor's cigar. Then he sat back in his chair and lit his own cigar with what remained of the now-worthless currency. Themen sat back and smoked without a word as they watched the fading embers in the ashtray. The contractor then stood up and left the office—without a contract. The meeting was over.

Dates & Places Used:

210

The Christmas Vampire

The world has claimed our holidays for its own, secularizing them by removing their spiritual foundations. I have felt for some time that the church needs to reclaim the true meaning of the holidays. My concerns were reinforced last year by my three-year-old daughter, Betsy. At the end of October she went trick-or-treating for the very first time. My wife had worked hard sewing a cute ladybug costume Betsy had picked out of a pattern book.

As the holiday approached, however, Betsy decided she would rather be a vampire. Her mother and I bargained with her, and she finally agreed to be a ladybug this year and a vampire next Halloween.

A few weeks after Halloween, the Sunday school class began rehearsing for the annual Christmas pageant. Betsy's teacher told her class that all the boys would be Christmas shepherds, and all the girls would be Christmas angels in the pageant. The teacher was perplexed when Betsy burst into tears and ran from the room searching for her father. When she found me, she sniffled through her tears, "My teacher says I'm going to be a Christmas angel in the pageant."

I asked what was wrong with an angel. She reminded me, "I don't want to be a Christmas angel, Daddy! I want to be a Christmas vampire!"

Dates & Places Used:

211

The Bigger Team

Legend has it that Knute Rockne was about to face the football team of USC—the University of Southern California—and knowing that was a far superior team, wondered if there was any way he could defeat them. Then he hit on this idea.

He scoured the city of South Bend, Indiana, for about a hundred of the biggest men he could find. When he had about a hundred men, each at least six-foot-five and weighing in at three hundred pounds or more, he put them all in Notre Dame uniforms. With the shoulder pads and the helmets, they looked even bigger.

Then, when it was time for the game to begin, he sent these men out of the locker room first. As the USC team watched, they just kept coming, and coming, and coming until these hundred men were all the USC team saw. The USC coach kept telling his team, "They can only field eleven men at a time." But the damage was done.

None of these men ever played one minute of the game. But USC had become so intimidated at the sight of them that they were unable to function, and Notre Dame won the game.

Kind of reminds us of the twelve spies and Israel as they lost out on "winning" the Promised Land even though they never engaged a single one of the "giants" in battle. How sad it is when we allow ourselves to see the enemy and lose sight of God.

Dates & Places Used:

212 TOPIC: Courage

Fear Conquered

Courage is fear that has been conquered by love.

Dates & Places Used:

213 TOPIC: Creation

Science and Milk

Science continues to do amazing things, but sitting under a tree, looking at cows in the meadow on a summer's day, one has to remember that the greatest scientists in the world have not yet figured out how to make grass into milk.

Dates & Places Used:

214

Creative Solution

The Sunday school teacher had just read the story of how God created man. She asked the class if they had any questions.

One of the little boys raised his hand and said, "My dad says we come from monkeys."

Sweetly the teacher replied, "Bobby, let's talk about your family problems after class."

Dates & Places Used:

215

Too Many Creators

Those who are amazed that God could create the earth in six days seem to have forgotten that he did not have theologians, politicians, and lawyers around to complicate the process.

Dates & Places Used:

216

First Jokes

Whatever problems Adam may have had in days of yore, when he cracked a joke, no one said, "I've heard that one before."

Dates & Places Used:

217

How Not to Find God

An astronomer was lecturing a group in France, and declared, "I have swept the universe with my telescope, and I find no God."

A musician appropriately rebuked the astronomer: "Your statement, sir, is as unreasonable as it is for me to say that I have taken my violin apart, have carefully examined each part with a microscope, and have found no music."

Dates & Places Used:

218

TOPIC: Creativity

Creative Distance

The songwriter Doc Palmas explaining his understanding of creativity in an interview on the National Public Radio program "All Things Considered":

You have to find the shortest distance between your insides and a pencil!

Dates & Places Used:

219

TOPIC: Criticism

A Lesson on Tact

A husband and wife were leaving the office of a marriage counselor. The husband turned to the wife as they walked to the car: "Well, did what the counselor say about tact and consideration finally get through your thick skull?"

Dates & Places Used:

220

TOPIC: Criticism

Who's Hard of Hearing?

A man was perplexed by his wife's refusal to admit her hearing problem. Speaking with his doctor one day, he exclaimed, "How can I get my wife to admit that she is hard of hearing?"

"I'll tell you what you need to do," his doctor replied. "When you arrive home this evening, peek your head through the door and ask, 'Honey, what's for dinner tonight?' If she doesn't answer, go into the living room and say, 'Honey, what's for dinner?' If she still does not answer, walk into the kitchen and ask, 'Honey, what's for dinner?' If she still does not hear you, then walk right up behind her and speak directly in her ear: 'Honey, what's for dinner?' Then you will be able to convince her of her need for a hearing exam."

"Great!" the man responded. "I think it will work!"

That evening the man arrived home from work. Just as he had been instructed, he opened the front door and called out: "Honey, what's for dinner tonight?" He listened carefully, but there was no reply. He walked into the living room and repeated, "Honey, what's for dinner?" He still received no answer. He then walked into the kitchen and asked, "Honey, what's for dinner?" Still there was no answer. The man walked right up behind his wife and spoke directly into her ear: "Honey, what's for dinner?"

At this the wife turned around and resolutely replied: "For the fourth time, I said we are having spaghetti!"

Dates & Places Used:

221

TOPIC: Criticism

Many Quarterbacks

At football games, other players are far outnumbered by quarterbacks: two on the field, four on the bench, and hundreds in the stands.

Dates & Places Used:

222

TOPIC: Criticism

Avoiding Criticism

It's easy to avoid criticism. All you have to do is say nothing, do nothing, and be nothing.

Dates & Places Used:

223

TOPIC: Criticism

Church Danger

A bishop was invited to dinner. During the meal he was astonished to hear the young daughter of the house state that a person must be very brave to go to church these days. "Why do you say that?" asked the bishop.

"Because," said the child, "I heard Papa tell Mama last Sunday that there was a big shot in the pulpit, the canon was in the vestry, the choir murdered the anthem, and the organist drowned everybody!"

Dates & Places Used:

224

TOPIC: Critics

Critical Exercise

The only exercise some folks get nowadays is jumping to conclusions, running down their friends, sidestepping responsibility, and pushing their luck.

Dates & Places Used:

225

TOPIC: Cultures

Clothes Don't Make the Kid

An American missionary and his family were returning from West Africa. So the children would not look conspicuous in homemade clothes, their mother outfitted them in the latest from a mail-order catalog.

As the family walked along a street in Paris, a stopover on their homeward journey, the parents realized everyone was staring at them. Turning around, they discovered the two little ones who tagged behind were casually walking along–carrying their suitcases on their heads!

Dates & Places Used:

226

A Cure for Splitting Headaches

Another new mixture: a combination of aspirin and glue, for people with splitting headaches.

Dates & Places Used:

227

The Curious Cat and Kid

Mom told her son, "Stop asking so many questions! Don't you know that curiosity killed the cat?"

Her son quickly responded, "What did the cat want to know?"

Dates & Places Used:

228

Hitting Bottom Is a Killer

Halfway down a steep, winding hill in the north of England a man stopped his car to ask a woman at her gate if the hill was dangerous. "Not 'ere it isn't," she said. "It's down at the bottom where they all kills themselves."

Dates & Places Used:

229

Rather Kiss Than Smoke

I kissed my first woman and smoked my first cigarette on the same day. I have never had time for tobacco since.

Dates & Places Used:

230

Free Girl Is Expensive

Nothing can be more expensive than a girl who happens to be free for the evening.

Dates & Places Used:

231

TOPIC: Death

Warm Feet

A man was gravely ill and was visited by a relative who looked at a very still body covered by a sheet. Assuming the worst, the relative asked, "Is he dead?"

The nurse who had been straightening the bed said, "No, his feet are warm. You don't die with warm feet."

Immediately there came a voice from beneath the sheets that said, "Joan of Arc did." And then he died.

Dates & Places Used:

232

TOPIC: Death

Bend Over and Die

The Irish Presbyterian Amy Carmichael's hope of heaven brightened during her long years as a semi-invalid until her death in 1951. A woman visited Amy and, during the course of the conversation, told Amy of how her doctor had warned her, "Don't even bend over suddenly, or you might die on the spot."

Amy gave a tart and twinkling reply: "However do you resist the temptation?"

Dates & Places Used:

233

TOPIC: Debt

Financial Plastic Surgery

One of the most needed types of surgery and the least practiced by the modern family is plastic surgery. The symptoms are too many possessions and not enough money to pay for them. The cure is plastic surgery—cut up the credit cards.

Dates & Places Used:

234

TOPIC: Deception

Begging Blind

A man on crutches hobbled over to a passerby and asked for money. The pedestrian handed him a dollar bill with the remark, "Cheer up, it would be much worse if you were blind."

"I know," he responded. "When I was blind, I kept getting phony money."

Dates & Places Used:

235

TOPIC: Deception

Our Shoes Will Find Us Out

Suspected drug dealer Alfred Acree thought he could escape the sheriff's deputies by running into a wooded area at night. But thanks to Alfred, the deputies had no difficulty at all tracking him.

He had a built-in tracking device. He was wearing a brand-new pair of L.A. Gear New Light tennis shoes. These shoes featured battery-operated lights that flashed every time the heel was depressed. "Every time he took a step, we knew exactly where he was," said investigator Anthony Anderson for the Charles City, Virginia, County Sheriff's Department.

We may think we can escape the consequences of our sins, but like the flashing shoes, our sins will eventually reveal us.

Dates & Places Used:

236

TOPIC: Deception

Listening to a Snake

One warm spring day we were driving on a road so thick with trees that we could not see the sun. Our four-year-old grandson Luke was with us, and he said, "There are so many trees here that I think I am in Eden."

My ears perked up and I said, "Eden?"

"Yes," Luke answered. "Don't you know about Eden?"

I just said, "Why don't you tell me about it."

So Luke did. "Well, there were lots of trees in the Garden of Eden, and in the middle of the garden was a fruit tree. God told Adam and Eve not to pick the fruit from that tree. But then a snake came along, and the snake said, 'It's okay, you can eat fruit from that tree.' And they did."

Then Luke said, "I would never listen to a snake. I would listen to God. Grandma, why would anyone listen to a snake?"

I never told Luke that I had ignored God many times and listened to a snake.

Dates & Places Used:

237

TOPIC: Decisions

Pick It Up Yourself

Murphy's Law reads, "If anything can go wrong, it will." But someone said, "Murphy was an optimist."

In 1916, Georgia Tech University in Atlanta played a football game against Cumberland University, a tiny law school. The Tech team was a mighty football powerhouse and rolled over

Cumberland by a score of 222 to 0. Tech pretty much beat the Cumberland players to a pulp, too. Toward the end of the game, Cumberland quarterback Ed Edwards fumbled a snap from center. As the Tech linemen charged into his backfield, Edwards yelled to his backs, "Pick it up! Pick it up!"

Edward's fullback, seeing the monsters rush in who had battered him all day, yelled back, "Pick it up yourself. You dropped it!"

Dates & Places Used:

238 TOPIC: Decisions
Monday Morning Coaches

A good example of not second-guessing your decisions comes from legendary football coach Paul "Bear" Bryant. After a tough loss on Saturday, Coach Bryant went to the barber shop for a haircut on Monday morning. After a few moments of silence, the barber said with some disgust, "Coach, I don't believe I would have put in that young quarterback just because the starter was not doing well. The turnovers of the young guy cost us the game."

Coach Bryant nodded and said, "Well, you know, if I'd had until Monday to decide, I don't think I would have either."

Dates & Places Used:

239 TOPIC: Decisions
Final Maybe

A sign seen on a businessman's desk: "MY DECISION IS MAYBE ... AND THAT'S FINAL!"

Dates & Places Used:

240 TOPIC: Defeat
Victory or Defeat

There are many victories worse than a defeat.

Dates & Places Used:

241

Christian Clichés

An *Eternity Magazine* article entitled "Bring on the Bromide Seltzer" poked a little fun at some of the Christian expressions commonly used in a 1984 Charles Swindoll tape. Here are a few of the clichés regarding money:

Share—Christians don't tell, they share. They don't criticize, they don't give, they don't testify, they don't talk, they share.

Opportunity to have a part—what radio preachers say when they want you to give money.

As the Lord leads—cliché for when your guilt becomes unbearable.

Further the ministry—another way of saying let's keep this baby afloat.

Love offering—opposite of a hate offering.

Dates & Places Used:

242

Reality of Words

It's an age of paradox when we have mobile homes that don't move, sports clothes for work, junk food that costs more than the real food, and sweatshirts to loaf in.

Dates & Places Used:

243

The Football Service

Quarterback Sneak: Church members who quietly exit following the Lord's Supper, a quarter of the way through the service, or near the last quarter of the service.

Draft Choice: Selection of a seat near the door.

Draw Play: What too many children and some adults do with the attendance cards and bulletins.

Halftime: Between Bible school and worship.

Benchwarmer: Those whose only participation is their attendance on Sunday morning.

Fumble: Dropping a songbook, singing the wrong verse, and general inattention during the service.

Backfield in Motion: Making two or three trips out of the worship service. (Public schools don't allow this.)

Stay in the Pocket: What happens to a lot of money that should go toward the Lord's work.

Two-Minute Warning: When the preacher begins extending the invitation, giving everyone time to shuffle books and gather belongings.

Sudden Death: The preacher goes overtime.

Blitz: The stampede for the doors after the service.

Halfback Option: When fifty percent of the congregation does not return Sunday evening.

Dates & Places Used:

244

TOPIC: Demons

The Origin of Deviled Ham

Religion teacher: "This Bible story tells how Jesus cast out demons from a possessed man and sent them into a herd of pigs."

Student: "Is that how we got deviled ham?"

Dates & Places Used:

245

TOPIC: Desire

Wrong Wish List

Little Johnny's parents were puzzled when he announced that he no longer wanted the list of toys he had included on his Christmas gift list. "Didn't you write Santa Claus asking for them?" his mother asked.

Little Johnny answered, "Yes, but I looked in the closet the other day, and I've already got them!"

Dates & Places Used:

246

Wrong Rut—Right Time

A frog was caught in a deep rut, so the fable goes. In spite of the help of his friends, he couldn't get out. They finally left him there in despair. The next day one of his friends saw him hopping about outside the rut as chipper as could be.

"What are you doing here?" the friend asked. "I thought you couldn't get out."

"I couldn't," the frog replied, "but a big truck came down the road and I had to get out."

Some of us are living beneath our capabilities. Because we cannot do great things, we are inclined not to do anything. Every Christian has at least one gift or capacity with which he can glorify God. Whatever it is, he should use it with all his heart.

Dates & Places Used:

247

TOPIC: Determination

A Ten-Year Schedule

A young woman made an appointment for an interview with a prestigious corporation. She asked if she could get into their well-respected training program. The very busy personnel manager, besieged by applications, said, "Impossible now. Come back in about ten years."

The applicant responded, "Would morning or afternoon be better?"

Dates & Places Used:

248

TOPIC: Determination

Not Learning to Quit

Somewhere I read the story of a young boy trying to learn to ice-skate. He had fallen so many times that his face was cut, and the blood and tears ran together.

Someone, out of sympathy, skated over to the boy, picked him up, and said, "Son, why don't you quit? You are going to kill yourself!"

The boy brushed the tears from his eyes and said, "I didn't buy these skates to learn how to quit; I bought them to learn how to skate."

Dates & Places Used:

249 TOPIC: Determination

I'll Die Trying

Here's some more bumper-sticker wisdom:
"I intend to live forever, or die trying!"

Dates & Places Used:

250 TOPIC: Diets

Dinners for Two

Doctor to overweight patient: "You'll have to give up those intimate little dinners for two unless you have another person with you."

Dates & Places Used:

251 TOPIC: Diets

Garlic Sandwich

Have you heard about the new garlic sandwich diet?
GARLIC sandwiches?
Yeah. You don't lose any weight, but you look a little smaller from a distance.

Dates & Places Used:

252

TOPIC: Diets

Methuselah's Food

Methuselah ate what he found on his plate,
and never, as people do now,
did he note the amount of the caloric count;
he ate it because it was chow.

He wasn't disturbed as at dinner he sat,
consuming a roast or a pie,
to think it was lacking in granular fat,
or a couple of vitamins shy.

He cheerfully chewed every species of food,
untroubled by worries or fears,
lest his health might be hurt by some fancy dessert,
and he lived over nine hundred years.

Dates & Places Used:

253

TOPIC: Differences

Mice and Elephants

Question: How are mice and elephants alike?
Answer: They are both extremely large animals, except for
one of them.

Dates & Places Used:

254

TOPIC: Diplomacy

The Art of Diplomacy

The art of diplomacy is saying, "Nice doggie, nice doggie,"
until you can find a stick.

Dates & Places Used:

TOPIC: Diplomacy

Diplomacy and Tact

Diplomacy gets you out of what tact would have kept you out of.
Dates & Places Used:

TOPIC: Direction

Just Checking

A man who had regularly prayed for many years began to wonder if God heard his prayers at all. During one of his routine times of prayer, he started this doubting pattern once again.

He stopped praying and thought for a moment. "Enough of this," he said. He then lifted his eyes toward heaven and yelled, "Hey up there, can you hear me?"

There was no response.

He continued, "Hey, God, if you can really hear me, tell me what you want me to do with my life."

A voice from above thundered a reply, "I WANT YOU TO HELP THE NEEDY AND GIVE YOUR LIFE FOR THE CAUSE OF PEACE!"

Faced with more of a challenge than the man wanted, he answered, "Actually, God, I was just checking to see if you were there."

The voice from above now answered with disappointment: "THAT'S ALRIGHT; I WAS ONLY CHECKING TO SEE IF *YOU* WERE THERE."
Dates & Places Used:

TOPIC: Directions

Disneyland Left

A family left on vacation headed for Disneyland. Three days later they returned home. Their curious neighbors immediately questioned them, "We thought you went to Disneyland. Why have you returned so soon?"

The weary travelers sadly reported, "As we approached Disneyland, we saw a sign that said: 'DISNEYLAND LEFT.' We were not sure where it had gone, but figured it was time to come home."

Dates & Places Used:

258 TOPIC: Disappointments

Conquered by Chicago

Former heavyweight boxer James "Quick" Tillis was a cowboy from Oklahoma who fought out of Chicago in the early 1980s. Years later, he still remembers his first day in the Windy City after his arrival from Tulsa.

"I got off the bus with two cardboard suitcases under my arms in downtown Chicago and stopped in front of the Sears Tower. I put my suitcases down and I looked up at the Tower and I said to myself, 'I'm going to conquer Chicago.'

"When I looked down, the suitcases were gone."

Dates & Places Used:

259 TOPIC: Discipline

Black Eye Prognosis

A doctor was examining an eyebrow laceration on a very active three-year-old. Two nurses and an orderly were required to restrain the screaming child. Noting the incipient swelling and discoloration, the doctor said to the mother, "Billy will be lucky if he comes through this without getting a black eye."

"Do what you have to, Doctor," she replied. "He's a terror at home too!"

Dates & Places Used:

260

Get the Stink Out

Disciplining children is a lot like taking out the garbage: If you don't do it, you have no right to complain later if something smells.
Dates & Places Used:

261

How Many Times

The little girl sat in her room after her mother had scolded her. Emotionally wounded, she had not yet been broken. The more she thought about the scolding, the madder she got. She finally stormed to her door and screamed out to her mother, "Alright, Mom, I give up! How many times **did you tell me** not to do it!?!"
Dates & Places Used:

262

Need New Mommy

"Daddy, I need a new mommy."
"Why do you need a new mommy?"
"Because Mommy spanks me."
"Why does Mommy spank you?"
"Because I'm naughty."
Dates & Places Used:

263

Well-Behaved Children

A condo committee was screening a couple interested in renting an apartment. "What kind of work do you do?" they asked.
"My husband is an engineer and I'm a schoolteacher."
"Any children?"

The applicant replied, "Two, one is seven, and the other is eight."

"Animals?"

"Oh, no!" she replied. "They're very well behaved."

Dates & Places Used:

264

TOPIC: Discovery

The Greater Discovery

We know about George Washington Carver and all he did for the peanut, but we have no idea who first put jelly with the peanut butter to make the perfect sandwich.

Dates & Places Used:

265

TOPIC: Discovery

Prince or Daddy

Watching a particular romantic ending to a Disney animated video, my five-year-old sighed, "I hope I meet my prince someday."

"Of course you will," I reassured her. "You know, I met my prince the day I met your daddy."

Puzzled, she turned to me. "Who was he?" she asked.

Dates & Places Used:

266

TOPIC: Discretion

Mistaken Genders

The vicar, awarding prizes at the local dog show, was scandalized by costumes worn by some members of the younger fair sex. "Look at that youngster," said he, "the one with the cropped hair, the cigarette, and breeches, holding two pops. Is it a boy or girl?"

"A girl," said his companion. "She's my daughter."

"My dear sir!" The vicar was flustered. "Do forgive me. I would never have been so outspoken had I known you were her father."

"I'm not," said the other. "I'm her mother."

Dates & Places Used:

267   TOPIC: Division

Left Foot Baptist Church

William P. Barker tells about a small town in Tennessee that had a place of worship with a sign in front that read: "LEFT FOOT BAPTIST CHURCH." A student had passed by it many times, chuckled to himself, and wondered about the meaning of the name of the church. Finally, one day, waiting for his bus, the student asked somebody in the town about the significance of the rather unusual name for the church.

It seems that a number of years ago, there had been a split in the local congregation, which practiced foot-washing. An argument broke out over which foot should be washed first. And the group insisting on the left foot taking precedence finally withdrew and split off to organize its own church and named its congregation accordingly! "LEFT FOOT BAPTIST CHURCH."

A division like that might be funny if it weren't so tragic.

Dates & Places Used:

268   TOPIC: Divorce

Alimony Can Be Avoided

While teaching a Sunday school class of single adults, one young man who was recently divorced complained about his alimony payments. A young woman in the class quickly responded, "I know a legal way out of paying alimony."

"What's that?" he asked.

With a slight grin she said, "Stay single or stay married!"

Dates & Places Used:

TOPIC: Doctors

Plumbers and Doctors

The brain surgeon returned from a European vacation to discover that his basement was filled with water–and rising. He called a plumber who arrived in a new Mercedes wearing an elegant business suit. The plumber opened the rear trunk, and donned a wet suit, oxygen tanks, diving mask, and flippers.

Moments later, he sloshed up from the basement. "Just a small problem. Someone left a faucet running in the laundry tub. I turned it off and opened the plug. Your basement should drain in less than half an hour."

"What's your fee?" asked the relieved brain surgeon.

"One thousand dollars," answered the plumber.

The surgeon was staggered. "One thousand dollars to turn off a faucet? I don't get that much for a series of consultations leading to major brain surgery."

"I know," answered the plumber. "I was once a brain surgeon myself."

Dates & Places Used:

270

TOPIC: Doctors

Both Returned

The physician phoned one of his delinquent patients. "Mrs. Taylor," he said, "I'm sorry to tell you this, but your check just came back."

"So did my arthritis," she replied. And hung up.

Dates & Places Used:

271

TOPIC: Doctors

New Lease on Life

Everyone has to learn to make adjustments in life. For example, the doctor who gave his patient just six months to live. When the patient didn't pay his bill, the doctor gave him another six months.

Dates & Places Used:

272

A Lack of Patients

Lawyer: "How do you deal with persons seeking free advice at cocktail parties, Doctor?"

Doctor: "I tell them to undress."

Dates & Places Used:

273

Surgical Powers

Three famous surgeons were bragging about their skills. "A man came to me who had his hand cut off," said one. "Today that man is a concert violinist."

"That's nothing," said another. "A guy came to me who had his legs cut off. I stitched them back on, and today that man is a marathon runner."

"I can top both of you," said the third. "One day I came on the scene of a terrible accident. There was nothing left but a horse's posterior and a pair of glasses. Today that man is seated in the United States Senate."

Dates & Places Used:

274

More Courageous Than Wise

Two little girls are sitting and talking about the first girl's dog. "My father has been training our dog to protect our house from strangers. He's been putting on disguises and getting her to attack him."

The second little girl asks, "Is she learning?"

The first girl answers, "She certainly is ... now every time a stranger comes to the house, she bites Daddy."

Dates & Places Used:

275

TOPIC: Doubt

Doubtful Confidence

An egoist is someone who is never in doubt, but is often in error.

Dates & Places Used:

276

TOPIC: Dreams

Interpreting Dreams

A wife said to her husband over breakfast, "I had a dream last night that you gave me a pearl necklace. What do you suppose that means?"

He answered, "You'll find out tonight."

And sure enough, that evening he gave her a book entitled *Interpreting Dreams*.

Dates & Places Used:

277

TOPIC: Drinking

Bars and Parking Lots

Since it is against the law to drink and drive, why are bars allowed to have parking lots?

Dates & Places Used:

278

TOPIC: Drinking

Communion Shots

A worship committee was recently planning for the changes that would occur when they went to two services on Sunday morning. One of the changes was the need for two Communion services. Some of the committee members were wondering how Communion cups were collected. Each of the members was telling what he knew about the collection of the cups after the service of Communion.

One member provided a novel answer in regard to this issue: "We always take ours home and use them for shot glasses."
Dates & Places Used:

279 TOPIC: Drinking

Drowning Sorrows

People who drink to drown their sorrow should be told that sorrow knows how to swim.
Dates & Places Used:

280 TOPIC: Driving

Just a Head Start

On a crowded street a motorist stopped for a red light and his rear bumper was bashed by the car behind him. He got out, looked for damage, glared at the man driving the other car, got back in his car, and drove off.

At the next light, the same thing happened again. This time the other driver got out and came over to him, holding up his driver's license.

"Look," the victim said, "never mind all that stuff. All I want from you is a five-minute head start."
Dates & Places Used:

281 TOPIC: Driving

Going to School Card

This fact is true,
That a snail goes slow,
But here is what I want
You to know;

Travel safe—make the speed
of a snail your goal,
For I never saw a snail,
'round a telephone pole!
Dates & Places Used:

TOPIC: Easter

Do It Again!

One time a father and his young son went on an overnight camping trip for the first time. While it was still quite dark, the father arose and started a fire. Then he aroused his sleeping son. After protesting a little, the boy got up. He stood near the fire trying to keep warm as they waited, for he knew they had come to witness the sunrise.

Soon it began! The blackness in the east gradually turned to gray, then the gray turned to blue. The image of a lake and shadowy trees began to emerge out of the darkness. The blue turned to a near-white color. Finally pink, violet, and orange hues emerged in the east over the pines! Suddenly the valley was flooded with light. They watched this spectacular display in silent awe.

Finally the boy could stand it no longer. He turned to his father and wistfully said, "Dad, do it again! Do it again!"

Don't you sometimes feel that way about Easter? To be sure it is a once-for-all happening in terms of the victory won in Christ. Yet Easter is needed many, many times in our lives. So we would say with the little boy, "Father, do it again. Do it again."

Dates & Places Used:

TOPIC: Easter

Which King?

Two little boys were sitting in the front row for an Easter pageant at their church. As Jesus was entering Jerusalem, one of the characters announced his entrance by shouting, "The

King is coming!" One of the boys in the front row jumped up in his seat, looked toward the back of the room, and shouted, "So that's Elvis!"
Dates & Places Used:

284 TOPIC: Economists
An Odd Thing About Economists

An economist is one who thinks he knows more about money than the people who actually have it.
Dates & Places Used:

285 TOPIC: Economists
Inconclusive Economists

If all economists were laid end to end, they still would not reach a conclusion.
Dates & Places Used:

286 TOPIC: Economy
The Sound of Money

Long ago money talked–then it whispered–now it's almost silent.
Dates & Places Used:

287 TOPIC: Economy
Jobs Without Work

Millions of Americans are not working ... but fortunately, they've got jobs!
Dates & Places Used:

288

Education Changes

Education takes you from cocksure ignorance to thoughtful uncertainty.

Dates & Places Used:

289

Correct the Problem

"I ain't had no fun all summer," wrote the teacher on the chalkboard. "How do you correct this?" she asked the class.

"Get a boyfriend," one student answered.

Dates & Places Used:

290

Unknown Math

To those who have no experience of guidance, denial will seem easy. But it is perilous to deny anything on that ground alone. One is reminded of the little girl who thought that she had exhausted mathematics when she had learned the twelve times tables. When her grandfather said with a twinkle in his eye, "What's thirteen times thirteen?" she turned on him with undisguised scorn and said, "Don't be silly, Grandpa, there's no such thing."

Dates & Places Used:

291

A Futile Quest to Learn

A father and his small son were out walking one afternoon when the youngster asked how the electricity went through the wires stretched between the telephone poles. "Don't know," said the father. "Never knew much about electricity."

A few blocks farther on the boy asked what caused lightning and thunder. "To tell the truth," said the father, "I never exactly understood that myself."

The boy continued to ask questions throughout the walk, none of which the father could explain. Finally, as they were nearing home, the boy asked, "Pop, I hope you don't mind my asking so many questions...."

"Of course not," replied the father. "How else are you going to learn?"

Dates & Places Used:

292

TOPIC: Education

School Is for Prisoners

One day my four-year-old daughter lined up all of her dolls on the couch in the living room.

"What are you doing?" I asked her.

"I'm playing school," she replied. "I'm the teacher and these are my prisoners."

Dates & Places Used:

293

TOPIC: Education

Educational Prejudices

Education is the process of driving a set of prejudices down your throat.

Dates & Places Used:

294

TOPIC: Egotists

Egotist Tongues

There's one good thing about egotists—they don't talk about other people.

Dates & Places Used:

295

TOPIC: Elections

Who Else?

The candidate had just finished what he felt was a stirring campaign speech. "Now, are there any questions?" he asked confidently.

"Yes," said a voice in the rear. "Who else is running?"

Dates & Places Used:

296

TOPIC: Electronics

Electronic Exceptions

On a recent flight to Washington, D.C., heard over the intercom system:

"Ladies and gentlemen, this is your captain speaking. We'll be reaching our cruising altitude of thirty thousand feet shortly, at which time I will turn off the fasten seat-belt sign. This will also indicate to you that you may turn on any portable electronic devices you may have.

"Please note that this does include any hearing aids or pacemakers you may be wearing. Thank you and enjoy the flight."

Dates & Places Used:

297

TOPIC: Emotions

Trouble with Women

The trouble with some women is that they get all excited about nothing—and then marry him.

Dates & Places Used:

298

Simultaneous Effectiveness

One employer said to his questioning employee: "The raise in salary will become effective just as soon as you do."
Dates & Places Used:

299

Better Than Mother

The boss was firing one of his employees. The irate employee demanded a reason for this harsh action. The boss did not agree with the accusation of being unfair. "I have treated you better than your own mother. She only carried you for nine months. I have been carrying you for two years."
Dates & Places Used:

300

More Power to You

A pastor began visiting a man on death row in a prison. The minister established a good rapport with this inmate and when it came time for the criminal to be executed by the electric chair, the reverend was asked to be there and console the man on the way to his death.

When the day arrived, the pastor went to be with the convict, but was very anxious about what to say. "Good-bye" seemed trite, "See you later" seemed inappropriate, and he became desperate for the right words. Just as they got to the electric chair, he blurted out, "More power to you!!"
Dates & Places Used:

301

TOPIC: Enthusiasm

Fired with Enthusiasm

If you are not fired with enthusiasm, you'll be fired with enthusiasm!

Dates & Places Used:

302

TOPIC: Enthusiasm

All Is Contagious

Enthusiasm is contagious—so is whatever else you may have.

Dates & Places Used:

303

TOPIC: Enthusiasm

Mark Twain's Excitement

Check this one in his lifeworks:
Asked about the reason for his success, Mark Twain replied, "I was born excited."

Dates & Places Used:

304

TOPIC: Errors

Errant Erasers

To err is human, but when the eraser wears out ahead of the pencil, you're overdoing it.

Dates & Places Used:

305

TOPIC: Eternity

Flight Training

A sign seen on a church bulletin board read: "Interested in going to heaven? Apply here for flight training."

Dates & Places Used:

306

TOPIC: Evangelism

Finger of God

An old deacon was leading in prayer using one of his stereotypical phrases, which was "Oh Lord, touch the unsaved with thy finger." As he intoned this phrase in this particular prayer, he stopped short. Other members came to his side and asked if he were ill.

"No," he replied, "but something seemed to say to me, 'Thou art the finger.'"

Dates & Places Used:

307

TOPIC: Evangelism

Woodpecker Evangelism

A woodpecker tapped his beak against the stem of a tree just as lightning struck the tree and destroyed it. He flew away and said, "I didn't know there was so much power in my beak!"

When we bring the gospel, there is a danger that we will think or say, "I have done a good job." Don't be a silly woodpecker. Know where your strength comes from. It is only God's Holy Spirit who can make a message good and fruitful.

Dates & Places Used:

308

TOPIC: Examples

Church Never Helped Dad

A lady says her seven-year-old son balked recently at going to church.

"Daddy doesn't go," the kid said.

"When Daddy was your age, he went every Sunday," the lady said.

"Is that true?" the lad asked his father. His father said it was.

"All right, then I'll go," the boy countered, "but it probably won't do me any good either."

Dates & Places Used:

309

TOPIC: Examples

Kids' Eyes Stay Open

Children may close their ears to advice, but they keep their eyes open to example.

Dates & Places Used:

310

TOPIC: Exceptions

No Exceptions

"I'm very sorry," said the personnel manager, "but if I let you take two hours off for lunch today, I'd have to do the same for every other employee whose wife gave birth to quadruplets."

Dates & Places Used:

311

TOPIC: Excuses

Grandfather Returns

"My boy," asked the boss, "do you believe in life after death?"

"Yes, sir."

"Then that makes everything fine," the employer continued softly. "About an hour after you left to attend your grandfather's funeral, he came in to see you."

Dates & Places Used:

312 TOPIC: Excuses

Stone-Cold Peas

Oh, Mama, please!
Don't make me eat these
Stone-cold peas!
They've grown eyes
And they're lookin' at
me!

I love to eat
Strawberries, oranges,
Broccoli with cheese,
Apples, pears that hang on
trees
Corn on the cob is really a
treat;
But peas on a plate
are not fun
to eat!

I've grown attached to these
peas,

We've both been here so long.
Would setting them free
Be so terribly
wrong?
Just look at them now
So green
And so lowly,
They will just sit here
And wrinkle up slowly.
If you listen carefully
You hear their pleas,
"Peas, oh peas, let us be frees!"

So, Mama,
Things will be just fine
If you don't
make me eat
these friends
of mine!

Dates & Places Used:

313 TOPIC: Excuses

Beyond Excuses

He who is good for making excuses is seldom good for anything else.

Dates & Places Used:

314

Very Newly Married

An older lady was busy at home one day when a knock was heard at the door. Upon opening the door, she was greeted by a five-year-old girl and a four-year-old boy whom she knew lived in the neighborhood.

The little girl stated that she and "her husband" were coming to visit. The lady played along with their little game and invited them in. She took them to the sofa just like they were grown up and asked them if they would like some lemonade and cookies. They said they would. After they had finished the lemonade, the lady asked them if they would like some more.

The little girl said, "No, thank you, we really must be leaving now. My husband has just wet his pants."

Dates & Places Used:

315

Deceptive Driver

Dr. Adrian Rogers after arriving slightly late to a prayer meeting: "I'm sorry I'm late, I had lost track of the time. I'll have you know that even though I was in a hurry to get here, I didn't break any speeding laws ... although I passed a number of people who were!"

Dates & Places Used:

316

Some Famous Last Words

1. I guess we've got enough gas to get to the next exit.
2. The state trooper never patrols this stretch of the interstate.
3. I hope you won't take this the wrong way, sir, but now that I've been here for a full week I've made a list of some things that should be changed.

4. I won't bother to set the alarm because I'm always wide awake by seven.
5. I can pick up this small screwdriver and walk out of the store with it and no one will see me.
6. I am smart enough to get by with my secret sin.

Dates & Places Used:

317

TOPIC: Expectancy

Live Every Day As If It Were the Last

Over Sunday dinner, a family discussed the sermon of the morning, "The Second Coming of Christ." The teenager said that he still had a lot of questions about the Lord's return. The father tried his best to answer him, but after a while he concluded by saying, "We do not have all the answers we might like, but we do have all we need to know. The best preparation is simply to live each day as if it were your last."

"I tried that once," the teenager replied, "and you grounded me for a month!"

Dates & Places Used:

318

TOPIC: Expectations

A Bad Yardstick

If people don't measure up to your standards, perhaps you should check your yardstick.

Dates & Places Used:

319

TOPIC: Expectations

So Much from a Nut

A minister gave an unusual sermon one day, using a peanut to make several important points about the wisdom of God in nature.

One of the members greeted him at the door and said, "Very interesting, Pastor. I never expected to learn so much from a nut."

Dates & Places Used:

320

TOPIC: Expediency

Just Jump the Fence

Colorado golfer Rick Riley was befriended by President Clinton who paired up with him for some golf. This gave Mr. Riley certain access privileges to the White House. When interviewed by KUSA television station on May 9, 1995, he told about his recent visit to the White House. The Secret Service checked his car twice, and when he got to the front door of the White House, he was checked one more time.

He was amused by this careful scrutiny and suggested, "Fellows, you didn't have to go to all this trouble–I could have just jumped the fence!"

They were not amused.

Dates & Places Used:

321

TOPIC: Experience

Carrying Cats

A man who carries a cat by the tail learns something he can learn in no other way.

Dates & Places Used:

322

TOPIC: Experience

Tests and Lessons in Life

Experience is a hard teacher; she gives the test first, and then the lesson.

Dates & Places Used:

323

Expensive Experience

*It seems like experience would be a better teacher
if it did not charge so much for tuition.*
Dates & Places Used:

324

Developing Experience

Experience is not what happens to a man. It's what a man
does with what happens to him.

Aldous Huxley, British author

Dates & Places Used:

325

Experience and Mistakes

Experience is what enables you to recognize a mistake when
you see it again.
Dates & Places Used:

326

School Never Ends

Just when you think you have graduated from the school of
experience, along comes a whole new course.
Dates & Places Used:

TOPIC: Experts

Educational Limits

There is nothing so stupid as an educated man, if you get off the thing that he was educated in.
Dates & Places Used:

TOPIC: Experts

Two Rules for Harvard's Success

A former treasurer of Harvard once told me that he had two golden rules for managing the Harvard portfolio:
1. Never consult the economics department.
2. Never consult the business school.
Dates & Places Used:

329

TOPIC: Extremes

Extreme Logic

Extremes are usually the antitheses of whatever they are the extremes of.
Dates & Places Used:

TOPIC: Failure

Educational Failure

There is no better education than one's own failures.
There is a true story about a project manager at IBM who lost the company ten million dollars. Dejectedly, he walked into the

president's office and said, "I'm sorry. I'm sure you'll want my resignation. I'll be gone by the end of the day."

The president's response showed his understanding of the value of failure. He said, "Are you kidding? We've just invested ten million dollars in your education. We're not about to let you go. Now get back to work."

Dates & Places Used:

331

TOPIC: Failure

Bungled Burglary

Carlos Carrasco, twenty-four, was sentenced to ten year's probation in San Antonio for a bungled burglary of a liquor store. According to records, Carrasco cut his hand badly when he broke through the store's roof; he tried to throw a bottle of whiskey out through the hole he had created but missed, causing the bottle to fall back to the floor, shatter, and set off a burglar alarm; he fell on the broken bottle, cutting himself again; he left his wallet in the store; once on the roof for his getaway, he fell off; and he left a trail of blood from the store to his home down the street.

Dates & Places Used:

332

TOPIC: Failure

Reasons for Departure

John Ralston, former coach of the Denver Broncos, explaining his departure: "I left because of illness and fatigue. The fans were sick and tired of me."

Dates & Places Used:

333

TOPIC: Failure

When It's Time for a Soaking

I hate to fail, but when it's time to take a bath, I get in the tub.

Dates & Places Used:

334

TOPIC: Faith

Give the Ball to Larry

Whether you are a basketball fan or not, you are probably familiar with the name Larry Bird–the former basketball great of the Boston Celtics.

During a retirement party for Larry Bird in Boston Garden, former Celtics coach K. C. Jones told of diagramming a play on the sidelines, only to have Bird dismiss it, saying: "Get the ball to me and get everyone out of my way."

Jones responded, "I'm the coach, and I will call the plays." Then Jones turned to the other players and said, "Get the ball to Larry, and get out of his way."

That's the church's message–Give the ball to Jesus, put your life in his hands, and get out of the way.

Dates & Places Used:

335

TOPIC: Fame

Self-Made the Easy Way

If you want to write your own ticket,
then print it yourself.
If you want to make a name for yourself,
then change the one you have.
If you want a place in the sun,
then don't forget your sunscreen.
Dates & Places Used:

336

TOPIC: Fame

Historical All-Stars

An American history instructor asked his class for a list of the eleven greatest Americans. As the students wrote, the professor strolled around the room. Finally, he asked one student if he had finished his list.

"Not yet," said the student. "I can't decide on a fullback."

Dates & Places Used:

337

TOPIC: Family

Input or Output

The often asked questions that preoccupy the time of reflective parents are questions like this: Do we hear too well or are our children just too noisy?

Dates & Places Used:

338

TOPIC: Family

The Cost of Kids

A young girl was once asked how many children there were in her family. She answered that there were seven children in her family. The inquirer was taken aback by such a high number of siblings in one family and suggested that seven children must cost a lot of money. The girl answered, "Oh no, we don't buy them, we just raise them."

Dates & Places Used:

339

TOPIC: Farmers

A Great Place for Eggs

A little boy was visiting friends who lived in the country. This was his first visit out of the city, and he was fascinated with how different life was on the farm. When it was time to gather eggs, the farmer invited the boy to go with him. The boy eagerly agreed. As the farmer began collecting the eggs, the boy

watched for a while and finally asked, "Why do you have to come all the way out here to get eggs? Why don't you just get them out of the refrigerator like my mom does?"
Dates & Places Used:

TOPIC: Fathers
Backward Training

You are being trained by your children when you hear yourself telling them the same thing more than once.
Dates & Places Used:

TOPIC: Fathers
The Riches of Fathers

A truly rich man is one whose children run into his arms when his hands are empty.
Dates & Places Used:

TOPIC: Fathers
Save It for Dad

Small boy to his mother: "Don't yell at me; I am not your husband."
Dates & Places Used:

TOPIC: Fathers
The Boy Way

A father became upset about the time his six-year-old son took to get home from school. He determined to make the trip himself to see how long it should take to cover that distance. He concluded that twenty minutes maximum was enough, but his son was taking well over an hour.

Finally the father decided to walk with his son. After that trip the man said, "The twenty minutes I thought reasonable was right, but I failed to consider such important things as a side trip to track down a trail of ants ... or a stop to watch a man fix a flat ... or the time it took to swing around a half-dozen telephone poles ... or how much time it took for a boy just to get acquainted with two stray dogs.

"In short, I had forgotten what it is like to be six years old."

Dates & Places Used:

344

TOPIC: Fathers

A Father's Image

4 years: My daddy can do anything!
7 years: My dad knows a lot ... a whole lot.
8 years: My father does not know quite everything.
12 years: O well, naturally, Father does not know that either.
14 years: Oh, Father? He's hopelessly old-fashioned.
21 years: Oh, that man—he's out-of-date!
25 years: He knows a little bit about it.
35 years: Before we decide, we'll get Dad's idea first.
50 years: What would Dad have thought about that?
60 years: My dad knew literally everything!
65 years: I wish I could talk it over with Dad once more.

Dates & Places Used:

345

TOPIC: Fear

Too Scared

With everyone concerned about the current random shootings, perhaps we have gotten more uptight than we realized. My father-in-law, a physician, related this account recently, from the Leake County area of Mississippi.

On a warm afternoon in late summer, a lady went to buy her groceries. After making her purchases, she placed the grocery bags in her backseat. Remembering some things she needed from a discount department store, she locked her car and went to finish shopping.

A little while later she got back to her car, started the engine, and drove home. As she drove down the highway, to her horror, she heard three POPS, then felt something hit her on the back of the head! Holding one hand over the wound, she managed to drive herself to the emergency room of the local hospital. Screaming for help that she had been shot, she got instant attention!

Upon arrival, the doctor said, "Move your hand so I can see the wound."

The woman answered, "I can't! My brains will fall out!"

Finally the doctor convinced her to let him examine the wound. As she removed her hand from the back of her head, the doctor discovered that she had been hit in the back of the head by canned biscuit dough!

After much laughter and relief, the doctor noted that he had seen a lot of "wounds" in his career, but never one inflicted by biscuit dough! Aside from acute embarrassment, the lady was sent home unharmed. Maybe one moral of this story is to be careful, but not to be uptight.

Dates & Places Used:

346

TOPIC: Fear

Backward About Forward

There are too many church members who can be described like the Missouri farmer describes his mule: "Awfully backward about going forward."

Dates & Places Used:

347

TOPIC: Feminists

Feminist Transformations

Some of us are becoming the men we want to marry.

Dates & Places Used:

348

TOPIC: Fighting

Fight for Kindness

The Sunday school teacher asked her small pupils to tell about their acts of kindness to helpless animals. After several heart-stirring stories, the teacher asked Tommy if he had anything to add. "Well," he replied proudly, "I beat up a guy once 'cause he kicked his dog."

Dates & Places Used:

349

TOPIC: Finances

Too Much of Not Enough

In reply to your request to send a check for my dues, I wish to inform you that the present condition of my bank account makes it almost impossible. My shattered financial condition is due to federal laws, state laws, county laws, city laws, corporate laws, liquor laws, in-laws, and outlaws.

Through these laws, I am expected to pay a business tax, amusement tax, head tax, school tax, gas tax, food tax, furniture tax, and excise tax; even my brains are taxed. I am required to get a business license, hunting and fishing license, car license, truck license, not to mention a marriage license and a dog license.

I am also required to contribute to every society and organization which the genius of man is capable to bring to life: Women's Relief, unemployment relief, and the gold digger's relief. Also to every hospital and charitable organization in the city.

For my own safety, I am required to carry life insurance, property insurance, liability insurance, burglary insurance, accident insurance, business insurance, earthquake insurance, unemployment insurance, fire insurance, and health insurance.

My business is so governed that it is no easy matter for me to find out who owns it. I am inspected, expected, disrespected, rejected, dejected, examined, reexamined, informed, required, summoned, commanded, and compelled, until I provide an inexhaustible supply of money for every known need of the human race.

Simply because I refuse to donate to something or other, I am boycotted, talked about, lied about, held up, held down, and robbed, until I am almost ruined.

The only reason I am clinging to life at all is to see what is coming next. I can tell you honestly that, except for a miracle that happened, I could not enclose this check. The wolf that comes to many doors nowadays just had pups in my kitchen; I sold them and here is the money.

Dates & Places Used:

TOPIC: Focus

No Loafing

Breadwinners can't afford to loaf.
Dates & Places Used:

TOPIC: Fools

Missing Heads

People who lose their heads are usually the last to miss them.
Dates & Places Used:

TOPIC: Fools

Stubborn Fools

A fool is someone who persists in holding his own views after we have enlightened him with ours.
Dates & Places Used:

353

TOPIC: Fools

The Half-Hearted and Half-Witted

Satan uses the tactics of the half-hearted,
to stifle the aspirations of the half-witted.
Dates & Places Used:

354

TOPIC: Forgiveness

The Paint of Love

Love is the only paint that will cover the faults of others.
Dates & Places Used:

355

TOPIC: Forgiveness

No-Fuss Forgiveness

Forgiveness warms the heart and cools the fuss.
Dates & Places Used:

356

TOPIC: Forgiveness

Not Too Buried

Those who say they will forgive but can't forget simply bury
the hatchet, but leave the handle out for immediate use.
Dates & Places Used:

357

TOPIC: Freedom

Freedom of Religion

Freedom of religion is the God-given right for each individual to choose to go to hell the human way or to go to heaven God's way.

Dates & Places Used:

358

TOPIC: Freedom

Forklift Power

Not long ago I was riding with a friend of mine when he was taking his eight-year-old son to school. While driving down the freeway the boy noticed a large flatbed truck with a forklift on the back. His eyes widened and he said, "Boy, I sure would like one of those."

Curious as to why an eight-year-old would want a forklift, I inquired, "Jonathon, what would you do with a forklift?"

With a real determined look on his face he said, "Anything I want to."

Dates & Places Used:

359

TOPIC: Friends

Good Friends and Bad Times

A friend is someone who is there when the good times aren't.

Dates & Places Used:

360

TOPIC: Friends

Friends Forgive Foolishness

Real friends are those who, when you've made a fool of yourself, don't feel you've done a permanent job.

Dates & Places Used:

361

TOPIC: Friends

All We Need

We really only need five things on this earth: Some food, some sun, some work, some fun, and someone.
Dates & Places Used:

362

TOPIC: Friends

New Friends and Old Stories

The nicest things about new friends is that they haven't heard your old stories yet.
Dates & Places Used:

363

TOPIC: Friends

A Replaced Friend

A man who was a bit paranoid walked into his apartment and found that everything in his apartment had been stolen and replaced with exact replicas. When he reported this crime to the police, the police thought he was crazy, told him to never bother them again, and left.

The lack of concern by the police bothered this man. He phoned his best friend and asked him to come to his apartment. He showed his friend these exact replicas of everything that had been stolen. He then asked his friend what he should do.

His friend's response was not too comforting. His friend said, "I'm sorry, sir, do I know you?"
Dates & Places Used:

364

TOPIC: Friends

A Friend Steps In

A friend is one who steps in when the world steps out.
Dates & Places Used:

365

TOPIC: Friends

A Friend Gets in the Way

A friend is one who never gets in the way, except when we are on the way down.
Dates & Places Used:

366

TOPIC: Friends

Friends and Enemies

The Bible tells us to love our neighbors, and also to love our enemies, probably because they are generally the same people.
Dates & Places Used:

367

TOPIC: Friends

Champagne and Sham Friends

Here is a toast to real friends: Here's <u>cham</u>pagne to <u>real</u> friends and <u>real</u> pain to <u>sham</u> friends.
Dates & Places Used:

368

TOPIC: Friends

Friendly Memories

If you want to establish long friendships, then you must develop a short memory.

Dates & Places Used:

369

TOPIC: Friends

Unsigned Cards

A really good friend is someone who mails you an unsigned birthday card—so you can mail it to someone else on short notice.

Dates & Places Used:

370

TOPIC: Fund-raising

Judy's Organ

There once was an organist named Judy,
Who, in order to fulfill her church duty,
Sat at the organ to play,
But discovered that day,
Nothing worked right—not even the tutti.

She called a repairman posthaste.
He said, "Repair would be fiscal waste.
A new organ is needed—
My words should be heeded."
(This news to the pastor was raced.)

The pastor once more repeated,
"The church budget is almost depleted.
If an organ's required
Funds must be acquired—
And help from outside will be needed!"

And so comes to you this fun letter,
And to you we could be a great debtor.
Your generous gift
Would give us a lift
And make our church music much better!
Dates & Places Used:

371

TOPIC: Funerals

The Wrong Virgin

A minister had run out of time to prepare for a sudden funeral. Using the latest technology, he went to his computer and found the funeral service he had used last, and doing a global "search and replace," had the computer put in the name of the newly deceased, "Edna," as a replacement for the woman in the previous funeral, "Mary."

Everything went fine until they came to the Apostles' Creed, wherein the minister confessed that Jesus was born of the Virgin Edna.

Dates & Places Used:

372

TOPIC: Funerals

The Yankees Shot Grandma

It was a military funeral on a hot, muggy day in central Mississippi. Grandpa, a war veteran, had passed away. The funeral had gone well, the family had gathered around the grave. The minister had finished the graveside service.

The honor guard from the local air base folded the flag and the presiding officer presented it to the widow with his condolences and those of the president of the United States. With perfect military precision he rose, stood at attention, and gave the special signal for the rest of the military escort to fire the first of three rounds of the twenty-one-gun salute.

The first volley rang out across the quiet countryside. The family had been facing toward the casket, away from the honor guard. Everyone jumped, except Grandma. She fainted, falling out of her chair. Seeing this, her grandson cried out, "Now they've done it! We haven't even buried Grandpa yet and those Yankees have shot Grandma in the back!"

Dates & Places Used:

373 TOPIC: Future

Shoveling Partly Cloudy

Late fall and early spring are the times when many must prepare to shovel a few inches of what the meteorologists predict as "partly cloudy" off the driveway.

Dates & Places Used:

374 TOPIC: Future

One Never Knows

A rabbi in a small town in Russia began to get very meditative after many years of searching for the ultimate purpose of life. He was getting old and had been in this village for many years and had begun to consider the status quo relatively unimportant. The constable decided to harass him one morning and asked him where he was going. He said he didn't know and thus was taken immediately to jail for not telling the truth. The constable yelled at him for insulting him, "You have gone to the synagogue at this time every day for the last twenty years, and now you mock me by saying you do not know where you are going?"

As the door to the cell was being closed on the rabbi, he said, "You see, one never knows what will happen next."

Dates & Places Used:

375

TOPIC: Gambling

A Bet a Day

A man's got to make one bet every day, else he could be walking around lucky and not even know it.
Dates & Places Used:

376

TOPIC: Gender

Stronger Women

If women are not as strong as men, how is it that a woman can put a cap on a fruit jar so it takes thirty minutes for her husband to get it off?
Dates & Places Used:

377

TOPIC: Gender

Men Must Ask

Do you know why the people of Israel wandered in the wilderness for forty years? Because, even back then, men wouldn't stop and ask for directions.
Dates & Places Used:

378

TOPIC: Generosity

A Generous Memory

A generous man forgets what he gives and remembers what he receives.
Dates & Places Used:

379

Theoretical Generosity

A peasant is applying to join the Communist party and appears before the local party secretary to answer questions as to his worthiness.

"If you have two cats, will you give one of them away?"

"Yes, I will."

"And if you have two tractors, will you give one away?"

"Certainly."

"And if you have two houses, will you give one away?"

"Absolutely."

"And if you have two cows, will you give one away?"

"No, I couldn't do that."

"Why on earth not?"

"Because I have two cows."

Dates & Places Used:

380

Too Late for a Diary

A young girl was telling her friend about all the Christmas gifts she had received: "I also got a diary. It's a nice diary—very expensive. The only thing is, it's a little late in my life for a diary. Everything has pretty well happened already!"

Dates & Places Used:

381

Culpable Hands of Children

Giving children chemistry sets and BB guns provides a wonderful education for the entire family. Both parents and children alike learn how foolish the parents were to place explosives, hazardous materials, and instruments of destruction in the "culpable hands" of children.

Dates & Places Used:

382

TOPIC: Gifts

Serious Business

A sign in a jewelry store window sold lots of diamonds. It read as follows:

A box of candy means friendship;
A bunch of flowers means love;
But a diamond means business!

Dates & Places Used:

383

TOPIC: Gifts

Keep the Dream

A week before Christmas, a wife told her husband, "I had a wonderful dream last night. I dreamed you gave me two hundred dollars on a new Christmas wardrobe. You wouldn't want to do anything to spoil a perfect dream like that, would you?"

"Of course not," he replied. "You may keep the two hundred dollars."

Dates & Places Used:

384

TOPIC: Giving

A Cheerful-er Giver

A six-year-old girl insisted that as a new first grader, she should be allowed to take part in the offering and put something in the offering plate during the worship service of her church. Mom and Dad agreed wholeheartedly. Dad even gave her a dollar and explained that God loves a cheerful giver.

When the usher stopped beside the little girl and held out the offering plate, the little girl's voice rang out in protest, "Hey, mister! Don't you have change for a dollar?"

Her very embarrassed father leaned down and whispered something in her ear. The whole congregation heard her reply:

145

"But, Daddy, I'd be a cheerful-er giver if I could give *some* to the Lord and buy a candy bar, too!"
Dates & Places Used:

385

TOPIC: Glory

Law of Destiny

Glory may be fleeting, but obscurity is forever.
Dates & Places Used:

386

TOPIC: Goals

Locate the Goal First

In life as in football, you won't get far unless you know where the goalposts are.
Dates & Places Used:

387

TOPIC: God

God and the Grocery Store Door

A young boy was listening to his teacher tell about the power of God–specifically that God is everywhere and would never leave us nor forsake us. She asked the class if they knew that this was true. The one boy agreed with his teacher and told the class, "God's the one that opens the door at the grocery store."
Dates & Places Used:

388

God as a Student

There's no poorer, lowlier, and more despised pupil on earth than God. He must be everybody's disciple. Everybody wants to be his schoolmaster and teacher.

Dates & Places Used:

389

Absolute Exception

If absolute power corrupts absolutely, where does that leave God?

Dates & Places Used:

390

Kid's-Eye View of God

Children's letters to God:

"Dear God: In Sunday school they told us what you do. Who does it for you when you are on vacation?"

"Dear God: Please put another holiday between Christmas and Easter. There is nothing good in there now."

"Dear God: Maybe Cain and Abel would not kill each other so much if they had their own rooms. It worked with my brother!"

"Dear God: I think about you sometimes even when I'm not praying."

Dates & Places Used:

391

God's Invisible Support

The problem with an atheist is that he has no invisible means of support.

Dates & Places Used:

392

Kids' Questions to God
What Do Kids Think About Him?

These questions were asked by elementary children and appeared in a newspaper article:

Dear God: Why isn't Mrs. God's name in the Bible? Weren't you married to her when you wrote it? Larry

Dear God: Why did you make people talk foreign languages? It would be easier if everybody could talk English like you and me. Alice

Dear God: If you made the sun and the moon and stars you must of had lots of equipment. Paul

Dear God: Instead of letting people die and having to make new ones why don't you just keep the ones you have now? Jane

Dear God: How come you only have 10 rules and our school has millions? Joy

Dear God: When you made the first man did he work as good as we do now? Tom

Dear God: There was no clouds Saturday so I think I saw your feet. Did I really? Kenny

Dear God: I know there's a God because I go to his house on Sunday and see all his cars parked there. George

Dear God: Where does yesterday go? Do you have it? Stanley

Dear God: I'm afraid of things at night more than in the day. So if you could keep the sun on longer that would a good thing. Joanne

Dates & Places Used:

393

TOPIC: God

Not That God

During his long career as pastor of New York's Riverside Church, the late Harry Emerson Fosdick spent many hours counseling students from nearby Columbia University. One evening a distraught young man burst into his study and announced, "I have decided that I cannot and do not believe in God!"

"All right," Dr. Fosdick replied. "But describe for me the God you don't believe in." The student proceeded to sketch his idea of God. When he finished, Dr. Fosdick said, "Well, we're in the same boat. I don't believe in *that* God either."

Dates & Places Used:

394

TOPIC: Golf

Communicating the Problem

Two golfers were annoyed by an unusually slow twosome in front of them. One of the offending pair was dawdling in the fairway while the other was searching diligently in the rough.

"Why don't you help your friend find his ball?" cried one of the impatient golfers.

"Oh," came the reply, "he's got his ball. He's looking for his club."

There are times of discouragement in the Christian life. But let us strive on as this golfer and never give up.

Dates & Places Used:

395

TOPIC: Golf

Golf Score

After years of golfing, I have finally gotten my score down to the low seventies. At this rate I am ready to try eighteen holes instead of my usual nine-hole game.

Dates & Places Used:

396

TOPIC: Golf

The End of Golf

At the seventeenth annual Pastors Conference at Moody Bible Institute, George Sweeting claimed that his father, a Scotsman, gave up golf at sixty-five years of age. The only reason he did so was because he finally lost his ball.

Dates & Places Used:

397

TOPIC: Golf

Practice Turf

Practice needed: A golfer who made a spectacularly bad shot and tore up a large piece of turf took the sod in his hand and looking wildly about, asked: "What do I do with this?"

"If I were you," said the caddy, "I'd take it home and practice on it."

Dates & Places Used:

398

TOPIC: Gossip

Gossip Relationships

Why must the phrase "It's none of my business" always be followed by the word "but"?

Dates & Places Used:

399

TOPIC: Gossip

That's Business

A business is too big when it takes a week for gossip to go from one end of the office to the other.

Dates & Places Used:

400

TOPIC: Gossip

Sour Grapevine

Gossip travels faster over the sour grapevine.
Dates & Places Used:

401

TOPIC: Gossip

Repeating Gossip

We hate to repeat gossip,
but what else can you do with it?
Dates & Places Used:

402

TOPIC: Government

Government Programs

Most government programs have three parts: a beginning, a muddle, and no end!
Dates & Places Used:

403

TOPIC: Gratitude

Always Reason to Praise

While on their honeymoon, the bride attempted to press the trousers of her husband's new suit with an iron received as a wedding present. When she applied the hot iron, part of the trousers went up in a puff of smoke, leaving a small but gaping hole.

The groom rushed in from the next room. "Is everything all right?"

Whereupon the bride burst into tears as she tried to relate what had happened.

"Honey," he replied, "let's get down on our knees and give thanks that my leg wasn't in those trousers!"

Dates & Places Used:

404

TOPIC: Gratitude

Reduction in Appreciation

Lucy asks Charlie Brown to help with her homework. "I'll be eternally grateful," she promises.

"Fair enough. I've never had anyone be eternally grateful before," replied Charlie. "Just subtract four from ten to get how many apples the farmer had left."

Lucy says, "That's it! That's it! I have to be eternally grateful for that? I was robbed! I can't be eternally grateful for this, it was too easy!"

With his blank stare, Charlie replies, "Well, whatever you think is fair."

"How about if I just say 'thanks, Bro?'" replied Lucy.

As Charlie leaves to go outside, he meets Linus. "Where've you been, Charlie Brown?"

"Helping Lucy with her homework."

Linus asks, "Did she appreciate it?"

Charlie answers, "At greatly reduced prices."

Dates & Places Used:

405

TOPIC: Greed

My Good Fortune

Remember the story of the lad whose thoughtful grandfather gave him two half-dollars one hot July day to purchase ice cream sundaes for himself and his little sister? On the way to the ice cream shop, one of the half-dollars somehow slipped out of his pocket and rolled into a gopher hole.

"How fortunate it was," the boy reported later on a positive note to his grandfather, "that although we lost Sister's half-dollar, I was able to hold on to mine!"
Dates & Places Used:

TOPIC: Growth

406 Think Green and Grow

If you think yourself green, you will grow.
If you think yourself ripe, you will rot.
Dates & Places Used:

TOPIC: Grudges

407 The Stings of a Grudge

To carry a grudge is like being stung to death by one bee.

William H. Walton

Dates & Places Used:

TOPIC: Guilt

408 The Real Problem

A friend of mine was driving through a school zone when a policeman pulled her over for speeding. As he was giving her the ticket, she said, "How come I always get a ticket, and everyone else gets a warning? Is it my face?"

"No, ma'am," said the officer. "It's your foot."
Dates & Places Used:

409

I Am Not Thou

A father was reading the Ten Commandments to his son. As he read, he was explaining what each one meant: "Thou shalt not ... Thou shalt not ..." When they came to a commandment that was particularly convicting to the three-year-old, his immediate response was, "Daddy, I'm not *thou*."

How often, when we read God's Word and his Spirit applies it to our lives, do we say in our hearts, "I'm not *thou*."

Dates & Places Used:

410

They've Lost God

There were two notoriously bad brothers, rascals from the cradle. Whenever anything out of line would happen around the little town they would catch the blame, and they were usually the guilty parties. After a fire at the school, the boys' parents, driven to the point of distraction, decided they would send the older boy, who was ten, down to counsel with their pastor.

The boy was frightened. The minister looked so austere in his black robe each Sunday. What would he be like one-on-one?

The minister looked at the young fellow somberly, then asked, "Young man, where is God?" The boy had no idea what to say, so he sat in silence. The minister repeated the question, "Young man, where is God?"

The boy still said nothing. The pastor thundered one last time, "Young man, I said, 'Where is God?'" The boy bolted out of the office at this tactic, raced home, and went upstairs to pack. Noticing his brother looking at him, he declared, "You'd better pack too, brother. They've lost God and I know they're gonna blame us!"

Dates & Places Used:

411

TOPIC: Habits

Winning or Losing

Winning is a habit. Unfortunately, so is losing.
Dates & Places Used:

412

TOPIC: Habits

Finding Habits

A habit is something you never knew you had until you tried to quit it.
Dates & Places Used:

413

TOPIC: Happiness

Happiness and Money

Happiness can't be measured by one's wealth. For instance, a person with eight million dollars may not be one bit happier than a person with seven million dollars!
Dates & Places Used:

414

TOPIC: Happiness

A Hundred-Dollar Wish

A man on the street said, "I'd be happy if only I had $100."
   A person passing by who heard him handed him $100. The man who received the $100 said, "I should have asked for $200."
Dates & Places Used:

415

Happiness, Health, and Memory

Happiness is nothing more than health and a poor memory.
Dates & Places Used:

416

Shock Therapy

A patient in a doctor's waiting room heard a scream from within the doctor's examining room, and saw an elderly woman come out and quickly depart in a state of agitation.

"What happened?" asked the waiting patient.

"I told her she was pregnant," replied the doctor.

"You couldn't be serious," remarked the patient.

"Of course not," he answered. "But it cured her hiccups."
Dates & Places Used:

417

God and the Doctor

God cures and the doctor gets the money.
Dates & Places Used:

418

Three Rules for Good Teeth

There are three proven rules for good teeth:
1. Brush after each meal.
2. See your dentist twice a year.
3. Mind your own business.
Dates & Places Used:

419

TOPIC: Hearing

An Unintended Listener

An elderly man who had been fitted with a hearing aid a week earlier returned to his doctor's office for a checkup.

"How do you like the hearing aid?" the doctor asked.

"Fine," the patient replied.

"How does the family like it?" the doctor inquired.

"Oh, I haven't told them yet," the patient answered, "but I've changed my will three times."

Dates & Places Used:

420

TOPIC: Heart

God's Measuring Tape

When God measures a man, he puts the tape measure around his heart, not his head.

Dates & Places Used:

421

TOPIC: Heart

A Pat on the Heart

"This is where your heart is!" said the teacher, pointing to the little boy's chest.

"My heart is where I sit down," said the little boy in her class.

"How did you get that idea?" asked the teacher.

The little guy said, "Because, every time I do something good, my grandma pats me there and says, 'Bless your little heart.'"

Dates & Places Used:

422

TOPIC: Heaven

Can't Go to Heaven

The teacher asked her preschool class, "Now, how many of you would like to go to heaven?" All the children raised their hands except Tommy.

The teacher asked Tommy why he wouldn't like to go to heaven. Tommy answered, "I'm sorry, but I can't. My mother told me to come right home after Sunday school."

Dates & Places Used:

423

TOPIC: Heaven

Heavenly Electrician

Their priest had asked Christine's husband, Sam, to do some rewiring in the confessionals.

The only way to reach the wiring was to enter the attic above the altar and crawl over the ceiling by balancing on the rafters. Concerned for her husband's safety, Christine waited in a pew.

Unbeknownst to Christine, some other parishioners were congregating in the vestibule. They paid little attention to her, probably assuming she was praying. Worried about her husband, she looked up toward the ceiling and yelled, "Sam, Sam, are you up there? Did you make it okay?"

There was quite an outburst from the vestibule when Sam's hearty voice echoed down, "Yes, I made it up here just fine!"

When a loved one dies, it's comforting to know they made it "up there" okay.

Dates & Places Used:

424

TOPIC: Heaven

No Money in Heaven

A pastor was preaching to his congregation concerning what heaven would be like. He explained that there would be no money in heaven—those things would no longer matter.

A little boy was sitting with his mother and listening intently. Upon hearing these words, he leaned toward his mother and whispered into her ear, "Hey, Mom, it sounds like we are already in heaven."

Dates & Places Used:

425

TOPIC: Heaven

Is Michigan Like Heaven?

A young three-year-old who lives in Phoenix, Arizona, enjoyed the winter visits from her grandparents and great-grandmother. One day in early summer she talked to her mother and asked, "Is Michigan like heaven?"

Her mother responded, "Well, no, Rachel, but why do you ask?"

The youngster responded with her keen insight, "When people go to Michigan, they never come back."

Dates & Places Used:

426

TOPIC: Heaven

The Problem with Florida

A minister in Florida lamented that it was difficult to get his message across to his congregation: "It's so beautiful here in the winter," he said, "that heaven doesn't interest them ... And it is so hot here in the summer ... that hell doesn't scare them."

Dates & Places Used:

427

TOPIC: Hecklers

Heckler Humor

Speaker to heckler: "Please–if I wanted a hard time I could have stayed home and talked to my kids."

Dates & Places Used:

428

TOPIC: Hell

A Rude Awakening

A man awakened in the hospital after an operation. It was dark in the room, all the curtains and blinds were drawn.

"Nurse! Nurse!" shouted the man, "why is it so dark in here? I want to see outside."

"Now, now, sir, be patient," she replied. "I drew the curtains because there's a terrible fire in the building next door and I didn't want you to think the operation was a failure."
Dates & Places Used:

429 TOPIC: Help

Helping In

Locksmith ad: "Let me help you out–or in."
Dates & Places Used:

430 TOPIC: Heritage

Genetic Equations

A ten-year-old boy was listening to his brother as he read about Handel's background: "Handel was half German, half Italian. and half English."
The ten-year-old exclaimed, "WOW, that's three quarters!"
No one's math seems too strong with this one!
Dates & Places Used:

431 TOPIC: Heroes

Heroes Are Made

John F. Kennedy was once asked how he became a war hero. His answer was straightforward and refreshingly honest: "It was entirely involuntary; someone sank my boat."
Dates & Places Used:

432

History's Timing

How come nearly all historical events happen next to a souvenir shop?

Dates & Places Used:

433

TOPIC: History

Fractured History

An English teacher at St. Paul's School, Concord, New Hampshire, writes the syndicated column, *Looking At Language*. In one of his columns, Mr. Lederer shows some bloopers from the eighth grade through college freshman level English classes he has taught. Again, let me stress that these are real statements from real students. These bloopers show the havoc students can wreak on the Bible and Western history.

"History calls people Romans because they never stayed in one place for very long. At Roman banquets, the guests wore garlics in their hair."

"Joan of Arc was canonized by Bernard Show."

"In 1658, the Pilgrims crossed the ocean, and this was known as Pilgrim's Progress."

And from the Bible:

"The Bible is full of interesting caricatures. In the first book of the Bible–Guinesses: Adam and Eve were created from an apple tree."

"God asked Abraham to sacrifice Isaac on Mount Montezuma.

"Jacob, son of Isaac, stole his brother's birth mark."

"Moses went up on Mount Cyanide to get the Ten Commandments."

Dates & Places Used:

434

TOPIC: History

Problems with History

History repeats itself. That's one of the things wrong with history.

Dates & Places Used:

435

TOPIC: Home

Generic Thanks for Children

Researcher: "If you had it all to do over again, would you have children again?"
Mother: "Yes, but not the same ones."
Dates & Places Used:

436

TOPIC: Home

Home Is Not a Nice Place

A cynic once observed that home is the place a fellow goes when he is tired of being nice to people.
Dates & Places Used:

437

TOPIC: Honesty

Lawyers or Good Guys

This is how Malcom Ford explains to his preschool class-mates what his father Harrison Ford does for a living:
"My daddy is a movie actor, and sometimes he plays the good guy, and sometimes he plays the lawyer."
Dates & Places Used:

438

TOPIC: Honesty

Not the Walkers

My wife and I decided to eat out one night, but failed to make reservations. When we arrived at our favorite restaurant, we learned that several people had signed up for a table ahead of us. I left our name with the hostess and we sat in the reception area.

Soon thereafter, a disgruntled couple left the restaurant, complaining that the wait was too long. Within minutes, the hostess called, "Walker?" No one responded. She called again but to no avail.

Quickly, I convinced my wife that if we told the hostess we were the Walkers, we'd get seated faster.

As we approached her, she said, "Walker?" I nodded. "We've been expecting you," she informed us. "Your family is waiting in the dining room."

Dates & Places Used:

439

TOPIC: Honesty

A Mugger's Match

It was recently reported that a young woman from abroad was accosted by a mugger while visiting New York. As the mugger grabbed the visitor's gold chain, he pushed her. She grabbed him to steady herself. During this somewhat convoluted movement, she inadvertently pulled off the gold chain he was wearing. The mugger ran off, unaware of his own loss. The next day, after consulting a jeweler, the visitor discovered she now owned an 18-karat gold chain. Hers was costume jewelry.

There seems to be some kind of divine recompense at work here . . .

Dates & Places Used:

440

TOPIC: Honesty

Fake License Stolen

A twenty-year-old University of Illinois student called the campus police to complain he had loaned his fake driver's license to a friend, which was confiscated at a Normal, Illinois, pub, and he was wondering how to get it back because he had paid fifty dollars for it.

And you were worried about the state of our educational system ...

Dates & Places Used:

441

TOPIC: Honesty

Grandma's Advice

Grandma had been sitting quietly in the backseat, but now she spoke up: "I told them, Constable, that we would never get far in a stolen car."

Dates & Places Used:

442

TOPIC: Honesty

All You Want

Dennis the Menace catches his friend Joey trying to get a paper out of a newspaper machine without putting in any money. He says, "Wait, Joey!! First you havta put in the money ... and then you can have as many papers as you want."

Dates & Places Used:

443

TOPIC: Honesty

Checkers by Phone

An honest person is someone you could play checkers with over the telephone.

Dates & Places Used:

TOPIC: Hope

Only Need to Bat

A Little Leaguer was playing the outfield in the first game of the season. After chasing a long hit and hustling the ball back into the infield, someone asked him how his team was doing and what the score was. The boy said his team was doing OK, but they were trailing seventeen to zero.

The person asked if he was discouraged about being so far behind, and if he was ready to admit defeat. He came back immediately with this retort: "We aren't beaten, we haven't even been up to bat yet!"

Hope is a vital element also in the battle with sin. We have good reason for confidence because God is in heaven and all power rests in him. And all who serve him can draw on his unlimited resources.

Dates & Places Used:

TOPIC: Hope

A Theology That Dirties Windows

Joseph Stowell told about the problem at Shepherd's Home. This institution in Union Grove, Wisconsin, was established to provide a loving home for the mentally impaired. Many children have been nurtured in Christian love through this home. Many have also come to know Christ as their Savior. They have also learned about the soon return of Jesus Christ. This is a teaching the children of Shepherd's Home have taken seriously. And that is the problem—each day the children run to the window to see if this is the day Jesus will return. They just can't keep their windows clean!

Dates & Places Used:

446

TOPIC: Hope

Cats Take Hope

When the country goes temporarily to the dogs, cats must learn to be circumspect, walk on fences, sleep in trees, and have faith that all this woofing is not the last word.

Dates & Places Used:

447

TOPIC: Hospitality

Limited Hospitality

Treat your guest as a guest for two days;
on the third day give him a hoe.

Dates & Places Used:

448

TOPIC: Humanity

Human Production Costs

At a meeting of air scientists and pilots, the scientists made it clear they would like to replace the pilot in the aircraft with instruments and servomechanisms. Scoot Crossfield, a U.S. test pilot, rejoined by asking: "Where can you find another nonlinear servomechanism weighing only 150 pounds and having great adaptability that can be produced so cheaply by unskilled labor?"

Dates & Places Used:

449

TOPIC: Humility

As Long As We Are Nothing

God created the world out of nothing,
and as long as we are nothing,
God can make something out of us.

Dates & Places Used:

450

TOPIC: Humility

Moms and Toilets

If you get an attack of importance, call your mother or scrub a toilet. Either one will put your talents in perspective.
Dates & Places Used:

451

TOPIC: Husbands

A Weighty Difference

What's the difference between a boyfriend and a husband? About thirty pounds!
Dates & Places Used:

452

TOPIC: Husbands

Decision-Making Husband

A husband once explained how he was the head of his household and took care of the major decisions: "I make all the big decisions in our family and my wife makes all the little decisions. She decides where we go on vacation, whether to buy a new car, what house we are going to buy, etc.... I make the big ones, like whether to admit the Eastern European nations into NATO."
Dates & Places Used:

453

TOPIC: Hypocrisy

Preaching Twin or Practicing Twin

Of the twin brothers, one became a minister and the other a physician. It was almost impossible to tell the twins apart. A man approached one of them on the street and asked, "Are you the twin who preaches?"

"No," came the answer, "I'm the one who practices."
Dates & Places Used:

454

Same Old Crowd

A saloon keeper sold his old tavern to a local church. Enthusiastic church members tore out the bar, added some lights, gave the whole place a fresh coat of paint, and installed some pews.

Somehow a parrot which belonged to the saloon keeper was left behind. On Sunday morning that colorful bird was watching from the rafters. When the minister appeared, he squawked, "New proprietor!" When the men who were to lead in worship marched in, the bird piped, "New floor show!" But when the bird looked out over the congregation, he screeched, "Same old crowd!"

God doesn't want us to be conformed to the world. He wants us to be transformed by our commitment to him. How about it? Different location but "same old crowd"? God forbid!

Dates & Places Used:

455

One-Sided Thinking

When two people agree on everything, one of them is doing all the thinking.

Dates & Places Used:

456

It's Not a Cow

A young woman from the city was visiting the farm. This was her first visit to the farm, and she was simply fascinated by the animals. She had never seen many of them before. Therefore, it was not unusual when she blurted out: "What a strange-looking cow. But why hasn't she any horns?"

The farmer explained, "Well, you see, some cows are born without horns and never have any. Others shed theirs, and

some we dehorn. And some breeds aren't supposed to have horns at all. But the reason this cow hasn't got any horns is because she ain't a cow ... she's a horse!"
Dates & Places Used:

457 TOPIC: Identity

Snail or Reindeer

A little girl was crawling in the grass while her mother was working in the yard. The child found a snail and watched its every move with fascination for the longest time. She was trying to figure out what kind of animal this was. And then it happened. The little snail raised its feelers. The little girl was now ready to announce her discovery to her mother: "Mommy, come look; I found a reindeer!"
Dates & Places Used:

458 TOPIC: In-laws

Opinions of His Mothers

The truest measure of a man is found somewhere between the opinion of his mother and the opinion of his mother-in-law.
Dates & Places Used:

459 TOPIC: Incarnation

It's a God

A group of first graders decided to produce their very own Christmas program. They produced their own updated nativity story. All the major characters were there—Joseph, the shepherds, the angels, the wise men from afar ... but where was Mary? Shortly after the production began, there was heard from behind some bales of straw moaning and groaning—Mary was in labor! A doctor with a white coat and black bag was then ushered onto the stage and disappeared with Joseph behind the bales of straw. After a few moments the doctor emerged from behind the bales of straw with a jubilant smile on his face and holding a baby in his arms. He then announced to the audience: "It's a GOD!"

Dates & Places Used:

460

TOPIC: Incarnation

His Only Forgotten Son

My five-year-old Stephen was practicing his memory verse for Bible Club. John 3:16, "For God so loved the world that he gave his only forgotten son ..." My wife laughed as she related this story, and so did I.

Yet far too often his slip is all too true. Jesus is ignored if not forgotten by the world. Even we Christians leave Jesus on the shelf until we can't handle things ourselves. In spite of this, God loved the world so much that he sent his Son knowing that he would be ignored, forgotten, put aside, and abused. What love God has for me. May I always remember that love and live accordingly.

Dates & Places Used:

461

TOPIC: Inconsistency

Self-Destructing Sticker

Bumper sticker: "Down with bumperstickers!"

Dates & Places Used:

462

TOPIC: Inflation

Value of a Dime

Inflation hasn't ruined everything. A dime can still be used as a screwdriver.

Dates & Places Used:

463

TOPIC: Inflation

Raising Sweet Cane

When the price of sugar goes up, customers raise cane.
Dates & Places Used:

464

TOPIC: Inheritance

Rich Ancestors

Misers aren't much fun to live with, but they make wonderful ancestors.
Dates & Places Used:

465

TOPIC: Insects

Single Mosquitoes

A Minnesotan was asked if the bugs were bad in his state.
"We don't have a single mosquito if that's what you're worried about," he replied.
"Really?" was the amazed response.
"That's right," retorted the Minnesotan. "They are all married and have large families!"
Dates & Places Used:

466

TOPIC: Instinct

In Stinked

A mama skunk had two little skunks named "In" and "Out." It seemed that when In was going out, that Out was coming in, and if Out was in, In was out. It was rare to find Out out if In wasn't in, and In in if Out wasn't out, because In and Out were never in or out together.

One day when Out was in and In was out, Mama told Out to go out and bring In in. So, Out went out to bring In in, and searched high and low, but couldn't find In. Mama sent Out out again, and this time Out brought In in. Mama skunk asked Out, "How did you find your brother In?"

"That was simple," responded Out. "In-stinct."

Dates & Places Used:

467

TOPIC: Insults

Insult upon Insult

A five-year-old girl was visiting her grandparents. She was an unruly child and showed very little respect for her grandparents. After yet another embarrassing episode with her grandmother, her humiliated mother sought to discipline the girl. Her mother said, "How dare you treat your grandmother like that; you wouldn't treat your other grandmother like that, would you?"

The little girl immediately changed her expression and became very serious. She looked up at her mother and innocently answered her, "Oh, no, Mother! I would never treat HER that way. She's too nice for that!"

Dates & Places Used:

468

TOPIC: Insults

Insult Carefully

Never insult an alligator until you've crossed the river.

Cordell Hull

Dates & Places Used:

469

TOPIC: Insults

Not Too Friendly

A woman at a grocery store was looking at the ice cream. Another woman came up behind her and grabbed hold of her hand. "Get away from there. You don't need that. You're already overweight."

The startled woman turned around to face her critic. The woman who had approached her realized she had confused this woman with a friend.

The woman gained her composure and responded to her critical assailant with these words: "You mean you have a friend!?!"

Dates & Places Used:

470 TOPIC: Insurance

Insured Cigars

A cigar smoker bought several hundred expensive cigars and had them insured against fire. After he'd smoked them all, he filed a claim, pointing out that the cigars had, in fact, been destroyed by fire.

The insurance company refused to pay, and then the man sued. The judge ruled that because the insurance company had agreed to insure the cigars against fire, it was legally responsible.

The company had no choice but to pay the claim. Then, when the man accepted the money, the company had him arrested for arson.

Dates & Places Used:

471 TOPIC: Insurance

Playing Doctor the Modern Way

Overheard: "Now I know health care really has become a major concern for everyone. The other day I saw a boy and a girl playing doctor. She asked for his Blue Cross card!"

Dates & Places Used:

472

Football Memory

The athletic department at Southern Methodist University had a tough time a few years ago due to overzealous alumni and their illegal gifts. When the new coach, Forrest Gregg, came on board, he had to begin building a new SMU football team. Shortly after he arrived at SMU, he was sitting in his office, studying the roster of students he had left and the ones he could draw from.

He was assessing their potential when all of a sudden the room got dark. It was caused by the shadow of a huge young man who was standing in the doorway of his office. Coach Gregg asked the young man what he wanted. This hulk of a boy said, "I want to play football."

Coach Gregg's eyes lit up, and he asked the young man to come into his office and have a seat. With excitement in his eyes he thought about the line and having this barn-size boy blocking the backfield. He got out his papers and asked the young man a few questions: "First, how old are you?"

The young man started counting on his fingers and then said, "Nineteen."

The coach looked at him a minute and said, "Okay," and asked, "how tall are you?"

The young man stood up, took his hand and measured up his leg, on up to his head, and then counted on his fingers again and said, "I'm six feet, eight inches tall."

Again the coach gave him a funny look, wrote down the answer, and asked, "Okay, what's your name?"

This time the young man paused, dazed off into space, nodded his head about fifteen times, and then said, "Charlie."

Well, that was too much for Coach Gregg, and he said, "All right, Charlie, I understand counting on your fingers to figure out how old you are. And I understand using your hand to measure how tall you are. But what was all the nodding of the head about when I asked you your name?"

Charlie answered, "Oh, that's simple, Coach. Happy Birthday to you! Happy Birthday to you! Happy Birthday, dear Charlie ..."

Dates & Places Used:

473

TOPIC: Intelligence

Not My Brains

Husband: "Junior must get his brains from one of us."
Wife: "It must be you. I still have mine."
Dates & Places Used:

474

TOPIC: Intelligence

Next to Die

Frustrated because of his wife ridiculing him for his stupidity, a man put a gun to his head and threatened suicide. When she burst out laughing at the apparent threat, he shouted, "Don't laugh, woman. After me, you're next!"
Dates & Places Used:

475

TOPIC: Interpretation

Decoding Messages

The ensign approached the captain of the ship as the captain was dining with his leading officers. The ensign reported that the captain had received a message from the admiral. The captain told the ensign to read the message aloud. The ensign did as he was told and read, "You idiot! It looks like you have bungled another mission! You're a poor excuse for a captain!"

The captain paused for a moment and responded: "Ensign, have that message decoded immediately!"
Dates & Places Used:

476

Native American Perspective

A benefactor wanted the Indian perspective on Little Big Horn. He asked an Indian artist to draw a picture illustrating it. After months of waiting, he received his picture. In the center was a large picture of General Custer. In the bottom right corner was a Jersey cow with a halo. In the left bottom corner was a southern plantation complete with cotton fields as far as the eye could see. Filling the cotton fields were Indians. When the benefactor asked the artist what the picture meant he explained, "General Custer: 'Holy cow! Where did all these cotton-pickin' Indians come from?'"

Dates & Places Used:

477

Wrong Resurrection Day

There was an alcoholic who kept putting off coming to grips with his habit of alcoholism. His family in desperation decided to frighten him into getting some help. One night he came home drunk, and they picked him up and carried him out to the cemetery. They buried him there, with only his head protruding from the ground.

When he finally came to, it was already morning. The birds were singing and the sun was shining. With his customary lack of concern, he looked all around at the forest of tombstones about him and said, "Well, imagine that. Resurrection day, and I'm the first one up."

Dates & Places Used:

478

Rewards of Interruptions

Do you know what happens to little boys who keep interrupting? They grow up and make a fortune doing commercials on television.

Dates & Places Used:

479

TOPIC: Introspection

A Good Sermon

The average man's idea of a good sermon is one that goes over his head and hits a neighbor.

Dates & Places Used:

480

TOPIC: Investments

Thar's Money in Them-Thar Teeth

My brother-in-law came for a visit last week. His father had worked as a dentist for years before he died. When the family went through his safe-deposit box, they found several bags of old teeth, filled or capped with gold. His father had often paid his patients for the old teeth and then put them away in his box.

Now usually when people have their teeth pulled, it is because the tooth is bad or rotten. These teeth were evidence of that fact. They looked awful and ugly. But my brother-in-law knew that the gold would be valuable so he made some contacts and found a company that would buy them. They were told that the tooth would be broken off and the gold would be refined with high heat and then tested to determine the value. The old, rotten teeth were brought in to the company and shortly after a check was issued for $4,000 ... well worth the effort.

God must look at us in the very same way. He sees us with all our old, ugly rottenness that has to be chipped away. He refines us to make us what he wants us to be. In the blood of his Son and in the power of the Holy Spirit, we are made new creations in Christ. The old has passed away and we become the children of God, with value and beauty restored in the image of God, gold as refined by fire.

Dates & Places Used:

481

TOPIC: Involvement

Wrong Side of the Boat

People who refuse to get involved in the problems of their community are like the two shipwrecked men in a lifeboat. From their end of the boat, the pair watched as those at the other end bailed frantically to keep the boat afloat.

The one said to the other, "Thank heaven, the hole is not on our end of the boat."

Dates & Places Used:

482

TOPIC: Jobs

Salary Security

The personnel manager said to the job applicant: "We keep salaries low so you won't have so much to lose if you get fired."

Dates & Places Used:

483

TOPIC: Jobs

Resumes and Irons in the Fire

An energetic young man entered the office of the personnel officer of a large corporation. As he entered the room, he approached the desk and plopped his resume onto the desk.

"You need look no further for candidates for this position. I am just the right person for this job."

During the course of their conversation, the young man proceeded to tell the personnel officer what was wrong with this corporation and how he would be able to fix these problems—probably within his first year of employment! As the young man concluded his presentation, he stood up and said, "But you had better hurry with your decision. Remember, I have other irons in the fire!"

With that the personnel officer stood, picked up the man's resume, handed it back to him, and said, "If you have other irons in the fire, I would suggest that you put this resume in with them!"

Dates & Places Used:

484 TOPIC: Jokes
Company Laughter

Brother: "I think we have company downstairs."
Sister: "How do you know that?"
Brother: "I just heard Mom laugh at one of Dad's jokes."
Dates & Places Used:

485 TOPIC: Judgment
Is Judgment Day a Holiday?

The preacher was waxing eloquent as he envisioned the Day of Judgment: "Lightning will flash, thunder will boom, rivers will overflow ... Fire will flame from the heavens ... The earth will quake violently ... darkness will fall upon the entire earth!"

A small boy's voice lifted from the congregation as he questioned his father, "Dad, do you think they'll let school out early that day?"
Dates & Places Used:

486

Wrong Jurors

There's one great flaw in our current jury system—it's scary to realize that your fate is in the hands of twelve people who could not figure out how to get excused from jury duty.

Dates & Places Used:

487

The Reason for Trials

A jury consists of twelve persons chosen to decide who has the best lawyer.

Dates & Places Used:

488

Dead Ducks

A hunter had spent the weekend hunting for ducks and had not even seen one. As he was driving home, he passed a farm with a pond filled with tame ducks. At the shore was a man feeding the ducks with a loaf of bread. The hunter stopped and approached the man. He explained his dilemma about finding no ducks and asked if the man would help him.

The man feeding the ducks said he would be delighted to help the hunter, but had no idea how he could do so. The hunter offered the man fifty dollars for just one shot at the ducks. Without hesitation, the man agreed. The hunter walked to the car and returned with his double-barrel shotgun. He shot both barrels at the ducks and killed twelve of them.

"I hope you don't mind that I killed so many of your ducks and only paid you fifty dollars, but a deal is a deal, right?"

"That's right sir—and I don't mind at all. These are not my ducks."

Dates & Places Used:

489

TOPIC: Justice

Justice Not Admissible

The problem with justice is that it is no longer admissible in a court of law.

Dates & Places Used:

490

TOPIC: Justice

Wrong Equation

Two wrongs might make a riot.

Dates & Places Used:

491

TOPIC: Kindness

Are You Jesus?

Several years ago a group of salesmen went to a regional sales meeting in Chicago. They assured their wives that they would be home in plenty of time for supper on Friday night.

One thing led to another and the meeting ran overtime. The men had to race to the airport, tickets in hand. As they barged through the terminal, one man inadvertently kicked over a table supporting a basket of apples. Without stopping they all reached the plane in time and boarded it with a sigh of relief. All but one. He paused, got in touch with his feelings, and experienced a twinge of compassion for the girl whose apple stand had been overturned. He waved good-bye to his companions and returned to the terminal. He was glad he did. The ten-year-old girl was blind.

The salesman gathered up the apples and noticed that several of the apples were battered and bruised. He reached into his wallet and said to the girl, "Here, please take this ten dollars for the damage we did. I hope it didn't spoil your day."

As the salesman started to walk away, the bewildered girl called out to him, "Are you Jesus?"

He stopped in mid-stride . . . and he wondered.

Dates & Places Used:

492

TOPIC: Kindness

Waiting to Do Good

He who waits to do a great deal of good at once, will never do anything.
Dates & Places Used:

493

TOPIC: Kindness

A Few Kind Words

Joe had been away from his family for two weeks and was lonely. As he sat down in a little cafe to eat, the waitress asked, "What would you like?"

Joe responded, "I want some lasagna and a few kind words."

The waitress soon returned with his order, set it in front of him, and turned to leave when Joe said, "Say, what about my kind words?"

She leaned down to his ear and whispered, "Don't eat the lasagna."

Dates & Places Used:

494

TOPIC: Kindness

Kind Words Better Than Wit

A word of kindness is seldom spoken in vain, while witty sayings are as easily lost as pearls slipping from a broken string.
Dates & Places Used:

495

TOPIC: Kindness

Kindness Echoes

Speak all kind words and you will hear kind echoes.
Dates & Places Used:

496

TOPIC: Kindness

The Kindest Word

*The kindest word ever said
is the unkind word
that was never said.*

Dates & Places Used:

497

TOPIC: Knowledge

Science and Common Sense

Science is a first-rate piece of furniture for a man's upper chamber, if he has common sense on the ground floor.

Dates & Places Used:

498

TOPIC: Knowledge

Too Much Knowledge

Nothing, with the possible exception of a fire or the whistle to quit work, can break up a discussion as quickly as a fellow who actually knows what he's talking about.

Dates & Places Used:

499

TOPIC: Law

The Patrol Is Against Us

On the walls of the men's room at a Kansas truck stop were scribbled the words from Romans 8: "If God be for us, who can be against us?"

Scrawled beneath someone had added:

"The Highway Patrol!"

Dates & Places Used:

500

Legal-Size Paper

The only reason for legal-size paper is that lawyers are unable to get all their mumbo jumbo on the same size of paper the rest of us use.

Dates & Places Used:

501

Lawyers Needed

It's a good thing there are lawyers, or there would be no one here to explain to the rest of the population why it is so important for us to have lawyers.

Dates & Places Used:

502

Christian and a Lawyer

Two New England farmers were walking through the cemetery when they saw a tombstone, "Here lies a Christian and a lawyer."

Said one, "They must have been hard up for ground 'round here, putting two men to a grave."

Dates & Places Used:

503

Milked by the Lawyer

Jewish parable: Two farmers claimed to own the same cow. While one pulled on the head and the other tugged at the tail, the cow was milked by a lawyer.

Dates & Places Used:

504

TOPIC: Lawyers

A Lawyer's Maxim

The big print giveth,
The small print taketh away!
Dates & Places Used:

505

TOPIC: Lawyers

Up to Their Necks

What do you do with ten lawyers buried up to their necks in cement?

Get more cement!
Dates & Places Used:

506

TOPIC: Laziness

Grandma Has the Brush

Dad telephoned his home. His teenage son answered.
"What are you doing, Son?"
"I'm just lying here in the living room watching television."
"Where is your mom?"
"She's out painting the house."
Dad was upset with his son's laziness. "Son, why don't you get out there and help your poor mother?"
"Well, I would," answered the boy, "but I can't."
"Why not?" asked his father.
"Because Grandma is using the other brush."
Dates & Places Used:

507

TOPIC: Leadership

Leadership Shortage

There is no shortage of leaders;
There is only a shortage of those willing to follow them.
Dates & Places Used:

508

TOPIC: Leadership

Leaders Who Move People

General Charles Gordon once asked Li Hung Chang, an old Chinese leader, a double question: "What is leadership?" and "How is humanity divided?"

He received this cryptic answer: "There are only three kinds of people in the world–those who are immovable, those who are movable, and those who move them!"

Dates & Places Used:

509

TOPIC: Leadership

Presidential Investment

It is reported that a few years back the president of the United States was trying to paint a brighter economic picture to the press than his administration had reason to take credit for. During a news conference, he was asked about the strength of the economy. The president answered, "If I wasn't the president of the United States, I would invest heavily in the stock market."

An unidentified voice from the back of the room responded, "If you weren't the president, we would all invest heavily in the stock market."

Dates & Places Used:

510

TOPIC: Leadership

Eisenhower's Art of Leadership

Leadership is the art of getting somebody else to do something you want done because he wants to do it.

Dates & Places Used:

511

TOPIC: Leadership

Access to Power

Access to power must be confined to men who are not in love with it.

Dates & Places Used:

512

TOPIC: Leadership

Leaders or Babies

In "The Last Days Newsletter," Leonard Ravenhill tells about a group of tourists visiting a picturesque village. They walked by an old man sitting beside a fence. In a rather patronizing way, one tourist asked, "Were any great men born in this village?"

The old man replied, "Nope, only babies."

The frothy question brought forth a profound answer. There are no instant heroes, whether in this world or in the kingdom of God. Growth takes time, and as 1 Timothy 3:6 and 5:22 point out, even spiritual leadership must be earned.

Dates & Places Used:

513

TOPIC: Leadership

No One Listens

Bill Clinton once told his wife Hillary that being president is kind of like running a cemetery–there are a lot of people under you, but no one is listening.

Dates & Places Used:

514

TOPIC: Leaven

Number Leaven

The children were receiving religious instruction. Their teacher told them that Christians are the light of the world, the salt of the earth, and the leaven of society.

The analogies of light and salt were obvious, but the children were confused about what leaven was. One of the children ventured a guess: "Leaven is what comes after the number ten!"

Dates & Places Used:

515

TOPIC: Lies

Wolf Pack Lies

Lies are like wolves;
They never travel alone.
They have learned that they do more damage
if they hunt in packs.

Dates & Places Used:

516

TOPIC: Lies

Born Storytellers

No one is a born storyteller, but if you work hard at it, you can avoid being one.

Dates & Places Used:

517

TOPIC: Lies

Liar Auctioneers

Auctioneers and lawyers will never tell lies, unless it is absolutely necessary.

Dates & Places Used:

518

TOPIC: Lies

Necessary Actions

A little boy's version of the Old Testament verse: "A lie is an abomination unto the Lord, and a very present help in trouble."

Dates & Places Used:

519

A Scoreless Life

Life is more fun if you don't keep score.

Dates & Places Used:

520

Shot by a Jealous Husband

Three elderly men were discussing the type of accidental death to be preferred:

The first man, who was eighty-years-old, said, "My preference would be to fall to earth suddenly in a plane."

The eighty-five-year-old man said, "I should prefer to go down with a ship in an ocean."

Then the ninety-year-old said, "I should like to be shot by a jealous husband."

That may be nothing more than wishful thinking! Be that as it may, we can't decide how we are going to die, but we can decide how we are going to live.

Dates & Places Used:

521

Calvin's Question

In the comic strip, *Calvin and Hobbes*, Calvin is at school, and his teacher is attempting to teach the class:

"If there are no questions, we'll move on to the next chapter."

"I have a question."

"Certainly, Calvin, what is it?"

"What's the point of human existence?"

"I meant any questions about the subject at hand."

"Oh—frankly, I'd like to have the issue resolved before I expend any more energy on this."

Dates & Places Used:

522

TOPIC: Life

Frog Lives

There is an animal that has more lives than a cat. This animal is a frog. He croaks every night!
Dates & Places Used:

523

TOPIC: Life

The Value of Birthdays

Learning to appreciate the unappreciated: Birthdays are good for you. Statistics show that the people who have the most live the longest.
Dates & Places Used:

524

TOPIC: Light

Reflecting the Light

On a street corner a small boy was holding a mirror in his hand, reflecting the light of the sun toward a house and centering the bright spot on one of the windows. "What are you doing?" asked a man who was passing by.

"My brother is sick in that house," said the little boy, "and since the sun never enters his room, I was trying to reflect a little of it in there with this mirror."

"Most Christians are talking when they should be listening."
Dates & Places Used:

525

TOPIC: Light

Saints Shine

A couple took their young son with them on a trip to Europe where they visited many of the cathedrals on the tourist trek.

When they returned home the little boy's Sunday school teacher asked him, "Did you learn what a saint is?"

He remembered the many stained glass windows which depicted the Christian saints so beautifully, and he said, "A saint is a man who the light shines through."

I wonder if that is not the best definition I've ever heard, and a good testimony to what we are trying to do ourselves here on earth.

Dates & Places Used:

526 TOPIC: Limitations

Positive Priorities

There have been a number of television programs and books produced by positive-thinking promoters who say you can be anything you want to be and do anything you want to do. It makes one curious what would happen if all of them decided to be the most popular program or the best-selling book.

Dates & Places Used:

527 TOPIC: Listening

Get the Message

A shipping company had advertised a job opening for a ship's radio operator and the outer office was crowded with applicants for the position. They were waiting to be called in turn, and were talking to each other loudly enough to be heard over the sound of a loudspeaker.

Another applicant entered, filled out an application, and sat quietly for a few moments. Suddenly, he rose and walked into the office marked "Private." A few minutes later, he came out wearing a broad grin—he had been hired.

A man in the waiting room protested. "Look here," he said. "We were here first, why did you go in there before us?"

The successful applicant replied, "Any one of you could have landed that job, but none of you were listening to the Morse code signals coming over the loudspeaker. The message was, 'We desire to fill this position with someone who is constantly alert. If you are getting this message, come into the private office immediately.'"

Dates & Places Used:

528
TOPIC: Loans
Better to Give Than Lend

It is better to give than to lend, and it costs about the same.

Dates & Places Used:

529
TOPIC: Logic
The Last Battle

Teacher: "In which of his battles was King Gustavus Adolphus of Sweden killed?"

Student: "I believe it was the last one."

Dates & Places Used:

530
TOPIC: Logic
Sun or Moon

The teacher asked his class, "Which is more important to us—the moon or the sun?"

One of the students answered, "The moon."

The teacher asked why the moon was more important than the sun.

The student explained, "The moon gives us light at night when we need it most. . . . The sun just gives us light in the daytime when we don't really need it."

Dates & Places Used:

531

T-Ball Strikeout

Gladys Thornapple is fixing lunch when in walks her son, Wilberforce, all decked out in his baseball outfit. Mom asks, "How did Little League go?"

Wilberforce growls, "Terrible. I struck out three times."

Trying to console her son, Mom says, "That's all part of the game, honey."

Wilberforce explodes with exasperation, "Mom, it's T-ball!"

Dates & Places Used:

532

Ocean of Emotion

Love is an ocean of emotion in a sea of expense.

Dates & Places Used:

533

Love Doesn't Always Fix It

One of the ladies in my church tells of helping her son with some schoolwork. Sean proudly handed his mother an essay he had written and asked her to read it. An educated lady with a master's degree, she read the paper with pen in hand. As she read she corrected the grammar and spelling and handed the paper back to him.

Sean looked the paper over and noticed all of the corrections. With tears in his eyes he looked up at his mother and said, "I didn't want you to fix it. I just wanted you to like it."

How often we busy ourselves trying to "fix" those closest to us—correct their mistakes and bad habits. We convince ourselves we are doing it for "their own good." And in reality, all they really want and need is for us to just like them.

Dates & Places Used:

534

TOPIC: Love

Love Sees What Is Not

Love is a state in which a man sees things most decidedly as they are not.

Dates & Places Used:

535

TOPIC: Loyalty

Fat and Pretty

The little boy loved his mother and loved to sit on her lap. One day the boy was sitting on his mother's lap while she was reading a book to him. After she finished the book, he cuddled up close to her and said, "I love you, Mommy!"

His mother was grateful for his love but mistakenly questioned the worth of its object. She asked, "How can you love a mother who is so fat and ugly?"

The son quickly protested, "Oh, Mommy, *you are not!* You're *fat* and *pretty!*"

Dates & Places Used:

536

TOPIC: Luck

Lucky Parents

Lucky parents who have fine children usually have lucky children who have fine parents.

Dates & Places Used:

537

TOPIC: Managers

Management Without Leadership

Efficient management without effective leadership is kind of like straightening the deck chairs on the Titanic.

Dates & Places Used:

194

538

TOPIC: Manners

Manners Are Not

Manners are the noises you don't make when eating soup.
Dates & Places Used:

539

TOPIC: Manners

Politically Correct Hecklers

A fan hollers at the official, "Yo, Ref! You intellectually challenged individual! That was a foul! Are you visually impaired or what?!"
Dates & Places Used:

540

TOPIC: Marriage

The Honeymoon Is Over

My wife, a registered nurse, once fussed over every pain or mishap that came my way. Recently, however, I got an indication that the honeymoon is over.

I was about to fix the attic fan, and as I lifted myself from the ladder into the attic, I scratched my forehead on a crossbeam. Crawling along, I picked up splinters in both hands, and I cut one hand replacing the fan belt. On the way down the ladder, I missed the last two rungs and turned my ankle.

When I limped into the kitchen, my wife took one look and said, "Are those your good pants?"
Dates & Places Used:

541

Wisdom in Marriage

The poet thus penned these words of wisdom:
"To keep a marriage brimming
with love in the loving cup,
whenever you're wrong, admit it.
Whenever you're right, shut up!"
Dates & Places Used:

542

Nonproductive Redecoration

A mother was showing a friend her house. As they entered the master bedroom she pointed out the twin beds and mentioned that she had redecorated after the birth of the twins.
Dates & Places Used:

543

Communication Line Is Busy

It's not that the husband does not want to reach out to his wife, but somehow there is interference. "I wanted to get in touch with her feelings," declared one social worker, "but since she was constantly getting in touch with her own feelings, the line was always busy."
Dates & Places Used:

544

Mr. Always Right

Just a word of wisdom for the woman who is looking for Mr. Right: Be sure that his first name is not Always!
Dates & Places Used:

545

TOPIC: Marriage

Doing Nothing for Each Other

"My husband and I have a very happy marriage," bragged one woman. "There's nothing I wouldn't do for him, there's nothing he wouldn't do for me—and that's the way we go through life—doing nothing for each other."
Dates & Places Used:

546

TOPIC: Marriage

Married Though Apart

Rodney Dangerfield had some advice about marriage. He said, "We eat apart, we take separate vacations. We never see each other. We're doing everything we can to keep our marriage together!"
Dates & Places Used:

547

TOPIC: Marriage

Ideal Waits for Ideal

When I was a young man I vowed never to marry until I found the ideal woman. Well, I found her—but, alas, she was waiting for the ideal man.
Dates & Places Used:

548

TOPIC: Marriage

Numerous Proposals

It's good when a woman is constantly being asked to get married . . .

It's not good when she is only asked by one or two people—HER PARENTS!
Dates & Places Used:

549

TOPIC: Marriage

Marry Well or Philosophize

By all means marry. If you get a good wife you will become happy, and if you get a bad one you will become a philosopher.
Dates & Places Used:

550

TOPIC: Marriage

Devil in the Family

An old Puritan once wrote, "If you marry a child of the devil, you can expect to have trouble with your father-in-law."
Dates & Places Used:

551

TOPIC: Marriage

Male Followership

There was a line of men standing in front of the Pearly Gates, waiting to get in. A sign overhead read:
"FOR MEN WHO HAVE BEEN DOMINATED ALL THEIR LIVES BY THEIR WIVES."
The line extended as far as the eye could see. There was another sign nearby:
"FOR MEN WHO HAVE NEVER BEEN DOMINATED BY THEIR WIVES."
One man was standing under it. St. Peter came over to him and said, "What are you standing here for?"
The man said, "I don't know. My wife told me to stand here."
Dates & Places Used:

552

TOPIC: Marriage

Make It Interesting

A man arrived home early to find his wife in the arms of his best friend. The friend admitted that they were in love, and he came up with a plan to quiet the enraged husband. "Let's play gin rummy," he suggested. "If I win, you get a divorce so I can marry your wife. If you win, I promise never to see her again. What do you say?"

"Okay, okay," the man agreed. "But how about if we play a penny a point just to make it interesting."

Dates & Places Used:

553

TOPIC: Marriage

Three-Ring Circus

Some people think marriage is a three-ring circus.
First there's the *engagement ring*.
Then there's the *wedding ring*.
And then there's the *suffer-ring*.

Dates & Places Used:

554

TOPIC: Marriage

Hard Work
for Long Marriage

A young student was telling his school teacher about his grandparents who were celebrating their fiftieth anniversary. His teacher was quite impressed and said, "Your grandparents are certainly lucky!"

The boy immediately objected, "Oh no, Grandma told me it wasn't luck; she said it took a lot of work!"

Dates & Places Used:

555

TOPIC: Marriage

Marriage Adventure

Marriage is an adventure—like going to war.
Dates & Places Used:

556

TOPIC: Marriage

One Runs Our Lives

A man explained how he and his wife learned to resolve their differences:

"My wife and I have a perfect understanding. I don't try to run her life, and I don't try to run mine!"
Dates & Places Used:

557

TOPIC: Marriage

The Cost of Marriage

A married couple may reach their golden wedding anniversary without ever having thought of divorce, but not without ever having thought of murder.

Statistics prove that single men die more quickly than married men. Therefore, if you are looking for a long, slow death—get married!
Dates & Places Used:

558

TOPIC: Marriage

Who Gets Missed?

"My wife ran off with my best friend," the man admitted. "And I sure do miss him."
Dates & Places Used:

559

TOPIC: Marriage

Temptation and Opportunity

Marriage is popular because it combines the maximum of temptation with the maximum of opportunity.

Dates & Places Used:

560

TOPIC: Marriage

Almost Thankful

Bigamy is having one husband too many. Monogamy is the same.

Dates & Places Used:

561

TOPIC: Marriage

What God Has Joined Together

A Sunday school teacher was showing pictures to her class and asking them what Bible verse each situation reminded them of. One of the pictures shown was that of two little boys, one pulling the head of a cat and the other pulling the cat's tail. She asked the class what verse this picture reminded them of.

One little fellow had recently attended a wedding and remembered something the pastor had read from the Bible. He raised his hand to volunteer his insight. When the teacher called upon the boy, he stood and reported: "What God has joined together let no man put asunder!"

Dates & Places Used:

562

TOPIC: Marriage

Honest Communication

A lifelong survivor of marriage once admitted to a friend: "OK, it's true, we fight. But, to be honest, we have never gone to bed mad. Of course one year we were up for three months."

Dates & Places Used:

563

TOPIC: Marriage

Mom Loves Him Most

One evening I drove my husband's car to the shopping mall. On my return, I noticed how dusty the outside of his car was and cleaned it up a bit. When I finally entered the house, I called out, "The woman who loves you the most in the world just cleaned your headlights and windshield."

My husband looked up and said, "Mom's here?"

Dates & Places Used:

564

TOPIC: Marriage

Some Authority

A marriage counselor was listening to a couple as they explained their conflicts. After listening for a while, he attempted to offer some hope to what seemed irreconcilable differences. He leaned forward and interjected, "The problem that you seem to have here is that you are both overreacting to minor problems. I know how you feel though, I had the same problem with my fifth wife."

Dates & Places Used:

TOPIC: Marriage

All but Three Qualities

A newspaper cartoon depicted a woman with folded arms and a superior expression on her face. She says to her husband, "A good husband needs to be strong, caring, and sensitive. You have all but three of those qualities."

Dates & Places Used:

TOPIC: Marriage

Honeymoons Are Not Fun

Heaven can be a bit perplexing to us as to its desirability. Perhaps this can be seen by the analogous conversation of a father with his four-year-old son on the issue of honeymoons.

"Andrew, when you grow up, if you get married, your honeymoon will be one of the most delightful times of your life."

"Oh, you mean I get to take my toy dinosaurs along?"

"Uh ... no ... you probably won't want to. But you'll still have a fantastic time!"

"Well then, can Jeffrey from next door come along on my honeymoon?"

"No, sorry; Jeffrey can't come."

"Then I don't know if I want to go on a honeymoon, Daddy. It doesn't sound like much fun to me."

Dates & Places Used:

TOPIC: Materialism

Impressive Consumption

Too many of us are spending money we haven't earned ... to buy things we don't need ... to impress people we don't like.

Dates & Places Used:

568

Beatles Wrote Swimming Pools

Somebody said to me, "But the Beatles were antimaterialistic."
That's a huge myth.

John and I literally used to sit down and say, "Now, let's write a swimming pool."   *Paul McCartney*

Dates & Places Used:

569

Where Is His Mommy?

One of those high-powered, take-charge corporation executives was checking into the hospital. Barking orders left and right, he had his own way until he reached the desk of a small, mild-mannered lady. She typed the man's name on a slip of paper and stuck the paper onto the man's wrist before he could react.

"What's *this* for?" demanded Mr. Big.

"*That*," replied the woman, "is so we won't give you to the wrong mother when you're ready to leave."

Dates & Places Used:

570

Uncertain Maturity

Maturity is when we change from cocksureness into thoughtful uncertainty ...

Dates & Places Used:

571

TOPIC: Media

News Coverage Better

It's not the world that's got so much worse, but the news coverage that's got so much better.

Dates & Places Used:

572

TOPIC: Mediocrity

More of the Same

If you always do what you always did, you'll always get what you always got.

Dates & Places Used:

573

TOPIC: Membership

Four Kinds of Bones

Membership in every association is made up of four kinds of bones:

1. The WISH BONES who spend their time wishing someone else would do the work;
2. The JAW BONES who do all the talking, but very little else;
3. The KNUCKLE BONES who knock everything that anyone else is trying to do;
4. The BACK BONES who get under the load and do the work.

Dates & Places Used:

574

TOPIC: Memory

Something to Remember

Not too long ago we received a memorial gift to the church. There was a short note written on a beautiful little card that described whom the memorial was for. It said the usual thing, "Enclosed you will find a check to be used as a memorial for …"

Unfortunately, the person who sent it forgot to sign the note AND to enclose the check. And to top it all off, the card had been purchased from the Alzheimer's Foundation.

Dates & Places Used:

575

TOPIC: Memory

God Remembers

A pupil once brought to the philosopher Hegel a passage of the philosopher's writings and asked for an interpretation. Hegel examined it and replied, "When that passage was written, there were two who knew its meaning–God and myself. Now alas! There is but one, and that one is God."

Dates & Places Used:

576

TOPIC: Mercy

You Need Mercy

A woman went to a photographer to get her picture taken. She insisted that this portrait do her justice.

The photographer studied his subject for a few moments and said, "May I suggest, madam, that what you need is not justice, but mercy?"

Dates & Places Used:

577

The Old Goat

A young couple invited their parson for Sunday dinner. While they were in the kitchen preparing the meal, the minister asked their son what they were having.

"Goat", the little boy replied.

"Goat?" replied the startled man of the cloth. "Are you sure about that?"

"Yep," said the youngster. "I heard Pa say to Ma, 'Might as well have the old goat for dinner today as any other day.'"

Dates & Places Used:

578

TOPIC: Miracles

Practicing Miracles

In Sunday school the minister was trying to illustrate the word "miracle." "Boys and girls," he said, "suppose I stood on the roof of a ten-story building, lost my balance, and fell off. Then all of a sudden, in midair, a whirlwind swept me up and brought me safely to the ground. Now what word would you use to describe this?"

After a long silence a boy raised his hand and said, "Luck?"

"True, true," replied the minister. "It could be luck–but that's not the word I wanted. I'll repeat the story. There I am on top of the ten-story building again, and I fall. A whirlwind catches me in midair and places me safely on the ground. Think now–what word would describe the situation?"

"Accident," cried out one girl.

"No, no," answered the minister. "Listen carefully for the third time. I'm on that same building, I fall and am swept to safety by a sudden whirlwind. What word could account for my safely reaching the ground?"

The boys and girls shouted in unison: "Practice!"

Dates & Places Used:

579

TOPIC: Miracles

When Dead Ducks Fly

Two friends were out hunting and one was always bragging about what a good shot he was. About that time a duck flew over. He took aim and fired ... the duck flew on unscathed.

He paused a minute and said, "My friend, you are now witnessing a miracle. There flies a dead duck."

We need to witness miracles! We need to experience miracles!

Dates & Places Used:

580

TOPIC: Miracles

Science and Miracles

We have published a similar illustration concerning the cooking of turkeys. Here is one that may be more relevant for travelers.

An incident at an airline counter in Philadelphia shows how our age takes miracles for granted. The clerk picked up the telephone and heard the caller ask, "How long does it take to go from Philadelphia to Phoenix?"

Because the clerk was busy with a customer and would have to look up the answer, she said, "Just a minute."

As she was about to put down the phone, the clerk heard the caller say, "Thank you," and hang up.

Dates & Places Used:

581

TOPIC: Miracles

Bible Mysteries

A retreat master once told an amusing story about a country preacher who announced that he would preach on Noah and the Ark on the following Sunday. He proceeded to give the scriptural reference for the congregation to read ahead of time.

A couple of ornery boys noticed something interesting about the placement of the story of the Flood in the Bible. They slipped into the church and glued two pages of the pulpit Bible together. On the next Sunday the preacher got up to read his text.

"Noah took himself a wife," the preacher read, "and she was ..." He turned the page to continue, "300 cubits long, 50 cubits wide, and 30 cubits high." He paused, scratched his head, turned the page back and read it silently, turned the page and continued reading. Then he looked up at the congregation and said, "I've been reading this old Bible for nigh on to fifty years, but there are some things that are hard to believe."

Dates & Places Used:

582 TOPIC: Miracles
Impossibility Takes Longer

"If it's difficult we do it immediately. If it's impossible it takes a little longer.

Miracles by appointment only."

Dates & Places Used:

583 TOPIC: Miracles
Allen's Swiss Sign

If only God would give me some clear sign–like making a large deposit in my name at a Swiss bank.   *Woody Allen*

Dates & Places Used:

584 TOPIC: Miracles
Strange Miracles

Have you ever thought about the everyday miracles?

How did God make a black cow that eats green grass to give white milk that makes yellow butter?

Dates & Places Used:

585

TOPIC: Mischief

Turn It Off First

I remember the last time I received a good spanking from one of my parents. My youngest brother and I were helping my mother bake a cake in the kitchen. We would often fight over who got to lick the beaters after the mixing was through. On this occasion my youngest brother had beaten me to the kitchen and asked first. When I had finished mixing, I did what I was told and handed the beaters to my little brother.

I was immediately grabbed by the arm, turned over my mother's knee, and spanked. After the spanking, my mother grabbed me by both shoulders, looked me squarely in the eyes, and in a stern voice said, "Next time, turn the mixer off first!"

Dates & Places Used:

586

TOPIC: Missionaries

Taste of Religion

Captured missionary to cannibals: "At least you get a taste of religion."

Dates & Places Used:

587

TOPIC: Missionaries

Eat Up the Prophet

It's difficult for missionaries to make a living working with cannibals–they keep eating up the prophet!

Dates & Places Used:

588

TOPIC: Mistakes

Mistaken Adjustment

A well-adjusted man is the fellow who can make the same mistake twice without getting nervous about it.

Dates & Places Used:

589

TOPIC: Mistakes

Mistakes Only the Beginning

If we learn nothing from our mistakes, they become the stepping-stones to utter failure.
Dates & Places Used:

590

TOPIC: Mistakes

Scientific Hindsight

Hindsight is an exact science.
Dates & Places Used:

591

TOPIC: Mistakes

Dear Dobonson

"Dear Dobonson: You are a mean and curle thing. You and your dumb sayings whon't take you to heaven. Kids don't like wippens."
Dates & Places Used:

592

TOPIC: Misunderstandings

Too Long to Wait

Two friends were talking together. The first man asked, "How did you enjoy the play last night?"

His friend, who was making a genuine attempt at raising his level of sophistication, answered, "Oh, it was fine, but we only got to stay for the first act."

"Why did you only stay for the first act?" his friend probed.

"Well, I wanted to stay for the whole thing, seeing this was the first play I ever attended, but the program said that the next act was taking place three days later."
Dates & Places Used:

593 TOPIC: Misunderstanding
Windy Window

Elderly woman at airline ticket counter: "No window seat, please. I don't want my new hairdo mussed up."
Dates & Places Used:

594 TOPIC: Misunderstanding
Elementary Logic

My wife, Mary, is a fifth grade teacher at Mary Moore Elementary School. They had just finished a short week due to a Monday holiday. She and a couple of her students were talking about how quick school had gone and Mary said it was because of the short week. One of the girls looked at Mary and said, "You mean if we had gone to school on Monday this wouldn't be Friday?"
Dates & Places Used:

595 TOPIC: Money
Barely Enough

A man went to the bank to cash a check. After receiving the money, he stood at the window and counted and recounted and recounted. The cashier finally said, "What's the matter? Didn't I give you enough?"

He answered, "Just barely."

Note the tremendous truth of Romans 8:32:"He who did not spare his own Son but gave him up for us all, will he not also give us all things with him?" If you allow that verse to get hold of you, it will have solved ninety-nine percent of your problem about desiring the will of God in your stewardship.

Dates & Places Used:

596

TOPIC: Money

Play Something Expensive

Parents who had invested a goodly amount in music lessons for their son admonished him in front of guests to "play something expensive."

Dates & Places Used:

597

TOPIC: Money

More Sounds of Money

Money may talk, but why can't it talk louder, speak with authority, and say what I want it to say?

Dates & Places Used:

598

TOPIC: Money

Give a Little Money

A wife asked her husband, "Can you give me a little money?" Her husband responded, "Yes, how little?"

Dates & Places Used:

599

Getting Your Money's Worth

A couple who were traveling along the interstate got hungry and decided to stop at a truck stop and have supper. They were not accustomed to eating at these remote diners, but were hungry enough to chance it. As they approached the door, a truck driver walked out of the restaurant. They asked the driver if the food was good.

The driver said he had eaten in this restaurant many times. He discouraged them from doing so with the following words: "The food is terrible, the mashed potatoes are watery, the meat is tough, the coffee is stale, and the pie is like cardboard. Oh, and one other thing—the portions are too small!"

Dates & Places Used:

600

Wallet Wounds

A Scotsman caught a taxi and they were hit by another car. The door flew open and the Scot was thrown to the pavement, bleeding and in great pain.

The cab driver jumped out, ran to the man, and asked if there was anything he could do for him.

"There sure is," moaned the Scot. "Shut off the meter."

Dates & Places Used:

601

Prior Earnings

It is especially hard to work for money you've already spent for something you didn't need.

Dates & Places Used:

214

602

TOPIC: Money

Money Never Listens

Money may talk, but have you ever noticed how hard of hearing it is when you call it?

Dates & Places Used:

603

TOPIC: Money

Misplaced Values

A child simply underestimates the proper worth of things. A number of years ago, I asked Marci (she was about five then) what she would buy if she had one hundred dollars to spend. She replied, " . . . a lot of toys, one horse, and one bird." That was it. That's the stuff dreams are made of–to a five-year-old child.

A little girl once approached her father and said, "Daddy, may I have a nickel?" The father drew out his wallet and, feeling generous, offered her a dollar bill. But the little girl, not knowing what it was, would not take it. "I don't want that," she said. "I want a nickel."

Dates & Places Used:

604

TOPIC: Money

Wealth Like a Viper

Wealth is like a viper, which is harmless if a person knows how to take hold of it; but if they do not, it will entwine round his hand and bite him.

Dates & Places Used:

605

TOPIC: Money

Money Helps You Look

Money doesn't bring you happiness, but it enables you to look for it in more places.

Dates & Places Used:

TOPIC: Money

Adjustments

A young couple had been married for about a year. They were struggling financially and decided to do something about it. They would develop a strategy. They sat down one day to talk about their finances, and the wife said to her husband, "If we miss two payments on the refrigerator and one payment on the washing machine, we'll have enough money to make a down payment on a new television set."

Dates & Places Used:

TOPIC: Money

Money Not Everything

Money is not everything ... there are also credit cards, debit cards, bankcards, money orders, certified checks, and traveler's checks.

Dates & Places Used:

TOPIC: Money

Minor Discrepancies

Recently I read about a reunion of those involved in the formation of the old American football league. The veterans and the owners swapped stories and enjoyed an evening of laughs and reflections together. Al Davis, currently the owner of the Los Angeles Raiders, remembers that those sitting at his table stared with envy at Nicky Hilton, who was to speak that evening in 1959. Nicky Hilton was introduced as having recently made $100,000 in the baseball business in Los Angeles.

Mr. Hilton stepped to the microphone and said he needed to correct what had been said. It was not he who had that experience, it was his brother Baron. And it wasn't Los Angeles, but

San Diego. And it wasn't baseball, it was football. And it wasn't $100,000, it was a million dollars ... and he didn't make it, he lost it!

Dates & Places Used:

609

TOPIC: Morals

Making Crooked Lines and Lives

The thing that makes men and rivers crooked is following the lines of least resistance.

Dates & Places Used:

610

TOPIC: Morals

The Teacher Has No Morals

A kindergarten teacher was suddenly taken ill and a replacement was hastily found. The substitute teacher was at a loss as to what to do with the children. She decided to tell them stories. And always, at the end of each story, she would say, "And the moral of that story is ..." After dozens of stories, the children had sat through dozens of morals.

The regular teacher recovered from her illness and returned to her class. One of her students greeted her with a smile and said, "Teacher, I'm glad you're back. I like you better than that other teacher."

The teacher was flattered by the child, but was curious. "Why do you like me better than the other teacher?"

The child looked into the teacher's eyes and said, "Because you don't have any morals."

Dates & Places Used:

611

TOPIC: Mothers

Mother Kneaded Him

The Pillsbury dough-boy was recently interviewed and asked how he could always maintain such a joyful disposition in spite of the fact he was a bit overweight and so pale in complexion. His answer was simple: He kept such a disposition because his mother always KNEADED him.

Guess he is just a slice off the old loaf!

Dates & Places Used:

612

TOPIC: Mothers

Mom and the Catsup

There was a father and son who went camping and spent the weekend together. On the way home, the father said, "There now, wasn't that fun?"

The boy responded, "I guess so, Dad. Only next time, could we bring Mom and the catsup?"

Dates & Places Used:

613

TOPIC: Mothers

Take Your Own Naps

When a frazzled mother sent her little boy to bed, she heard him grumbling to himself, "Every time she gets tired, I'm the one who ends up having to take a nap."

Dates & Places Used:

614

TOPIC: Mothers

Too Hard on Mom

A father and his son were talking together when the father asked the son what he wanted for his birthday. The boy said he wanted a baby brother. His birthday wish came true–he got a baby brother.

Prior to his next birthday his father asked his son again, "What would you like for your birthday?"

The little boy hesitantly told his father, "Dad, what I would really like is a pony, but I'm afraid that would be too hard on Mom."

Dates & Places Used:

615

TOPIC: Mothers

Children Start with Labor

A mother was considering her plight in life: "I guess if it was going to be easy, it would not have started with something the doctor called 'labor.'"

Dates & Places Used:

616

TOPIC: Mothers

When Without a Tissue

One day I looked out the door to check on my four-year-old and two-year-old playing outside. My two-year-old, Ellen, was on the ground facedown and four-year-old Noah was on his knees beside her. Thinking she might be hurt, I raced out to check on them. "What's the matter with Ellen?" I called.

Noah answered, "I was getting her to blow her nose on the ground because we didn't have a Kleenex!"

Dates & Places Used:

617

Mom's Been Home Too Long

A mother knows she's been home too long for the following reasons:

1. She begins to talk to Barney as a real person.
2. She forgets which one is real—Mister Rogers or King Friday.
3. She cries for a wedding on Sesame Street.
4. She is one of the congregation that JUST laughed at the first three reasons—because she knew what all three of them was about.

Dates & Places Used:

618

Keep Mom Running Smoothly

Perhaps mothers should come with a maintenance agreement which provides for a complete overhaul every five years, three kids, or 300,000 miles, whichever comes first. Here are several points which ought to be included:

Fuel—While most mothers will run indefinitely on hot coffee, pizza, and hamburgers, an occasional gourmet meal for two in elegant surroundings will add immeasurably to increased efficiency.

Motor—A mother's motor is probably one of the most dependable anywhere. A mother can start and reach top speed from a prone position at a single cry from a sleeping child. To keep that motor at peak efficiency, regular breaks are recommended. A leisurely bath and nap every 1,000 miles, a baby-sitter every 10,000 miles, and a two-week live-in sitter every 100,000 miles will do wonders.

Battery—Batteries should be recharged regularly. Roses, candy, or other thoughtful and unexpected gifts often do the trick.

Chassis–A mother operates best when her chassis is properly maintained. Her wardrobe would be changed as needed every fall and spring. Regular exercise should be encouraged and provided for. A complete change of hairdo and makeup should be part of the regular maintenance. When the chassis begins to sag, there are a number of possible remedies, including racquetball and Weight Watchers.

Tune-ups–Mothers need regular tune-ups. Compliments are both the cheapest and most appreciated.

By following these simple instructions, the average mother would last a lifetime, providing love and caring to those who need her most.

Dates & Places Used:

619

TOPIC: Mothers

Mom Knows the Swing

Minor leaguer Pete Rose, Jr., son of baseball's all-time hits leader, on why he calls his mother when he is in a slump: "My dad was such a great hitter, he didn't bother with technical stuff. But my mom knows my swing."

Dates & Places Used:

620

TOPIC: Mothers

The Old Mom

A sign in a restaurant revealed the harsh reality: "Our pies are like the ones your mother used to bake–before she entered the workforce."

Dates & Places Used:

621

Silent Suffering

The other day when our little girl was being particularly cute, I exclaimed, "Oh, Chris, what do people without a two-year-old do!" Her response: "They suffer . . . *IN SILENCE.*"

Dates & Places Used:

622

More Than Her Car

Police don't know where Deborah Kemp found the strength. But Kemp knows. Six-year-old daughter Ashleye was in the backseat, and Kemp wasn't going to let the man steal her car after she pumped gas. The thirty-four-year-old mother was dragged on her knees for several blocks as she clung to the door and steering wheel of the moving car.

"I wasn't trying to be a hero," she said. "I was concerned about my baby . . . that was part of me in that car." Kemp eventually pulled the suspect from the car and beat him with an anti theft club device while he apologized and begged her to stop.

The driverless car went out of control and smashed into a restaurant, breaking a gas line. That's when the child woke up. Kemp suffered only ripped pants and bloody knees. The child was not injured. The suspect can't walk: One leg is broken, the other fractured. He also suffered head injuries.

Dates & Places Used:

623

A Prayer for Mom

Johnny had been misbehaving and was sent to his room. After a while he emerged and informed his mother that he had thought it over and then said a prayer.

"Fine," said the pleased mother. "If you ask God to help you not misbehave, he will help you."

"Oh, I didn't ask him to help me not misbehave," said Johnny. "I asked him to help you put up with me."

Dates & Places Used:

624

TOPIC: Mothers

Sleeping with God

The burst of thunder sent a three-year-old flying into her parents' bedroom. "Mommy, I'm scared," she said. The mother, half awake and half unconscious, replied, "Go back to your bed. God will be there with you."

The small figure stood in the unlit doorway for a moment and then said softly, "Mommy, I'll sleep here with Daddy, and you go in there and sleep with God."

Dates & Places Used:

625

TOPIC: Mothers

Mom's Old Daughters

A one hundred-year-old woman was honored at a birthday celebration by her four daughters. She was asked if she felt that old.

She looked around the room and then gave her answer. "I really don't feel this old, except that I look around the room and see these white-haired ladies and realize they are all my daughters!"

Dates & Places Used:

626

A Child's Cause and Effect

Every time I put my pajamas on, it gets dark.
Every time the phone rings, I have this urge to make noise.
Every time I go to bed, I need a drink of water.
Every time I get a drink of water, I need to go to the bathroom.
Every time I need a friend, my mom is always there!

Dates & Places Used:

627

Teens Give Wrinkles

On her forty-first birthday, a woman received, among other presents, an extravagantly expensive wrinkle-removing cream from her teenage daughter. "And what did she give you last year?" a guest asked the mom.

Her reply, without hesitation, was: "The wrinkles!"

Dates & Places Used:

628

The Goal Is the Goal

Bobby Dodd, the former great football coach of Georgia Tech, tells the story of a game in which his team was leading 7–6 with just a minute to go. He instructed his quarterback not to pass the ball under any conditions. He said, "Whatever you do, hold on to that football; do not pass the ball."

In the next ten or fifteen seconds of play, they moved the ball down the field to within ten yards of the opposing team's goal line. As the quarterback began to execute the next play, with the seconds ticking away, he just couldn't resist, and he threw a pass.

As it often happens, the pass was intercepted by a player on the other team. This opponent rushed toward the Georgia Tech goal line. The entire team had given up the chase–except the quarterback who had thrown the pass. He had continued to chase his opponent and somehow was able to tackle him. The ball was fumbled and the quarterback recovered the ball.

Georgia Tech won the game 7–6. After the game, the losing coach said to Coach Dodd, "I will never understand how that quarterback was able to do what he did."

Dodd explained, "Well, it's actually quite simple—your boy was running for a touchdown; my boy was running for his life."

Dates & Places Used:

TOPIC: Motivation

629

Gotta Try It

There was a young man hitchhiking through the southern portion of the United States. A farmer driving an old pickup truck stopped to give him a lift. As they rode along, they got to talking about the local moonshine whiskey. The young man said he didn't drink very much. Moonshine would probably be too strong for his taste.

"Nonsense!" said the farmer. "You gotta try some." He fished around behind him and finally produced a small jug. "Here," he said handing the jar to the lad. "Take a drink!"

"Oh, no, thanks," said the young man. "I really don't think I care for any."

"No, I insist," pressed the farmer. "Have some."

"No, thanks—really," said the young man.

The farmer wasn't going to take no for an answer. He stopped the truck and grabbed his shotgun from the rack in back. He pointed the gun at the lad and roared, "I said, take a drink!"

"Okay! Okay!" said the young man. "I've changed my mind! I guess I will have some after all." The young man took a few swallows before he realized how powerful the stuff was. His throat muscles tightened, his eyes watered, and he made a choking sound.

"What do you think of it?" asked the farmer. "Good, ain't it?"

"Yeah," gasped the lad, "I guess so."

Then the farmer handed the young man the shotgun and grinned. "Here! Now you hold the gun on me and make me take a drink!"

Dates & Places Used:

630

TOPIC: Motivations

The Measure of Fear

Remember the fellow who found himself in the middle of a pasture with an angry bull charging him? The only escape in sight was a tree, but the nearest limb was ten feet off the ground. The fellow ran for it and made a tremendous leap. He missed it on the way up, but caught it on the way down.

Dates & Places Used:

631

TOPIC: Motives

Taxi Courtesy

A man was riding in a taxi in New York City when he noticed that the driver slowed down to avoid a pedestrian. Trying to compliment the driver's actions he said, "I noticed you slowed down?"

The driver responded, "Yea, if you hit them, you've got to fill out a report!"

Dates & Places Used:

632

TOPIC: Names

Names or Numbers

A census taker stopped at the door of a woman who had six children. He asked her how many children she had. She began to name each of her children. The census taker interrupted her and explained that he only needed the numbers.

The insulted lady responded angrily, "I love each and every one of my children; they each have NAMES and I have never considered giving them NUMBERS!" She then slammed the door shut.

Dates & Places Used:

TOPIC: Nationality

Nation of Eden

An Englishman, a Frenchman, and a Russian were discussing the nationality of Adam and Eve. Each said that Adam and Eve were of their own nationality with supporting reasons:

The Frenchman: "Because who but a Frenchman would be so romantic as to have a boy and girl sharing an apple in a garden?"

Englishman: "Who but an Englishman would have the propriety to give the woman the first bite?"

Russian: "Who but a Russian would have only one apple to divide between two people, not even enough clothes to wear, and have the audacity to call it Paradise?"

Dates & Places Used:

TOPIC: Needs

Needed Junk

Junk is something you throw away about three weeks before you need it.

Dates & Places Used:

TOPIC: Needs

Needful Luxuries

I don't need the essentials,
It's the luxuries I can't live without.
Dates & Places Used:

TOPIC: Negotiations

Talking or Fighting

Jaw, Jaw, Jaw is better than War, War, War.
Dates & Places Used:

637

Lack of Obedience

A husband and wife were discussing the possibility of taking a trip to the Holy Land. "Wouldn't it be fantastic to go to the Holy Land and stand and shout the Ten Commandments from Mt. Sinai?" the husband asked his wife.

"It would be better if you stayed home and kept them," the wife replied.

Dates & Places Used:

638

Commandment for Siblings

A third grade Sunday school teacher was giving a Bible lesson on the commandment "Honor thy father and mother."

"Now, does anyone know a commandment for brothers and sisters?" the teacher asked.

One particularly perceptive child raised her hand and confidently responded, "Thou shalt not kill!"

Dates & Places Used:

639

Third Time Alarm

When I was a kid, I was watching television in the basement one evening. My dad called down to me, "Mike! Come up for dinner!"

Twice I ignored his calls. Just as the show ended, he shouted, "Mike! Get up here now!"

As I leaped to the top of the stairs, he yelled, "Where have you been?!"

I looked at him innocently and said, "I didn't hear you when you called me the first two times."

Dates & Places Used:

640

TOPIC: Obedience

Watch Out for Mom

An exasperated mother sent her naughty son to his room to discipline him. He stormed up to his room and defiantly hid under the bed. When the boy's father got home, he went up to check on his wayward son.

He entered the room but did not see the little guy. He wandered around the room for a moment and then looked under the bed. When he looked under the bed, he saw a couple of eyes looking out from under the bed. Then he heard his son's voice: "Hi, Daddy. Is Mommy trying to get you, too?"

Dates & Places Used:

641

TOPIC: Offerings

Empty-Handed Givers

There are too many church attendees who could appropriately begin all church services by singing: "Nothing in my hand I bring. Simply to the cross I cling."

Dates & Places Used:

642

TOPIC: Omnipresence

God in the Bathroom

A Sunday school teacher asked her class of preschoolers if they knew where God lives.

One little boy raised his hand, and the teacher called on him.

"God lives in my bathroom," the boy confidently answered.

"Why do you say that God lives in your bathroom?" inquired the teacher.

"Because every morning my dad pounds on the bathroom door and says, 'Good Lord, are you still in there?'"

Dates & Places Used:

643

Well-Timed Blunders

A blunder at the right moment is better than cleverness at the wrong time.
Dates & Places Used:

644

Opportunity or Problem

Barb and her husband Chuck were youth leaders who had just arrived at a campground for a weekend retreat with a youth group. While Chuck unloaded the van, Barb handed out room assignments. On the bulletin board of the lobby in the main lodge was a poster declaring, "There are no problems, only opportunities."

One boy came over to her and said, "Uh, Barb, I've got a problem."

Barb pointed to the sign, "Jeff, there are no problems, just opportunities."

"Well, if that's the way you want it," said Jeff, "but there's a girl in my room."
Dates & Places Used:

645

Opportunity Honks

For the modern girl, opportunity doesn't knock anymore; it parks in front of her house and honks the horn.
Dates & Places Used:

646

Grandma's Glasses

One day two little boys were playing, and one asked the other, "Wouldn't you hate to wear glasses all the time?"

The other little boy responded, "No-o-o, not if I had the kind Grandma wears. She sees how to fix a lot of things, and she sees lots of nice things to do on rainy days, and she sees when folks are tired and sorry, and what will make them feel better, and she always sees what you meant to do even if you haven't gotten things just right. I asked her one day how she could see that way all the time, and she said it was the way she had learned to look at things as she grew older. So it must be her glasses."
Dates & Places Used:

647

TOPIC: Optimism

Never Give Up!

We never lose, but sometimes the clock runs out on us.
Dates & Places Used:

648

TOPIC: Optimism

Worse Than Bad Breath

Bad breath is better than no breath at all.
Dates & Places Used:

649

TOPIC: Optimism

Three Out of Four Ain't Bad

A husband came home from work after a very long and terrible day. Everything had gone wrong. He said to his wife, "I've had nothing but bad news at the office today. If there is one thing I don't want, it is more bad news."

His wife gently replied, "In that case, you'll be glad to know that three out of four of your children did not break their arms today."
Dates & Places Used:

650

TOPIC: Optimism

The Oldest Optimist

An optimist is an eighty-year-old man who marries a thirty-year-old woman and buys a house next to a grade school.
Dates & Places Used:

651

TOPIC: Ownership

Wrong Name on the Ball

A golfer hit a drive straight down the middle and longer than his usual distance. Pleased, he strode off after the ball, but found another golfer about to hit it. "Pardon me," he said, "but that's my ball."

The other insisted, "This is my ball."

The other golfer persisted, "If you pick up the ball you will see that it has my name on it."

The stranger scooped up the ball, examined it, and haughtily said, "And what is your name doing on my ball?"
Dates & Places Used:

652

TOPIC: Ownership

All Is in Her Name

A woman went into the office of a cemetery manager and complained, "I can't find my husband's grave. I know he's buried here."

"What is the name?" the manager asked.

"John Jones," she replied.

Referring to his card index, the manager said, "Madam, we have no John Jones. We just have a Mary Jones."

"That's my husband," she said. "Everything is in my name."
Dates & Places Used:

653

The Beauty Remains

The French painter Renoir (Ren-wah) continued his painting, even when he experienced excruciating pain from rheumatoid arthritis. When asked why he continued to torture himself in this way, his answer revealed his heart. He said, "The pain passes, but the beauty remains."

Dates & Places Used:

654

Multiple Maladies

A little girl was riding along on her bike when she bumped her head on the low hanging branch of a tree. She ran into the house hollering, "Mom! Mom, Joey hurt me!"

Mom looked up from what she was doing and said, "Sissy, Joey didn't hurt you. Joey's not even here. He went to the grocery store with your daddy."

The little girl got this startled look on her face. Then in a bewildered sort of voice she said, "That means stuff like this can happen on its own at anytime. Whoa, bummer!"

Dates & Places Used:

655

Just Two Times

A young mother left her two preschool children for the day in the care of their less experienced father on his day off from work. At the end of the day, she returned home to find her husband exhausted from a day with his children but trying to hide the fact.

The mother gently asked her husband: "Did everything go okay?"

The father answered, "Oh, sure, it was fine."

"Did you have any trouble?" she explored.

"Just a couple of times the kids were a bit unmanageable."

"And when did these episodes take place?"

Her husband confessed, "The first time was the first four hours after you left, and the second was the five hours before you returned."

Dates & Places Used:

656

TOPIC: Parents

Free as a Chicken

Some parents would like to be as carefree as chickens on a modern chicken farm. The chickens have all the fun of laying eggs and none of the bother of raising a family.

Dates & Places Used:

657

TOPIC: Parents

Sometimes Two Parents

One trouble with juvenile delinquency nowadays is not always apparent ... sometimes it's two parents!

Dates & Places Used:

658

TOPIC: Parents

Parental Diets

Children are like our stomachs. They do not need all that we can afford to give them.

Dates & Places Used:

659

TOPIC: Parents

Parental Disadvantage

The secret of dealing successfully with a child is not to be the child's parent.
Dates & Places Used:

660

TOPIC: Parents

Photo Finishes

Parents: People who have pictures in their wallets where money used to be.
Dates & Places Used:

661

TOPIC: Parents

Our Lives Are Controlled

The first half of our lives is controlled by our parents;
The second half of our lives is controlled by our children.
Dates & Places Used:

662

TOPIC: Parents

Theories or Experience

Child-raising theories did abound,
Before my children were around,
Then one day I had my own,
Now, all those theories I disown.

Energy was once my friend,
Now I am at my strength's end.
Fortune gone, the fridge is clean,
My child has now become a teen!
Dates & Places Used:

663

Passion and Control

Passion is the mob of the man that commits a riot upon his reason.
Dates & Places Used:

664

Busier Than Isaiah

One minister remarked sorrowfully:
"The prophet Isaiah wrote, 'In the year that King Uzziah died I saw the Lord.' If he were a modern minister, he would write, 'In the year that Uzziah died I made a thousand pastoral calls, dictated two thousand letters, and held five thousand telephone conversations. I reviewed a book a week, pronounced sixty-three invocations at public functions, put my name on twenty-five committee letterheads, served as chairman of the Community Chest, and didn't have time to say my prayers.'"
Dates & Places Used:

665

The Smell of Sheep

If you can't stand the smell of sheep, you shouldn't be a shepherd.
Dates & Places Used:

666

Pastoral Kissing

An Episcopalian priest was wearing his clerical collar while visiting his wife who was in the hospital for minor surgery. He stopped in to see her and chatted with her for quite some while.

Before leaving, he leaned down and gave his wife a great passionate kiss and left the room. The woman in the next bed over stared in disbelief. After the priest left, the stunned woman spoke to her roommate, "You know, I've been a faithful member of the United Methodist Church all my life, but my pastor has never even come close to treating me as well as yours does."
Dates & Places Used:

667 TOPIC: Pastors
Pastoral Holding

A successful and eloquent pastor attended a reunion at the first church he had ever pastored. During the reception, one of the longtime members of the church approached her former pastor and shared some of the changes that had taken place since his departure.

She concluded her discourse with the intent of complimenting her former pastor, "Regardless of all the changes and blessings God has bestowed upon our church, none of the pastors have been able to HOLD ME the way you did."
Dates & Places Used:

668 TOPIC: Pastors
Pastors and Lawyers in Heaven

A couple in Southern California were planning to get married, but before they were able to get married, they were swallowed up by an earthquake. The next thing they knew, they were standing together in heaven. As soon as they were presented to St. Peter for processing, they asked Peter if they could still get married. Peter hesitated for a moment and then answered, "Let me think about it–I'll get back to you on this."

A week passed, then a month, then six months, but still no word back from St. Peter. Then, after seven months of waiting, they were approached by St. Peter with a pastor following closely behind. "All right, you can get married now!"

The couple thanked Peter for his granting of their request, but they now had a second request. Over the seven months of waiting, they felt that it would be wise to draw up a prenuptial agreement.

St. Peter was upset, and he told the couple so: "Listen, it took me seven months to find a pastor up here; how long do you think it's going to take me to find a lawyer?"

Dates & Places Used:

669

TOPIC: Pastors

The Butcher Is Not the Shepherd

A man observed a fellow driving a group of sheep across a field, beating a stick, and yelling at them. "I thought shepherds led their sheep," said the observer.

"I'm not the shepherd," came the answer. "I'm the butcher."

Dates & Places Used:

670

TOPIC: Pastors

Pastors of a Feather

People expect the clergy to have the grace of a swan, the friendliness of a sparrow, the strength of an eagle, and the night hours of an owl—and some people expect such a bird to live on the food of a canary.

Dates & Places Used:

671

TOPIC: Patience

Development of Long-Suffering

In order to be long-suffering a person has to suffer long.

Dates & Places Used:

672

TOPIC: Patience

Ice Cream Today

Mom asked her preschool daughter: "Would you like an ice cream sundae?"

Her daughter thought for a moment and answered: "No, I think I would rather have one today."

Dates & Places Used:

673

TOPIC: Peers

The Jesus Fashion

Dad was tired of hearing his son complain about what his friends had and he did not have. Dad had an idea: set a higher standard for his son. The next time his son began his complaining, the father stopped him: "Is this what Jesus would do? Would Jesus complain about the clothes he had and want to wear the same thing your friends are wearing? Is it so important that you wear just what your friends are wearing? Why can't you be more like Jesus?"

The son waited for his father to catch his breath and then interrupted, "All right, Dad, I give up; just tell me what Jesus is wearing, and I'll wear it too!"

Dates & Places Used:

674

TOPIC: Peers

Bad Influence on Self

One adolescent confided to another: "The trouble with me is, I'm the sort of person my mother doesn't want me to associate with."

Dates & Places Used:

675

Insults Are Not Free

If we come to view ourselves as working for an external reward, we will no longer find the activity worth doing in its own right.

There is an old joke that illustrates this. An elderly man, harassed by the taunts of the neighborhood children, devised a scheme. He offered to pay them a dollar each if they would return on Tuesday and yell their insults again. The children did so eagerly and received the money.

Then he told them he would pay only twenty-five cents on Wednesday.

When they returned, insulted him again, and collected their quarters, he informed them that Thursday's rate would be just a penny.

"Forget it," they said—and never taunted him again.

Dates & Places Used:

676

TOPIC: Perfectionism

Not a Fanatic

Secretary to irate boss: "Of course I can spell correctly. But I'm not a fanatic about it."

Dates & Places Used:

677

TOPIC: Perfectionism

Who Does Jesus Think He Is

Jesus, Moses, Elijah, and St. Peter are playing a round of golf in heaven. Jesus is playing an absolutely perfect game well below par.

By the sixteenth hole, the other three heavenly golfers are discouraged and grumbling a little.

Right after Jesus gets a hole in one on the sixteenth hole, Moses turns to Elijah and whispers, "Who does he think he is, Arnold Palmer?"

Dates & Places Used:

678 TOPIC: Performance
Wrong Information

I knew this fellow who went to seminary. He was brilliant, was first in his class, Phi Beta Kappa, about as bright as anybody who'd ever graduated from the seminary, but he had one failing. He couldn't remember names. So he had to have these cheat cards in his coat pocket.

He got up to preach his first sermon, looked out over the congregation, and started his sermon. "In the days when ...," he pulled back the lapel of his suit coat and looked at the card, " ... Nebuchadnezzar was king of ...," he looked at the card sticking up out of his inside suit coat pocket, " ... Babylon, he made a great statue of himself and ordered all the people of the realm to bow down and worship the golden statue. But among the people were three captives, three ...," and he consulted the coat pocket again, " ... Hebrews who were held as slaves, captives, who refused to bow down at the sounding of the trumpets! Their names were ...," but in the excitement of getting started, the card had slipped down into the pocket and he mistakenly read the label on the pocket: " ... Hart, Shaffner, and Marx ..."

Dates & Places Used:

679 TOPIC: Persistence
Nelson Quit

Our gasoline was getting low as we drove through the Salt River Canyon toward Phoenix. I asked my wife what was the next town on the map.

"Nelsonville," she replied.

We drove on and on, but there was no sign of a town. At last, we came upon a building with a gas pump in front, and I pulled in.

"Is this Nelsonville?" I asked the attendant.

"No, Bensonville," he replied.

"But where is Nelsonville? It shows on the map. We should have passed it."

"Oh, him," the attendant said. "He quit."

Dates & Places Used:

680

TOPIC: Persistence

Wrestling a Gorilla

Persistence is like wrestling a gorilla. You don't quit when you get tired. You quit when the gorilla gets tired!

Dates & Places Used:

681

TOPIC: Persistence

Path of Least Persistence

Those who fail in life often pursue the path of *least persistence.*

Dates & Places Used:

682

TOPIC: Perspective

The Search in the Wrong Direction

When my children and I had finished unpacking in our new home, we noticed our poodle was missing. Concerned that she couldn't find her way back in the unfamiliar surroundings, I loaded the kids into the car and went to look for her. We drove up and down the neighborhood without any luck.

Not far from our house I noticed a man sitting on his front porch. I asked him if he'd seen our dog. "Yes," he replied. "She's been following your car for the past ten minutes."

Sometimes we look so hard for God's blessings that we fail to notice what is in our own backyard, following us through life.

Dates & Places Used:

683

TOPIC: Perspective

Fair Exchanges

The husband's idea of a gift exchange:
  His gift is a new set of golf clubs
  Her gift is a new pair of dishwashing gloves
The wife's idea of a gift exchange:
  His gift is a new snow shovel
  Her gift is a new coat
The child's idea of a gift exchange:
  The child gets some new clothes and some baseball cards
  Dad gets a new video game
  Mom gets a new race car set

Dates & Places Used:

684

TOPIC: Perspective

No View

A Colorado native moved to Texas and built a house with a large picture window from which he could view hundreds of miles of rangeland. "The only problem is," he said, "there's nothing to see."

About the same time, a Texan moved to Colorado and built a house with a large picture window overlooking the Rocky Mountains. "The only problem is I can't see anything," he said. "The mountains are in the way."

People have a way of missing what is right before them. They go to a city and see lights and glitter, but miss the lonely people. They hear a person's critical comments, but miss the cry for love and friendship.

Dates & Places Used:

685

TOPIC: Perspective

A Boy's Essay on Anatomy

Your head is kind of round and hard, and your branes are in it and your hair on it. Your face is the front of your head where you eat and make faces. Your neck is what keeps your head out of your collar. It's hard to keep clean.

Your shoulders are sort of shelves where you hook your suspenders on them. Your stummick is something that if you do not eat often enough, it hurts, and spinach don't hep it none.

Your spine is a long bone in your back that keeps you from folding up. Your back is behind you always, no matter how quick you turn around.

Your arms you got to have to pitch with, and so you can reach the butter. Your fingers stick out of your hand so that you can throw a curve and add up 'rithmatick.

Your legs is what—if you have not got two of—you cannot run to first base, neither can your sister. Your feet are what you run on. Your toes are what always get stubbed. And that's all there is of you except what's inside, and I never saw it.

Dates & Places Used:

686

TOPIC: Perspective

The Early Worm

The early bird gets the worm. But let us not forget, the early worm gets gotten.

Dates & Places Used:

687

TOPIC: Perspective

Giant Flies

Missionaries were showing a graphic film on hygiene to the Masaii in Kenya, Africa.

The film started out with the camera zoomed in on an ugly fly the size of a Volkswagen Beetle. It filled the screen. Then the fly was shown walking in and out of the putrid body of a dead animal, the moist mucus of the carcass sticking to the feet and legs of the fly. The insect is then shown feeding on the fresh feces of a cow, noting how the dung was sticking to the fly. Then the fly was seen walking across a fresh loaf of bread about to be served to the family.

After the film was shown, the missionaries asked the audience what they thought of the film. The Masaii thought the flies were terrible, but ... they considered themselves fortunate they did not have flies THAT BIG in Africa!

Dates & Places Used:

688

TOPIC: Perspectives

Look at the Bright Side

There has never been a case of eyestrain which was caused by looking on the bright side of things.

Dates & Places Used:

689

TOPIC: Pessimism

Final Inevitability

Dustin Hoffman said that he would want the following words put on his tombstone:

"I knew this was going to happen!"

Dates & Places Used:

690

TOPIC: Pessimism

Unhealthy Timing

From under a beach umbrella: "Just when I can afford to lie in the sun, they decide it's hazardous to my health."
Dates & Places Used:

691

TOPIC: Pests

Causing Happiness

Certain people cause happiness wherever they go.
Other people cause happiness whenever they go.
Dates & Places Used:

692

TOPIC: Phones

Phone Fantasies

Mommy was teaching her young son to use the phone. She showed him which numbers to push and explained about the dial tone and the sound of the other phone ringing. The process had begun. The son waited anxiously for the call to be completed, but no one picked up the phone on the other end.

The mother told him to hang up the phone. "We'll try again later, Son."

The boy was not so easily discouraged. "Wait a minute, Mommy, I think I hear someone coming!"
Dates & Places Used:

693

TOPIC: Pity

Boyhood Compassion

A young boy let the offering plate pass him without putting his offering in it. After the service was over, he approached the pastor and gave him his offering. The pastor asked him why he did not put the money in the offering plate.

246

The boy explained, "I wanted to be sure that you got it. My parents said that you are the poorest preacher this church has ever had—I just didn't want to take any chances."
Dates & Places Used:

694 TOPIC: Planning

Best Time to Plant

I remember visiting a nursery, looking for a certain type of tree for the front yard of the last parsonage in which we lived. While there I saw a sign that said, "The best time to plant a tree was 15 years ago."

The next line stated, "The second best time is today."
Dates & Places Used:

695 TOPIC: Pledges

Stolen Pledges

The sexton ran into the rabbi's apartment near the temple and said excitedly, "Rabbi, somebody broke into the synagogue office yesterday and stole $80,000 in pledges!"
Dates & Places Used:

696 TOPIC: Politicians

Politics Is

Politics is the art of looking for trouble, finding it everywhere, diagnosing it incorrectly, and applying the wrong remedies.
Dates & Places Used:

697

TOPIC: Politicians

Political Promises

Politicians are the same all over. They promise to build a bridge even when there's no river.
Dates & Places Used:

698

TOPIC: Politicians

Free Family Tree

The cheapest way to have your family tree traced is to run for public office.
Dates & Places Used:

699

TOPIC: Politicians

Political Positions

A politician is an animal that can sit on a fence and keep both ears to the ground.
Dates & Places Used:

700

TOPIC: Politicians

Politician or Statesman

When you're abroad you're a statesman; when you're at home, you're just a politician.
Dates & Places Used:

701

TOPIC: Politicians

Getting All the Votes

Politics is the gentle art of getting votes from the poor and campaign funds from the rich by promising to protect each from the other.
Dates & Places Used:

702

TOPIC: Politicians

Political Publicity

Ninety-eight percent of the adults in this country are decent, hard working, honest Americans. It's the other lousy two percent that get all the publicity. But then, we elected them.
Dates & Places Used:

703

TOPIC: Politicians

A Friend in Washington, D.C.

If you need a friend in Washington, get a dog.
Dates & Places Used:

704

TOPIC: Politicians

Introduction to Politics

Harry Truman, talking politics with a group of Yale students, was asked by one earnest youth, "How do I start in politics, sir?"

Replied the former president, "You've already started. You're spending somebody else's money, aren't you?"
Dates & Places Used:

705

Political Blame

Ninety percent of all politics is deciding who to blame.
Dates & Places Used:

706

TOPIC: Politics

No Preparation for Politics

Politics is perhaps the only profession for which no preparation is thought necessary.
Dates & Places Used:

707

TOPIC: Population

Standing Room Only

Those who are too concerned about the overpopulation of the earth have no reason to worry. Eventually there will be standing room only. At that point, births will decrease dramatically.
Dates & Places Used:

708

TOPIC: Possessions

Premature Ownership

A bishop was being entertained by a wealthy landowner in Iowa. He had preached in his host's church on God's ownership. Looking over his broad acres and remembering the morning sermon, the owner asked the bishop, "Do you mean to tell me, Bishop, that this land does not belong to me?"

The bishop said the answer came to him in a flash: "Ask me that one hundred years from now."
Dates & Places Used:

TOPIC: Possessions

Keep Moving

The place was Bethel, Vermont, nestled in the vast expanse of the Green Mountains. It was a hot day, a perfect day for a walk to enjoy the view of the river and the surrounding mountains. My trail was the railroad tracks that seemed to endlessly imitate the direction of the river.

By the tracks stood an old mill that was being converted into some kind of a workshop. From my vantage point on the tracks, I could see a stop sign on one of the windows of the shop. No doubt it said, "NO TRESPASSING!" but I had to check it out just to make sure.

I was right. But the sign said a lot more than I had expected. There in black and white on that dusty window were these words:

"Trespassers will be shot;

Survivors will be shot again."

Without letting on how I felt at that point, I glanced over my shoulders and scouted the bush and the riverbank for signs of life, particularly property owners who carried loaded guns. I rapidly came to the conclusion that I did not belong in that place, that I was passing through. *I kept moving!*

Sometimes (maybe more than we would like to admit) we find ourselves preoccupied with the beauty of the world around us, including those things that may attract our attention, saying to us, *"Come and see what I am all about."*

Often in the midst of the beautiful and the interesting, there lies the quiet, yet very real, warning of danger. *We need to keep moving!*

The apostle Peter no doubt had this in mind when he reminded his readers that they were only "aliens and strangers" here on earth. The apostle Paul shared this concern as he prompted the Philippians to remember that their "citizenship is in heaven."

As we walk where God has placed us, may we walk while enjoying the beauty, avoiding the dangers, seeking our promised home, and all the while pressing on, heeding the call that says, KEEP MOVING!

Dates & Places Used:

710

I Don't Get It

Sam Goldsmith went out with his wife during the Depression. They would often go window-shopping because they didn't have money to purchase anything.

One night, looking in a fur store, the wife saw a beautiful jacket and exclaimed: "Sam, I really would like it. Don't you think you could purchase it for me?"

Sam thought for a moment and replied, "Dearest, extenuating circumstances perforce me to preclude you from such a multiple extravagance."

She replied, "I don't get it."

To which Sam answered, "Exactly."

Dates & Places Used:

711

Powerless Money

Thomas Aquinas was once speaking with Pope Innocent II while the pope was counting a large sum of money from the Vatican treasury. The pope turned to Aquinas and noted that the church no longer needs to say, "Silver and gold have I none."

"True, Holy Father," Aquinas observed. "Neither can the church any longer say, 'Arise and walk.'"

Dates & Places Used:

712

The Bride Won't Obey

"How did the wedding go?" asked the minister's wife.

"Fine, my dear, until I asked the bride if she would obey, and she said, 'Do you think I'm crazy?' and the bridegroom,

who was in sort of a stupor, mumbled, 'I do,'—then things
began to happen."
Dates & Places Used:

713 TOPIC: Power

Evaluating the Enemy

*It is never safe to assume
that our enemy is as strong as we are.
Our enemy may be much stronger.*
Dates & Places Used:

714 TOPIC: Power

A Snake in the Powerhouse

At about eleven o'clock on Saturday night, as many people
were preparing to turn out lights, the lights in our community
all went out by themselves. Air conditioners suddenly quit running. Houses all over were without power. It seemed strange
that this would happen on a night when there were no storms in
the area. People wondered what had caused the power outage
as their homes grew warm in the July heat and their patience
grew thinner.

The power was off most of the night, and it was the next
morning before we found out what had caused the problem. A
whole community had lost power for most of the night because
a snake had gotten into the powerhouse and fouled things up.

If we experience a Christian life that is ineffective and
without power, the problem is not that our God lacks power.
The problem may be a snake in the powerhouse, something
in our life, some debilitating sin that does not belong in the
life of a Christian. We must be careful what we allow to creep
into our lives.
Dates & Places Used:

715

TOPIC: Praise

Vocal Encouragement

If there is something laudable,
Make sure that it is audible.
Dates & Places Used:

716

TOPIC: Praise

A Louder Horn of Praise

Get someone else to blow your horn and the sound will carry twice as far.
Dates & Places Used:

717

TOPIC: Praise

Mark Twain on Praise

I like compliments. I like to go home and tell them all over again to the members of my family. They don't believe them, but I like to tell them in the home circle, all the same. I like to dream of them if I can. I thank everybody for their compliments, but I don't think that I am praised any more than I am entitled to be.
Dates & Places Used:

718

TOPIC: Prayer

Cellular Link to God

A pastor was on his way to church with his three-year-old daughter. On the way the pastor remembered an urgent message he was supposed to give his wife. He reached for his cellular phone and notified his wife.

As he was hanging up the phone, his daughter inquired with fascination, "Who did you call, Daddy? Did you call God?"

Prayer is the cellular link to God for every Christian. How often do we use this ready resource? It is on-line whenever and wherever we need to communicate with our heavenly Father.

Dates & Places Used:

719

TOPIC: Prayer

Praying Past the President

The story is told around Washington about former presidential assistant Bill Moyers who has a strong Baptist heritage and is presently a popular political commentator. Moyers was at a lunch with President Johnson and was giving thanks. His prayer was interrupted by the president, who said, "Speak up, I can't hear you."

Muttered Moyers, "I wasn't speaking to you, Mr. President."

Dates & Places Used:

720

TOPIC: Prayer

God's Delays Are Not Denials

Never think that God's delays are God's denials. A lone shipwreck survivor on an uninhabited island managed to build a rude hut in which he placed all that he had saved from his sinking ship. He prayed to God for deliverance, and anxiously watched the horizon each day to hail any passing ship.

One day he was horrified to find his hut in flames. All that he had was gone. To the man's limited vision, it was the worst that could happen, and he cursed God. Yet the very next day a ship arrived.

"We saw your smoke signal!" the captain told him.

Dates & Places Used:

TOPIC: Prayer

Leftover Prayers

A little boy was asked to pray before the meal. The boy looked over the meal set on the table before bowing his head. He picked up his fork instead and began to eat. His parents asked him why he didn't pray before his meal.

The boy answered, "I already prayed for this food; these are leftovers!"

Dates & Places Used:

TOPIC: Prayer

Time to Run

The kindergarten Sunday school class was learning about how God cares for us in times of trouble. The teacher asked the class to draw pictures of things that make them afraid. After they finished drawing, each child explained to the others what he or she had drawn.

Five-year-old Scott had created in vivid crayon a looming funnel cloud, a car, and a man. He described how the man could not get his car started and a tornado was coming toward him.

"The man really needs to pray, doesn't he?" asked the teacher.

"No," Scott disagreed. "He needs to run!"

We need balance in our lives. There is a time for prayer and a time for deeds.

Dates & Places Used:

TOPIC: Prayer

What Did God Say?

My wife and I try to make prayer something we do for all our needs, concerns, and joys. Our three-year-old daughter recently got an "ouchy." Jenny said, "Mommy, will you pray to Jesus to make it better?"

So, Mommy prayed a brief and simplistic prayer. As soon as she said "Amen," Jenny said, "Well, what'd he say?"

Oh, for the faith of a child to want and expect such clear and direct answers. Out of the mouth of babes ...

Dates & Places Used:

724

TOPIC: Prayer

Talk to the Plate

A pastor was visiting in the home of one of his parishioners. A small boy in the home started reaching for the potatoes before the blessing was said. His mother gently scolded him.

The boy was confused. Why were they at the table, except to eat? As the adults bowed their heads to say grace, the child suddenly caught on. As his father started to pray, the boy shouted, "Hey, Dad! Could I be the one who talks to the plate this time?"

There are times when prayers have so little forethought and passion that those who are offering these prayers could easily be talking to their plates.

Dates & Places Used:

725

TOPIC: Prayer

Singing During Prayers

Dwight L. Moody had a practical mind that never let a meeting get out of hand. Long public prayers particularly irritated him. Once he told his song leader, Sankey, "Lead us in a hymn while our brother is finishing his prayer."

Dates & Places Used:

726

TOPIC: Prayer

Prayer Rates

The daughter of a telephone operator was asked in religion class to define prayer. "Prayer," said the child, "is messages sent up at night and on Sundays when the rates are lowest."

Dates & Places Used:

727

Wake Up and Help

A father and mother were teaching their little girl to pray before meals. Before every meal the girl would ask if she could pray, but she was still having a little trouble remembering the words. On one occasion she stopped in the middle of her prayer, looked up at her parents, who had their eyes closed, and demanded, "Mommy, wake up and tell me the words!"

Dates & Places Used:

728

TOPIC: Prayer

Talking to His Plate

A little boy went to dine with his parents at the home of an elderly gentleman. After watching the old man bow his head and speak in a soft voice, the boy asked his mother, "What did Mr. Bryan say to his plate?"

Dates & Places Used:

729

TOPIC: Prayer

Criminal Kid's Prayer

Dennis the Menace is kneeling at his bedside, hands folded, his eyes looking toward heaven. With an imploring look on his face he prays, "I'm here to turn myself in!"

Dates & Places Used:

730

TOPIC: Prayer

All That Is Within Me

At a recent community dinner, the organizers realized halfway through the meal that they had forgotten to say grace. A pastor who was also in the middle of his meal was asked to say the prayer. He began by instructing those present that when you remember in the middle of a meal to ask your blessing, remember that the psalmist David did the same. David began his prayer by saying, "Bless the Lord, O my soul, and all that is *WITHIN* me . . ."

Dates & Places Used:

731
TOPIC: Preaching
Reason for the Coffee

A church that loved good fellowship always served coffee after the sermon. The pastor asked a little boy if he knew why they served the coffee.

"I think," said the boy, "it's to get the people awake before they drive home."

Dates & Places Used:

732
TOPIC: Preaching
A Suspicious Congregation

When a minister steps behind the pulpit, he dare not assume that his congregation sits expectantly on the edge of the pews, waiting for his sermon. In reality, they are probably a bit bored . . . and harbor suspicion that he will make matters worse.

Dates & Places Used:

733
TOPIC: Preaching
Preaching Like Fighting Bees

I don't like to hear cut, canned, dried sermons. When I hear a man preach, I like to see him act like he was fighting bees.

Abraham Lincoln

Dates & Places Used:

734

Pregnancy Questions

For several months a little boy had been watching his mother's stomach increase in size. It was becoming harder and harder to sit on her lap.

"Mommy, why is your stomach getting so big?"

He was told that his little sister was inside her stomach.

"Mommy, why is my little sister inside your stomach?"

He was told that he used to be in her stomach too.

When the boy's father got home, the boy asked his father if he could talk to him in private. They went to the boy's room.

"Daddy, I need answers to two questions:

First, why does Mommy keep eating little kids?

And second, how did I escape?"

Dates & Places Used:

735

Prejudice Saves Time

Prejudice is a great time-saver ...
It allows one to form opinions
without having to know the facts.

Dates & Places Used:

736

Prepared for Thirst

Dig the well before you get thirsty.

Dates & Places Used:

737

Centipede Football

The story is told about a football game between the big animals and the little animals. At the start of the second half the big animals were ahead and gave Tiger the ball. When he reached the scrimmage line, down he went. He hobbled back to the huddle and the big animals asked him, "What hit you?"

The tiger said, "That centipede."

Next they gave the ball to Lion. With a roar he ran to the line of scrimmage, but down he went. The other animals asked him, "What happened?"

The lion answered, "It was that centipede!"

So they gave the ball to Rhino. When he too tumbled to the ground at the scrimmage line, they asked, "What happened?"

He said, "It was that centipede!"

"Where was that centipede the first half?" the big animals asked the coach of the little animals. "Putting on his shoes," the coach said.

Dates & Places Used:

738

Truman on Presidential Leadership

All the president is, is a glorified public relations man who spends his time flattering, kissing, and kicking people to get them to do what they are supposed to do anyway.

Dates & Places Used:

739

Presidential Risk

In America any boy may become president. I suppose it's just one of the risks he takes.

Dates & Places Used:

740

TOPIC: Prices

Prices or Values

It is possible to know the price of everything and the value of nothing.

Dates & Places Used:

741

TOPIC: Pride

Conceit

A young pastor often boasted in public that all the time he needed to prepare his Sunday sermon was the few minutes it took him to walk to the church from the parsonage next door. After a few weeks of hearing his sermons, the congregation bought a new parsonage–five miles away!

Dates & Places Used:

742

TOPIC: Pride

Glue Down the Audience

Dustin Farnumm, a talented but conceited actor, once crooned on to his dinner host, writer Oliver Herford, about a play he was doing at the time. "Why, yesterday," boasted Farnumm, "I had the audience glued to their seats."

To which Herford replied, "How clever of you to think of it!"

Dates & Places Used:

743

TOPIC: Pride

I for an I

When two egoists meet, it's an "I for an I."

Dates & Places Used:

744

TOPIC: Pride

Doctor Imminence

On the first day of graduate school at a Christian university, the instructor was introduced to the students as "Doctor." The head of the school made many references to "Dr. Smith has done this ..." and "Dr. Smith has achieved that."

When the teacher rose to speak, he immediately said, "I want you to know that I do not insist that we go by this 'Doctor' title. I'm not interested in such things." And then with a sly smile he added, "If you want to call me anything, just call me 'Your Imminence.'"

Dates & Places Used:

745

TOPIC: Pride

Reputable Character

If you spend too much time on polishing your reputation, your character will become tarnished.

Dates & Places Used:

746

TOPIC: Pride

Wrong Weight As Well

There is a story about a woman who had been trying for years to persuade her egotistical husband to put an end to the idea that he and he alone was number one. This man was obsessed with being number one.

He never stopped talking about being first in sales at the office, and first on the list for the next promotion. He enjoyed playing tennis and golf, but only when he won. He had to be first in line to buy tickets for a game and first to hit the parking lot after the event. Does he sound like anyone you and I know? Or does he sound like you or me?

In any case, this man's long-suffering wife watched with interest one day when he stepped on one of those fortune-telling scales. He dropped a coin into the slot and out came a little "fortune-telling" card which read: "You are a born leader, with superior intelligence, quick wit and charming manner–magnetic personality and attractive to the opposite sex."

"Read that!" the man said to her triumphantly. She did. Then she turned it over and said, "It has your weight wrong too!"
Dates & Places Used:

747

TOPIC: Pride

Swallow Pride

Swallow your pride occasionally. It's nonfattening.
Dates & Places Used:

748

TOPIC: Pride

Disease of Pride

Pride is the only disease that makes everyone sick, except the one who has it.
Dates & Places Used:

749

TOPIC: Pride

Chicago Bedbugs

There once was a Texas rancher who visited colleagues in Chicago. They decided to show him the big city. When he saw the stockyards, he said, "That ain't much. We've got branding corrals on my ranch bigger than that." When he saw skyscrapers, he commented, "We've got tombstones at home taller than that."

That night, the annoyed Chicago hosts decided to get even. They left rats in the Texan's bed. When the rancher climbed under the sheets, the unpleasant surprise brought him quickly to his feet, screaming, "What was *that?*"

"Those are Chicago bedbugs," they answered.

Gaining his composure, the Texan replied, "You're right . . . young'uns, aren't they!"

Dates & Places Used:

---

750 TOPIC: Principles

Principles and Practice

When a man says he approves of something in principle, it means he hasn't the slightest intention of putting it into practice.

Dates & Places Used:

---

751 TOPIC: Priorities

Torn Pants Better

A young boy came into the house covered with mud after finishing a rough day at play. "Mom," he shouted at the top of his voice, "if I fell out of a tree, would you rather I broke a leg or tore my pants?"

"What a silly question," his mother answered from the next room. "I'd rather you tore your pants!"

"Well, I got good news for you then," the boy replied triumphantly. "That's exactly what happened!"

Dates & Places Used:

---

752 TOPIC: Priorities

Room for the Birds to Fly

There is a fascinating little story about a certain Japanese artist who painted a picture on a fairly large canvas. Down in one corner was a tree, and on the limbs of the tree were some birds—but all the rest of the canvas was bare. When he was asked if he was not going to paint something more to fill the rest of the canvas, he said, "Oh, no, I have to leave room for the birds to fly."

We so often fill our lives so full that there is not room for the birds to fly.

Dates & Places Used:

753 TOPIC: Priorities

The Parrot's Doom

Ernest Campbell tells about the woman who went to a pet store to purchase a parrot to keep her company. She took her new pet home but returned the next day to report, "That parrot hasn't said a word yet!"

"Does it have a mirror?" asked the storekeeper. "Parrots like to be able to look at themselves in the mirror." So she bought the mirror and returned home.

The next day she was back, announcing that the bird still wasn't speaking. "What about a ladder?" the storekeeper said. "Parrots enjoy walking up and down a ladder." So she bought a ladder and returned home.

Sure enough, the next day she was back with the same story— still no talk. "Does the parrot have a swing? Birds enjoy relaxing on a swing." She bought the swing and went home.

The next day she returned to the store to announce the bird had died. "I'm terribly sorry to hear that," said the storekeeper. "Did the bird ever say anything before it died?"

"Yes," said the lady. "It said, 'Don't they sell any food down there?'"

Dates & Places Used:

754 TOPIC: Profanity

Removal of Profanity

A stranger called on the phone and began, "I represent the Society for the Suppression of Profanity." He continued, "I want to take profanity out of your life."

"Hey, Mom," Bobby interrupted, "a man is here who wants to buy your car."
Dates & Places Used:

TOPIC: Progress

Things Could Be Better

Alteration is not always improvement, as the pigeon said when it got out of the net and into the pie.
Dates & Places Used:

TOPIC: Purity

A Little Impurity Pollutes

Schopenhauer's Law of Entropy: If you put a spoonful of wine in a barrel full of sewage you get sewage. If you put a spoonful of sewage in a barrel of wine, you get sewage.
Dates & Places Used:

TOPIC: Purity

Snow White's Snowdrift

I used to be Snow White—but I drifted.
Dates & Places Used:

TOPIC: Purpose

Minding One's Own Business

Here are a couple of reasons why some people do not mind their own business:

They may not have minds, and they may not have any business.
Dates & Places Used:

267

759

TOPIC: Purpose

Busy Bugs

It isn't so much how busy you are, but why you are busy. The bee is praised; the mosquito is swatted.

Dates & Places Used:

760

TOPIC: Purpose

Salt and Sugar of the Earth

You are the salt of the earth, but remember, the world needs some sugar too.

Dates & Places Used:

761

TOPIC: Quality

Five Mistakes

A businesswoman stopped at a coffee shop and ordered a cup of coffee. The waitress grudgingly delivered it and asked, "Anything else?"

"Yes," said the businesswoman, "I'd like some sugar, cream, a spoon, a napkin, and a saucer for the cup."

"Well, aren't you the demanding one," snapped the waitress.

"Look at it from my point of view," said the businesswoman. "You served a cup of coffee and made five mistakes."

Dates & Places Used:

762

TOPIC: Questions

Dumb Questions Are Better

Asking dumb questions is easier than correcting dumb mistakes.

Dates & Places Used:

763

TOPIC: Questions

The Age of Questions and Answers

A toddler seems to know all the questions.... A teenager seems to know all the answers.
Dates & Places Used:

764

TOPIC: Questions

Fool Forever

One who asks a question is a fool for a moment.
One who does not ask questions is a fool forever.
Dates & Places Used:

765

TOPIC: Reactions

Dandruff Treatment

Here is some good advice for those who are prone to overreacting: "Don't treat dandruff with a guillotine."
Dates & Places Used:

766

TOPIC: Reading

Books Break Ice

A book should serve as the ax for the frozen sea within us.
Dates & Places Used:

767

TOPIC: Reading

Books of Worth

The chief knowledge that a man gets from reading books is the knowledge that very few of them are worth reading.
Dates & Places Used:

768

TOPIC: Reality

What Elephants?

A great religious leader was teaching his followers in the jungles of India. Devotees from around the world came to hear his teaching. He taught that which most people considered reality was only an illusion.

During one of his discourses, his lecture was stampeded by a herd of wild elephants. He and his followers immediately climbed trees to protect themselves for certain destruction. As they gathered composure and returned to their circle, one doubting disciple asked his religious master why, if the elephants were only illusions and not real, the religious leader joined the rest of the group in the trees.

The religious leader's answer: "WHAT ELEPHANTS?"
Dates & Places Used:

769

TOPIC: Recovery

Never Felt Better

A farmer was coming out of his field along the back roads of a remote area. Just as he pulled out on the road, a city slicker came speeding over the hilltop and hit his rig. The farmer is lying there pinned under his wagon ... his dog not far away ... and his mule across the road in the other ditch.

About that time a car pulled up and the farmer thought, "Thank God, someone is going to help me." When he saw that it was the sheriff, he was even more relieved. The sheriff looked over the situation at a glance. Seeing the mule had a broken leg and suffering, he pulled out his revolver and shot it to end its misery. He walked across the road and saw the dog was just as bad off, so he shot him to end his misery.

Then he walked back over to the farmer and asked if he was in pain. "Never felt better in my life!" the farmer said.

Dates & Places Used:

770

TOPIC: Relatives

Marriage Is Relative

An eight-year-old boy asked his girlfriend to marry him. She turned him down, saying that in her family only relatives married. She explained, "If you and me were relatives we could get married, but we're not. In my family my daddy married my mother. My grandpa married my grandma, and all my uncles married my aunts. So you see, we can't get married, 'cause we're not relatives."

Dates & Places Used:

771

TOPIC: Relevance

Put Saints into Circulation

The story is told that during the reign of Oliver Cromwell the government ran out of silver coinage. Cromwell sent his men to a cathedral to see if they could find any silver. They reported: "The only silver we can find is in the statues of the Saints standing in the corners."

"Good," he replied. "We'll melt down the Saints and put them into circulation!"

Dates & Places Used:

772

Just One Camel

A church group traveled through Turkey to visit the sites of the seven churches of Revelation. As their bus went down a dusty road, they noticed up ahead a man riding a camel. The group stopped their bus to take a picture. It was only after they stopped that they noticed that behind the rider and the camel was his wife walking along. With the help of their interpreter they asked the man, "Why are you riding while your wife walks?"

"It is simple," he replied, "she doesn't own a camel."

That is the problem with many in the church. We say, "What's mine is mine. Too bad about the other guy. That's his problem."

Dates & Places Used:

773

TOPIC: Responses

Explosive Motto

Two explosive experts told what their motto was: "If you see us running, you had better catch up."

Dates & Places Used:

774

TOPIC: Responses

When God Calls

I was listening to every preschooler recite their memory verse for the week: "Call unto me and I will answer thee" (Jeremiah 33:3).

One little girl, trying very hard to remember the verse the way she had been taught, twisted and turned as she cautiously recited, "Call unto me ...," she paused briefly and then hurriedly finished, "and I will call you right back!"

Dates & Places Used:

775

TOPIC: **Responses**

Who, Me?

The English teacher asked Ted to name two pronouns. Taken aback and without the answer, Ted answered, "Who, me?!?"

Without hesitation, the teacher agreed, "That's correct, Ted. You're doing much better in this class."

Dates & Places Used:

776

TOPIC: **Responsibilities**

Feet and Shoulders

If you want your children to keep their feet on the ground, put some responsibility on their shoulders.

Dates & Places Used:

777

TOPIC: **Results**

Things Turn Out

Things seem to turn out best for those who make the best of the way things turn out.

Dates & Places Used:

778

TOPIC: **Results**

Yes–No–Yes–No

The careful driver was not sure his blinkers were working. He asked his son to get out of the car and tell him when his blinkers were working.

His son got out of the car, walked to the front of the car, and looked at the front of the car. The father turned on the blinker. The son responded immediately: "Yes–no–yes–no–yes–no."

Dates & Places Used:

779

Believe the One Who Rose

An agnostic professor condescendingly confronted a little girl who believed in Jesus: "There are many throughout history who have claimed they were God. How can you be sure who told the truth? Which one of these men can you believe?"

The girl responded without hesitation: "I believe in the ONE who rose from the dead!"

Dates & Places Used:

780

TOPIC: Resurrection

Easter on Memorial Day

Every day we would pass the cemetery as I drove my two preschoolers to their day care. As we passed each day, my son Tim would remind his younger sister, "Janna, that's where the dead people are."

Janna was almost three years of age, and the idea of death was somewhat confusing to her. Her brother explained that the cemetery is where they bury people's bodies in the ground when they are dead, and their spirits go back to God.

Several months later, on Memorial Day, our family went for a bike ride. Janna rode behind me in a bike trailer. With helmet on and her eyes darting from site to site, we all enjoyed the fresh air and sunshine of that day. We rode by the cemetery. It was filled with flowers and flags, people everywhere. Some were huddled in groups. Others knelt alone in front of headstones.

Janna saw this site and from the bike trailer behind me began to shout, "They're alive! They're alive! Daddy, they're alive!" It may have been Memorial Day, but for Janna, it was Easter.

Dates & Places Used:

781

TOPIC: Revenge

Bite Them Back

A businessman was once bitten by a rabid dog. The man rushed to see his doctor. The entire time the doctor examined him, the man wrote feverishly on a legal pad.

274

The doctor tried to calm the man and told him that with proper treatment there was no immediate need for a will.

"Oh, Doctor, I'm not writing a will," the businessman explained. "I'm making a list of competitors I want to bite."

Dates & Places Used:

782

TOPIC: Revenge

Matrimonial Vengeance

The war-torn husband finally found a way to get his wife to not use his razor to scrape paint.

He began to use her toothbrush to clean his whitewall tires.

Dates & Places Used:

783

TOPIC: Revenge

Grave Revenge

The person who pursues revenge should dig two graves.

Dates & Places Used:

784

TOPIC: Revenge

Alimony Vengeance

Banks have long printed checks in a wide spectrum of colors; some have offered checks with floral or scenic backgrounds. The modest-sized Bank of Marin in Marin County, California, has gone one step further. A customer can simply bring in a personal photograph or drawing and have it printed onto a standard check form.

Undeterred by the higher cost, more than five hundred customers signed up for the illustrated checks. But perhaps the most imaginative—and vindictive—customer is the one who ordered special checks to be used solely for making his alimony payments. They show him kissing his new—and beautiful—wife.

Dates & Places Used:

785

TOPIC: Revenge

Try Kindness

There was a sheep-raising farmer. Next to him there was another farmer who was raising wheat, children, and large dogs. The dogs were scaring the sheep. The sheep farmer did not know what to do. He could shoot the dogs or poison them, be nasty to his neighbor, or even take him to court.

He prayed about it ...

As soon as some new lambs were born he gave each of his neighbor's children one of the lambs as a pet. The children were thrilled. But their father could no longer allow his dogs to run rampant as before. He restrained them for the sake of the pet lambs. The two farmers became friends. Kindness won.

Dates & Places Used:

786

TOPIC: Revenge

Injury Responses

Doing an injury puts one below his enemy.
Revenging an injury makes one even with him,
But forgiving an injury sets one above his enemy!
Dates & Places Used:

787

TOPIC: Rules

Seat Belts
and Driver's Licenses

A car headed out of Calgary was stopped by a Canadian Mountie. He told the driver: "Congratulations, you have just won a $100 prize for the hundredth car passing through here today with all occupants buckled up with seat belts. Now, what are you going to do with the money?"

"Well," said the motorist, "I think I'll go and get a driver's license, now that I can afford it."

Dates & Places Used:

788

TOPIC: Rules

Ignore the Roberts Boys

In our church, we have a very large and active family by the name of Roberts. The family spans several generations. They are involved in almost every aspect of the church, including the women's groups. As a consequence, most people in the church know who the Roberts are.

One of the women's groups in our church is filled with older women who are all just as sweet as they could be. They are all very experienced adults and time has been at work. Many of them are a little hard of hearing. One day during one of their regular business meetings, an argument broke out over some issue. The chairperson was attempting to bring some order to this discussion and kept making reference to "Roberts' Rules of Order".

Time and again she said that Roberts' Rules of Order wouldn't allow them to do such and such.

Finally in exasperation, one of the other women said, "Well, why do we have to listen to those Roberts boys anyway? They're not part of the women's group."

Dates & Places Used:

789

TOPIC: Sacrifice

Will You Wash My Dishes?

Sometimes we get a distorted idea about what love is. One night, a man decided to show his wife how much he loved her. After dinner he began to recite romantic poetry, telling her he would climb high mountains to be near her, swim wide oceans, cross deserts in the burning heat of day, and even sit at her window and sing love songs to her in the moonlight.

After listening to him go on for some time about this immense love he had, she ended the conversation when she asked, "But will you wash the dishes for me?"

Dates & Places Used:

790

TOPIC: Saints

Circus Saint

He may be a saint, but if he is, he was canonized by the Ringling Brothers Circus.
Dates & Places Used:

791

TOPIC: Sales

Unbreakable Comb Sales

A man was selling "unbreakable combs" in front of a department store. To convince his skeptical audience, he bent two ends of a comb together until they touched. There was a loud crack, and the salesman was left with two pieces of plastic in his hand. Undaunted, he held them up and said, "And this, ladies and gentlemen, is what the comb looks like on the inside."
Dates & Places Used:

792

TOPIC: Sales

Persuasive Country Boy

Lyndon Johnson once said that when anyone tells you he's just a dumb old country boy, put your hand on your wallet.
Dates & Places Used:

793

TOPIC: Sales

Rudolph Versus the Wolves

Robert L. May was the creator of Rudolph the Red-Nosed Reindeer. This lovable creature was created in a book for the

Montgomery Ward Santas to give to children. May's comment concerning the popularity of dear Rudolph: "Rudolph is the first reindeer that ever kept the wolf from the door."

Dates & Places Used:

794 TOPIC: Sales

Undelivered Pizza

Two businessmen were flying from Cleveland to Minneapolis. As they flew over Chicago, one of the men picked up the air phone and ordered a pizza. The other fellow next to him asked him how he was going to get the pizza. He said he wasn't. The curious fellow asked him why he ordered the pizza, then.

He said that he lived in Chicago and ordered the pizza to make some money. He was asked how he was going to make money by ordering a pizza from a plane. He said that the pizzeria offered delivery anywhere in less than thirty minutes within a twelve mile radius or they would double your money back. He was only three miles away when he called for his pizza. He would be returning to Chicago at the end of the week and would go to the pizzeria and collect twice the price of the pizza.

Dates & Places Used:

795 TOPIC: Sales

Phone Sales Answers

The next time one of those telephone salespeople calls during dinner to sell you something you don't need, ask for his phone number and say you would like to call him back at *his* number– when you are a bit more free. Or say you'll buy the item if the telemarketer will fold up that scripted sales pitch he's reading and be able to recite it from memory. Or say you'll take ten of his products, but first you have to check with the executor handling your bankruptcy case.

Dates & Places Used:

796

TOPIC: Salvation

The Way in the Manger

My three-year-old son, Tommy, and I were singing Christmas songs together. Instead of singing "away" in a manger, Tommy kept singing "the way" in a manger.

Tommy was right! Jesus is the way, the truth, and the life. Once again, I received a glimpse of the kingdom through the mouth of a babe!

Dates & Places Used:

797

TOPIC: Sanity

Catching Imaginary Curveballs

An executive who passed a mental hospital on his way to work used to stop every once in a while to watch one of the patients going through the motions of winding up and pitching an imaginary ball. A friend asked the executive what he found so interesting about the man's performance.

"Well," said the executive, "if things keep on going the way they are, I'll be there some day catching for that guy, and I want to get on to his curves."

Dates & Places Used:

798

TOPIC: Santa

Santa Realities

Some second graders were talking about Santa—whether old Saint Nick was real or not. One child said that he had thought at one time that Santa was not real. His cousins had told him this. And so the next time he was at the shopping mall, he ran up to

Santa and kicked him in the leg. Santa let out a resounding scream. He then knew for sure that Santa was real.

Another child confessed that she was not sure if Santa was real. But she added that she would never tell anyone about her doubts. She explained that as soon as her older sister announced that she no longer believed in Santa, she stopped getting toys and started getting clothes. It looked like Santa had turned on her sister and that was not going to happen to her.

Dates & Places Used:

799

TOPIC: School

Drive to School and Learn

School is never the same when you get your driver's license. A teenage son got back home from his first day at school as a driver. His mother asked him what he learned at school today.

"I learned," said the son, "that if I don't get to school early, I don't get a good parking place."

Dates & Places Used:

800

TOPIC: School

Stick It Out

A little boy was goofing around all day long, paying no attention to his schoolwork. After repeated warnings the teacher sent him to the principal's office.

The boy came back and paid careful attention to the teacher for several minutes. But then he was back to his earlier inattentiveness. His impatient teacher approached him, "What was the last thing the principal told you?"

The boy replied, "If I can stick it out for five more minutes, school will be over."

Dates & Places Used:

801

TOPIC: School

Look at the Legs

A student in a biology class was given the assignment to learn about birds. He was to learn the classification, the scientific name, the common name, and characteristics of all the birds. The professor said, "Learn everything about them."

The day of the exam, the student was horrified when he looked at the test giving the birds pictured from their knees down. He knew the birds well but he couldn't identify any of them from their knees down. He tossed his paper onto the pile of exams on the instructor's table and explained his frustration.

The unsympathetic professor said, "Well, you'll just have to take a zero. I told you to learn everything about them. What's your name, Son?"

The boy reached down and pulled up his pants to his knees and said, "You tell me!"

Dates & Places Used:

802

TOPIC: School

Reluctant Student

A little boy was experiencing his first day of first grade. At lunchtime, he packed up his crayons, papers, scissors, and paste and was ready to head out the door.

His teacher stopped him and said, "It's time for lunch, Tommy. Why aren't you with the other children?"

"I always go home when the other kids go to eat," he replied. "I'll come back tomorrow."

"No, Tommy, that was last year when you were in kindergarten. This year you get to stay all day. You go to lunch, then come back here in the afternoon to study and do more work. You're only half through for the day ... there's lots more," so said the teacher.

Tommy thought about this for a moment, then shook his head in frustration. "Who signed me up for that?" he demanded.

Dates & Places Used:

803

No Need for School

A six-year-old boy came home dejected from his first day at school and announced, "I am not going to school tomorrow."

"Why not?" his mother inquired.

The boy answered, "I can't read, I can't write, and they won't let me talk–so what's the use?"

Dates & Places Used:

804

Suspension Stands Up

A ten-year-old girl had heard about some students getting expelled or suspended from school and did not understand what this meant. She went to her father and asked, "Dad, what does it mean to get suspended from school?"

Her father answered, "It means that you have to do your schoolwork at home standing up."

This answer led to another question, "But, Dad, why standing up?"

The father concluded, "Because a certain portion of your body is too sore to sit on."

Dates & Places Used:

805

How to Keep a Secret

The only way to keep a secret among three people is for two of them to be dead.

Dates & Places Used:

806

Security

The manager and one of his salesmen stood before a map on which colored pins indicated the representative in each area.

"I'm not going to fire you, Cartwright," the manager said, "but just to emphasize the insecurity of your position, I'm loosening your pin a little."

Dates & Places Used:

807

Through the Rough Spots

A husband and wife were discussing old times, when the husband said, "My dear, I have taken you safely over all the rough spots of life."

"Yes, dear," said the wife, "and I don't think you missed a one of them."

Dates & Places Used:

808

Me-Deep Conversation

An egotist is someone who is always me-deep in conversation.

Dates & Places Used:

809

The Only Regret

My one regret in life is that I'm not someone else.

Dates & Places Used:

Woody Allen

810

TOPIC: Self-Image

A Lot of Dirty Skunks

One day a gangster rushed into a store, shooting right and left and hollered, "All you dirty skunks get out of here."

They all left except one Englishman.

"Well," hollered the gangster, "what do you have to say for yourself?"

That's when the Englishman answered, "There sure were a lot of them, eh?"

Dates & Places Used:

811

TOPIC: Self-Image

Not Without Consent

No one can make us inferior without our consent.

Dates & Places Used:

812

TOPIC: Self-Image

He Can Dance a Little

Fred Astaire was without dispute one of the top singers, dancers, and actors of all time. In *Top Hat, Swing Time, Holiday Inn,* and other famous movies, he danced and crooned his way into people's hearts worldwide.

But in 1932, when Astaire was starting out, a Hollywood talent judge wrote on his screen test: "Can't act. Can't sing. Can dance a little."

As Christians, we may fail badly. "What kind of a Christian would do that?" we think. "How can I ever serve Christ again?"

But we develop in the Christian life when we leave those failures behind and daily use our God-given gifts for him. In time, those failures will be forgotten footnotes.

Dates & Places Used:

813

TOPIC: Self-Image

Just a Spare

A neighbor was befriending a new child in the neighborhood. "I understand you have twins in your home."

"Yes, sir, that's correct," the boy replied.

"And are you one of those twins?"

The little boy looked down to the ground sadly and answered, "No, sir, I'm just a spare."

Dates & Places Used:

814

TOPIC: Self-Image

Misplaced Inferiority

The trouble with inferiority complexes is the right people don't have them.

Dates & Places Used:

815

TOPIC: Self-Image

All Men Frauds

All men are frauds. The only difference between them is that some admit it. I myself deny it.

Dates & Places Used:

816

TOPIC: Self-Control

Stop the Pig in You

Don't go hog-wild and make a pig of yourself.

Dates & Places Used:

817

TOPIC: Self-Righteousness

Righteousness Is Dangerous

Sin doesn't harm us as much as our own righteousness.

Dates & Places Used:

818

TOPIC: Sensitivity

Communication Involves Listening

The sociologist on an African jungle expedition held up her camera to take pictures of the native children at play. Suddenly the youngsters began to yell in protest. Turning red, the sociologist apologized to the chief for her insensitivity and told him she had forgotten that certain tribes believed a person lost his soul if his picture was taken. She explained to him, in long-winded detail, the operation of the camera. Several times the chief tried to get a word in, but to no avail.

Certain she had put all the chief's fears to rest, the sociologist then allowed him to speak. Smiling, he said, "The children were trying to tell you that you forgot to take off the lens cap."

Dates & Places Used:

819

TOPIC: Separation

Too Separated

A church had a sign in front: JESUS ONLY. One night a storm blew out the first three letters and left US ONLY. Too many churches have come to that.

Dates & Places Used:

820

Sermon Feed

An old farmer said to the preacher, "I see at the Minister's Seminar you discussed how to get people to attend church. I've been to a lot of meetings for farmers, but I have never heard a single speech on how to get the cattle to eat. We spend our time discussing the right kind of feed."

Dates & Places Used:

821

Oil Field Wisdom

An oil field worker once offered some great advice to a speaker who had trouble concluding his public address: "Once we start drilling, if we haven't struck oil in thirty minutes, then we should stop boring."

Dates & Places Used:

822

Louder, Preacher

One Sunday evening after our choir had sung a particularly lively tune, they invited the pastor to take his place at the drums. Then they repeated the song. He had a great time and ended with an earsplitting solo. When the pastor returned to the pulpit, he said, "Playing the drums is like preaching. If you don't know what you're doing, you just do it a little louder."

Dates & Places Used:

823

TOPIC: Sermons

Sleepy Sermon Omen

Just before time for his sermon, a pastor commented to one of the church deacons that he had been so tired during the preparation of his sermon that he had fallen asleep while preparing it.

The deacon thought for a moment and suggested, "I guess that's not a very good omen for this morning, is it?"

Dates & Places Used:

824

TOPIC: Sermons

Preach Them to the Rear

A stranger came to church, and the minister was pleased to see him come forward to sit in one of the empty seats. Afterwards he greeted the newcomer and said, "I'm glad you felt free to sit well forward, even though you are a visitor."

"Well," said the man, "I'm a bus driver, and I just wanted to see if I could learn how you can get everyone to the rear all the time."

Dates & Places Used:

825

TOPIC: Sermons

Died in Service

A seven-year-old boy attending church with his parents noticed a white flag with gold stars on it, and asked, "What's that, Daddy?"

His father whispered, "That's a reminder of all those who have died in service."

The youngster thought a moment, and in a loud whisper asked, "Daddy, did they die in the nine or the eleven o'clock service?"

Dates & Places Used:

826

TOPIC: Sermons

Church Commercial Too Long

The little boy returned from his first time in church and was asked how it went. He said, "The music was nice but the commercial was too long."
Dates & Places Used:

827

TOPIC: Sermons

Sermon Subjects

The new minister asked, "What should I preach about?"
"About heaven and fifteen minutes!" was the reply.
Dates & Places Used:

828

TOPIC: Service

Lose the Blues Rules

Ten rules for getting rid of the blues: Go out and do something for someone else—and repeat it nine times.
Dates & Places Used:

829

TOPIC: Service

Service Pays Rent

The service we render to others
is really the rent we pay for our room on earth.
Dates & Places Used:

830

TOPIC: Service

Without Customers

Anyone who thinks the customer is not important should try doing without him for a period of ninety days.
Dates & Places Used:

831

TOPIC: Sex

The Bottom Line

A three-year-old boy went with his dad to see a new litter of kittens. On returning home, he breathlessly informed his mother, "There were two boy kittens and two girl kittens."

"How did you know that?" his mother asked.

"Daddy picked them up and looked underneath," he replied. "I think it's printed on the bottom."
Dates & Places Used:

832

TOPIC: Sex

Too Much Explanation

A little boy ran into the living room where his father was reading. "Dad, where did I come from?"

The boy's mother cleared her throat and excused herself to let Father answer this long-feared question. Father cleared his throat and went through a long, careful explanation of how children are born.

When he was finally through, Junior commented, "That's OK, Dad; but my pal Joe down the street says he comes from Omaha, and I just wanted to know where I came from."
Dates & Places Used:

833

God Knows the Facts of Life

A father was telling his little boy about the facts of life. About half of the way through the father's discourse, the son asked, "Do you think God knows about this?"

Dates & Places Used:

834

TOPIC: Sharing

Size Determines Size

The Sunday school teacher turned to eight-year-old Tommy; "Tommy, if you had a big apple and little apple, which one would you give to your brother?"

Tommy thought for a moment and asked, "Do you mean my big brother or my little brother?"

Dates & Places Used:

835

TOPIC: Shopping

The Nest Egg Is Gone

A woman returned home from a holiday shopping spree with her arms loaded with packages. Her husband met her at the door and said, "What did you buy? With prices as high as they are, I'll bet you spent a fortune. I hate to think what has happened to our nest egg."

"I'll tell you what happened to our nest egg," his wife said defensively as she began to put her packages on the dining-room table. "The old hen got tired of sitting on it."

Dates & Places Used:

836

TOPIC: Sickness

Nothing Serious

The doctor was giving a physical exam for a life insurance policy and asked, "What did your father die of?"

The worried patient wanted to pass this exam. The patient paused, "I don't know exactly, but I'm sure it wasn't anything serious."

Dates & Places Used:

837

TOPIC: Silence

Silence Is Dreadful

I went home for lunch. While sitting at the table, I watched my twenty-one-month-old child spill a half gallon of bleach. It's been said that children are like mosquitoes—when it gets quiet, the trouble is about to begin ...

Dates & Places Used:

838

TOPIC: Sin

Before Forgiveness

A Sunday school teacher had just concluded her lesson and wanted to make sure she had made her point. She said, "Can anyone tell me what you must do before you can obtain forgiveness of sin?"

There was a short interval of silence and then, from the back of the room, a small boy spoke up. "Sin," he said.

Dates & Places Used:

839

TOPIC: Sin

Forbidden Fruit Spoils Faster

While forbidden fruit is said to taste sweeter, it usually spoils faster.
Dates & Places Used:

840

TOPIC: Sin

Our Job Is to Sin

A young boy was explaining basic Christian theology to his younger sister: "You see, it was Jesus' job to die for our sins; it's our job to sin."
Dates & Places Used:

841

TOPIC: Sin

To Stop Sinning

It's not really that hard to stop sinning all at once. All you have to do is die.
Dates & Places Used:

842

TOPIC: Sin

Leaders Should Sin Less

Leaders aren't sinless, but they should sin less!
Dates & Places Used:

843

TOPIC: Sin

Can't Let Go

Two mountain boys spotted a bobcat up a tree and decided to have some fun. One said, "I'll shinny up that tree and chase him down, and you put him in a sack."

The other agreed, and the first fellow climbed up the tree. When he reached the right limb, he started shaking, and the cat came tumbling down. The other fellow grabbed the varmint by the back of the neck and tried to put him into a sack. There was a terrible commotion. Dust and fur and skin were flying in all directions. The fellow in the tree called down, "What's the matter, you need help catching one little ol' bobcat?"

"No," replied his friend. "I don't need help catchin' him. I need help turnin' him a-loose."

Dates & Places Used:

844

TOPIC: Sin

How Sin Feels

To err is human, but it feels divine.
Dates & Places Used:

845

TOPIC: Sin

A Tab with the Devil

If you spend your life running up a tab with the devil, don't expect him to forget on payday!
Dates & Places Used:

846

TOPIC: Sincerity

Impersonal Confrontation

The boss is talking to his secretary and says, "I'm afraid I've lost touch with the employees, Miss Jones. Do you think a personal letter from the heart would help?"

Miss Jones looks pleased and says, "Why, that's a wonderful idea, sir."

The boss smiles and says, "Good! Write something up for me, will you?"

Dates & Places Used:

847

TOPIC: Singles

Wrong Question

Lady widowed at age 30 . . .
Man called her . . . Good man . . .
Said he would eventually ask important question . . .
Went out . . .
Will ask important question . . .
Called . . .
Said was ready to ask important question . . .
Daughter answered . . .
"Will you really be our daddy?"
Man never asked a very important question.

Dates & Places Used:

848

TOPIC: Skeptic

Ongoing Prophecy

A skeptical American dropped in a coin and out of the speaker of this inventive Japanese device came the following announcement:

"You are an American. You are 5'10" tall. You weigh 150 pounds and you are booked on flight 408 to Los Angeles, California."

The man was totally incredulous. He was sure someone was playing a practical joke on him. So he slipped into a rest room, changed his clothes, put on a different coat, and pulled his hat over his ears so it hid his face. Hobbling like a shrunken old man, the American stepped onto the machine, dropped in his dime, and waited for the announcement. It wasn't long in coming.

"You are an American. You are 5'10" tall. You weigh 150 pounds, and while you were changing clothes, your plane left for Los Angeles."

Dates & Places Used:

849

TOPIC: Slander

Intelligent Talk

People of high intelligence talk about ideas.
People of average intelligence talk about things.
People with no intelligence talk about other people.
Where are you in the lineup?

Dates & Places Used:

850

TOPIC: Sleep

Eight Plus Eight

The key to getting ahead is setting aside eight hours a day for work and eight hours a day for sleep, and making sure they're not the same eight hours.

Dates & Places Used:

851

TOPIC: Sleep

Pastoral Wake-Up Call

A cartoon depicts a pastor holding the phone while the clock reads 2:00 A.M. The voice from the phone says, "I know it's early, Pastor, but I figured you'd be up praying."

Dates & Places Used:

852

TOPIC: Sloth

Mark Twain on Spiders in Papers

Peace is not always a good thing. Mark Twain, while editing a newspaper in Missouri, received a letter from a subscriber who wrote that he found a spider in his paper. The subscriber wanted to know whether finding the spider was good or bad luck.

Twain answered the letter by telling the subscriber that it was neither good luck nor bad. "The spider was merely looking over our paper to see which merchant was not advertising, so that he could go to that store, spin his web across the door, and lead a life of undisturbed peace ever afterward!"

Dates & Places Used:

853

TOPIC: Solutions

If Noah Had Been Wise

If Noah had been truly wise,
he would have swatted those two flies.

Dates & Places Used:

854

TOPIC: Solutions

Ask the Right Questions

"I beg your pardon," said the man returning to his seat in the theater, "but did I step on your toes when I left?"

"You certainly did!" answered the annoyed patron.

The man turned to his companion. "Honey, come on through," he said. "We're in the right row!"

Dates & Places Used:

TOPIC: Solutions

She's Out of Sight

Uncle Arky tells about the couple up the road who got into a fight a while back: The husband didn't see his wife for more than a week–then he got so he could see her just a little out of one eye.

Dates & Places Used:

TOPIC: Solutions

Gum Solution

An elderly man was taking his first flight on an airplane. He was much more relaxed than he had expected–but there was one problem. His ears would not stop popping. He mentioned this to the airline steward. The steward returned momentarily and explained that chewing gum would keep his ears from popping and handed the man some gum.

At the end of the flight the man thanked the steward: "The gum worked fine; I did not notice any more pressure in my ears, but I have another problem now. I'm having a terrible time getting this gum out of my ears. Could you help me?"

Dates & Places Used:

TOPIC: Solutions

Deal with the Source

Two farmers were fascinated by a booth where little celluloid balls bobbed on top of water jets. Customers were offered substantial prizes if they succeeded in shooting any one of the balls off its perch. One of the farmers spent six quarters in a vain effort to pick off one ball. Finally his friend pushed him aside and picked up the rifle.

"Watch how I do it," he said. He took a single shot. All six balls disappeared.

As they walked away from the booth, laden with prizes, the unsuccessful one marveled. "How did you ever do it?" he asked.

"It just took knowing how," explained the winner. "I shot the man working the pump."

Dates & Places Used:

858 TOPIC: Solutions

Living with Solutions

Solving problems is simple. Living with the solutions is difficult.

Dates & Places Used:

859 TOPIC: Solutions

Creative Solutions

Not all creative ideas become effective solutions.

It seems that a whale washed up on a beach in Florida. But all efforts to save it failed. Then they had to decide what to do with this dead whale carcass.

Nobody wanted it or knew what to do with it. Someone decided, for some reason, that it was a Highway Department problem and that they should clean it up. The Highway Department took on the job in a most creative way. Don't ask me why, but they decided that their best course of action would be to blow it up.

Word got out, and people showed up from miles around to watch. Do you remember the old adage, "What goes up must come down"? Well, the whale was blown up, and bits and parts rained down on the crowds, the surrounding homes, and the cars.

How do you explain to your insurance agent that the dents in your car are from a whale? It wasn't a hailstorm, it was a whale storm. Not all creative ideas become effective solutions.

Dates & Places Used:

860

TOPIC: Solutions

One Needed It More

Two men stood in front of a taxi cab and heatedly argued about who had the right to the cab. While they argued, the wife of one of the men looked on. After the men had argued for a couple of minutes, the one man became calm, opened the door for his opponent, and returned to his wife.

His wife immediately asked him why he had suddenly allowed the other man to take the cab. Her husband explained, "You see, dear, he needed the cab more than we did. He was late for his martial arts class. He's the teacher!"

Dates & Places Used:

861

TOPIC: Spectators

Worn-Out End Zone

I've watched so much football, I've worn out my end zone!
Dates & Places Used:

862

TOPIC: Speech

Those Who Don't Say Much

There are two kinds of people who don't say much
... those who are quiet
... and those who talk a lot.
Dates & Places Used:

863

TOPIC: Speech

Never Outspoken

There was a man at the party who seemed a self-appointed authority on every subject. One of the guests approached the host of the party and told the host, "He certainly is outspoken, isn't he?"

The host disagreed, "Not by anyone I know."

Dates & Places Used:

864

TOPIC: Speech

Tongues on Tap

Any faucet can turn the water on, but after a few years, only a good faucet will turn it off. The same thing applies to human tongues.

Dates & Places Used:

865

TOPIC: Speeches

Listeners' Advantage

Listeners have the advantage. They know when the speaker should stop, but the speaker seldom does.

Dates & Places Used:

866

TOPIC: Spite

Spite House

Joseph Richardson, a New York millionaire, lived and died in a house only five feet wide. It was called the "Spite House" and deserved its name.

Owning the narrow lot of land on which it was built, Mr. Richardson wished to sell it to the neighboring property owners. They would not pay him what he asked, and so he put up this house, which disfigured the block—and then condemned himself to a life of discomfort in it.

Dates & Places Used:

867

TOPIC: Sports

Football Fanatic

A man was seated next to a woman at a football game. This woman was following the game with full enthusiasm. She seemed to be there by herself, but there was an empty seat next to her. The curious man asked her if the seat was taken.

The woman answered, "It was my husband's seat."

"Oh, I'm sorry," the man said and then asked, "isn't there someone else in the family who could use the ticket?"

"No," she said, "they're all at the funeral."

Dates & Places Used:

868

TOPIC: Sports

The Toil of Tennis

Ruth Graham tells the story of the early days of missionary work in China. The missionaries knew the importance of relaxation and built a tennis court of dirt. They played for fun.

On one occasion, a group of Chinese gentlemen came calling in the middle of a game. With hands tucked up their sleeves, Oriental fashion, they watched first with interest, then with growing concern. As the game drew to a conclusion and the overheated players, mopping their foreheads, joined their Chinese friends, they were greeted with genuine sympathy. "We were talking among ourselves," they said, feeling their way so not to offend. "But can you Americans not afford to hire people to bat that ball back and forth for you?"

Dates & Places Used:

869

Sports and Education

Abraham Lincoln had difficulty getting an education, but what do you expect from a guy who didn't play football, basketball, or baseball?
Dates & Places Used:

870

Every Third Car Empty

Statistics show that in 1940 each car on the road had an average of 2.2 persons; in 1950 it was 1.4. It won't be long until every third car on the road will be empty.
Dates & Places Used:

871

Phenomenal Odds

If the odds are a million to one against something bad occurring, chances are 50–50 it will.
Dates & Places Used:

872

Pure Rabbit Burgers

A man was driving through the country when he saw a sign in front of a country store: "Rabbit Burgers—25 cents." Intrigued by both the idea and the price, he stopped, went inside, and purchased one.

While he was eating, he spoke with the proprietor: "I stopped because I saw your sign and your price. Are these made completely from rabbit meat?"

"They're mostly rabbit," the proprietor said.

"What do you mean by 'mostly'?"

"I put in a little mule, too."

"What do you mean by 'a little'?"

"Fifty-fifty," replied the storekeeper.

"What do you mean by 'fifty-fifty'?"

The storekeeper answered, "You know, you put in one rabbit, and you put in one mule."

Dates & Places Used:

873

TOPIC: Stewardship

Givers Who Stop at Nothing

The minister prayed, "Protect us from members of this church who, when it comes to giving, stop at nothing."

Dates & Places Used:

874

TOPIC: Stewardship

Too Many Obligations

A pastor approached one of the wealthiest members of his congregation about making a pledge to the church. The man informed the pastor that he had many obligations already. He asked if the pastor knew that the man's father was about to have his farm foreclosed, and that his mother needed surgery. The pastor said that he had not known these things.

The wealthy man then asked if the pastor knew that his brother had been badly injured in an automobile accident and needed reconstructive surgery ... and that his brother-in-law was going to prison unless he was able to come up with the money to make up a shortage in his accounts by next Tuesday. The embarrassed pastor admitted that he had not known of any of these tragic circumstances in the life of this man.

305

The pastor apologized for taking up the time of this man and started to leave. But the wealthy man was not finished with his tirade against the pastor: "Well, Pastor, if I'm not going to give a single dime to my family in their times of need, what makes you think I'm going to give any to the church?"

Dates & Places Used:

875 TOPIC: Strategy

The Best Offense

The best way to tackle Herschel Walker is to gang-tackle him from behind ... while he's sitting on the bench!

Dates & Places Used:

876 TOPIC: Strength

Too Tough to Keep

A burly construction foreman lined up his crew and told them, "The first thing I want you fellows to know is that I can lick any man in this gang."

A husky young man stepped forward and said, "You can't lick me."

The foreman looked him over carefully and replied, "You're probably right! You're fired!"

Dates & Places Used:

877 TOPIC: Strength

Pointing with Plows

Bernie Bierman had a classic answer to the frequent question, "How do you get such big men for your Minnesota football teams?"

"It's like this, friend. When I go driving along country roads, I look for boys walking behind plows.

"When I see one, I stop and ask him the way to Minneapolis. If he leaves the plow and points the way in the usual manner, I thank him and drive on.

"But if he picks up the plow and points with it, I just load him in the car and head straight for the registrar's office."

Dates & Places Used:

878

TOPIC: Stress

Get It Right This Time

Lisa was in a hurry. She had been shopping, and it was time to get home. But she still needed to get some gas for her car. She pulled into a service station to fill her tank with gas. She stopped the car and got out. She then realized the wrong side of her car was by the fuel pump. She got back in her car and drove to the other side of the pump. Once again she realized that in her haste she had simply moved the wrong side of the car to the other side of the pump! She jumped back in the car and began her third attempt. Her preschool son who had been watching this whole process from his car seat now asked his mother, "Are you gonna get it right this time, Mommy?"

There are times we get behind and perhaps try a little too hard to catch up–only to find ourselves going around in futile circles. The best advice may very well come to us in the form of this young boy's question, "Are you going to get it right this time?"

Dates & Places Used:

879

TOPIC: Stress

Losing Their Heads

A few hundred years ago two men were talking in France. The one asked the other what he did for a living. The man said that he kept his head, while all around him others were losing theirs. The inquiring man asked his acquaintance what type of job that was. The answer: the man operated a guillotine!

Dates & Places Used:

880

TOPIC: Stress

Diamonds Take Time and Stress

Diamonds are produced from coal that outlasted the pressures placed upon them.

Dates & Places Used:

881

TOPIC: Stress

Those Who Keep Their Heads

If you can keep your head when all about you others are losing theirs, it's just possible that you haven't grasped the situation.

Dates & Places Used:

882

TOPIC: Stubbornness

Self-righteous Neighbors

Stubbornness we deprecate, firmness we condone.
The former is our neighbor's trait, the latter is our own.

Dates & Places Used:

883

TOPIC: Students

One Less Test

Mike was studying for a test one evening. He was very quiet for a long time. So naturally his parents became curious. When they checked on him, they overheard this prayer: "Now I lay me down to rest, and hope to pass tomorrow's test. If I should die before I wake, that's one less test I have to take."

Dates & Places Used:

884

TOPIC: Students

The Wrong Test

A young woman, home from college for the weekend, was complaining about how tough the exams were. She was especially worried about the one coming up the next week. Her mother gave her the standard lecture, saying, "You should try studying this time."

Rena took her advice this time and studied intensely for three days, only coming out of her studies to eat and sleep. When she came home the following weekend, her mother asked her how she had done.

"Mom," she replied, "I don't know why I bothered to study. That was the easiest test I've ever taken."

Isn't it funny how, after finding how well prayer and meditation works for us, we decide things are going so well we don't need them?

Dates & Places Used:

885

TOPIC: Stupidity

Lucky Guess

A farmer was walking down the road carrying a sack. His neighbor was driving his pickup and pulled alongside of him and asked him what was in his bag. "Chickens," the farmer answered. The neighbor then asked how many were in the sack. The farmer replied with a challenge, "You guess how many chickens are in this sack and I will give you both of them."

Guess who got the chickens?

Dates & Places Used:

886

Confident Stupidity

The trouble with the world is that the stupid are cocksure and the intelligent are full of doubt.
Dates & Places Used:

887

Successful Failures

Success has made failures of many people.
Dates & Places Used:

888

Quality of Success

Nothing recedes like success!
Dates & Places Used:

889

Preparation Helps Luck

Chance favors the prepared mind.
Dates & Places Used:

890

A Sign of Success

Three men were riding to work, and the subject of success came up. One said, "Success is being asked to the White House to consult with the president."

The second commented, "No, success is being asked to the White House to consult with the president, and the red phone rings, but the president won't answer because he is listening to you."

Finally the third added, "No, success is when you're at the White House consulting with the president, and the red phone rings, the president picks it up, listens, then says 'It's for you.'"
Dates & Places Used:

891

TOPIC: Success

Successful Failures

I'd rather be a failure at something I enjoy than be a success at something I hate.
Dates & Places Used:

892

TOPIC: Success

Two Aspects of Success

Every important life story has two aspects: the things a man has energy enough to do, and the things a man has stability enough to stand.
Dates & Places Used:

893

TOPIC: Success

Always Room at the Top

There's always some room at the top because some people who get there fall asleep and roll off.
Dates & Places Used:

894

A New Approach for the Boss

It wasn't exactly what the boss expected when he asked his employees to put suggestions in a box as to how the business could be improved. "When I come in each morning, I like to see everyone in his or her place and started on the day's work. Anyone have any suggestions?"

The next day he found only one suggestion in the box. It read, "Wear squeaky shoes."

Dates & Places Used:

895

Watchful as a Whale

Consider the whale. Whenever he spouts off, he takes the chance of being harpooned.

Dates & Places Used:

896

Wordy Intellectuals

An intellectual is someone who takes more words than necessary to tell more than he knows.

Dates & Places Used:

897

The Taxing Side of Our Government

There is one difference between a tax collector and a taxidermist—the taxidermist leaves the hide.

Dates & Places Used:

898

Money Still Goes Far

They say that money doesn't go as far as it used to. That's not necessarily true. It's just that more of it goes in a different direction: to Washington, D.C.

Dates & Places Used:

899

Peter Pays Paul

A government which robs Peter to pay Paul can always depend on the support of Paul.

Dates & Places Used:

900

Unloading Your Financial Ship

In the United States, April is always a difficult month. Even if your ship does come in, the IRS is right there to help you unload it.

Dates & Places Used:

901

Partial Tax Payment

A man sent a check to the IRS for $100.00 with a note. It read: "I just have not been able to sleep so here is $100.00 I owe you. If I still can't sleep after that, I'll send you the rest."

Dates & Places Used:

902

TOPIC: Taxes

Tax Refunds

Next to being shot at and missed, nothing is quite as satisfying as an income tax refund.

Dates & Places Used:

903

TOPIC: Teaching

Lemon Pie Learning

Good teaching practices reinforcement: "Hit students in the face with a lemon pie enough times and sooner or later they will lick some of it off."

Dates & Places Used:

904

TOPIC: Teaching

A Teacher's Axiom

A teacher hasn't taught until the student has learned.

Dates & Places Used:

905

TOPIC: Teamwork

Hunch for a Team

Notre Dame had a fullback, halfback, quarterback, and a hunchback.

Dates & Places Used:

906

Together with Michael Jordan

Chicago Bulls rookie forward Stacy King scored one point in a basketball game in which Michael Jordan scored sixty-nine points. His analysis of the game was: "I'll always remember this as the night that Michael Jordan and I combined to score seventy points."

Dates & Places Used:

907

Church Builders

There is a game that is occasionally played in business management and quality control seminars to emphasize the way we may think and what changes in thought would serve us well. The game goes like this. The participants are teamed into two or three teams of at least three people on each team. The teams are then given building materials–the kind of building materials really do not matter. Each of the teams is then told to build the largest building possible in a given amount of time.

What happens in the next few minutes is fascinating. Some teams just go to work. Others appoint a leader–or the leader is self-appointed–and take orders in the construction process. Sometimes a team will spend most of its time planning. The team may not even have enough time left for the actual building stage of the game.

All the teams stay busy, all build a building. There is always a comparative winner among the teams, but not one team succeeds. No team has ever built the largest building possible. The rules of the game never told the teams they cannot work together on one building. But they never come together and work as one team. The teams just never think to cooperate.

So it is with the church. Christ gave us a commission–a construction process. All we have to do is do it. We accomplish our task in various ways. We may spend most of our time organizing, or following the leader, or arguing among ourselves, or competing with other churches—and perhaps a little time actually doing the job. But there may be other models or paradigms that we have excluded from our thoughts—like cooperation, teamwork, unity, and love. Perhaps, then, the world would know we were his disciples, by our love for one another.

Dates & Places Used:

908

TOPIC: Teamwork

Someone Else Died

I know that all of you were saddened to learn this week of the death of one of our church's most valuable members—Someone Else. Someone's passing created a vacancy that will be difficult to fill.

Else has been with us for many years, and for every one of those years, Someone did far more than the normal person's share of the work. Whenever leadership was mentioned, this wonderful person was looked to for inspiration as well as results. Someone Else can work with that group.

Whenever there was a job to do, a class to teach, or a meeting to attend, one name was on everyone's lips, "Let Someone Else do it." It was common knowledge that Someone Else was among the largest givers in the church. Whenever there was a financial need, everyone just assumed that Someone Else would make up the difference. Someone Else was a wonderful person, sometimes appearing superhuman, but a person can only do so much.

Were the truth known, everyone expected too much of Someone Else. Now Someone Else is gone. We wonder what we are going to do. Someone Else left a wonderful example to follow, but who is going to follow it? Who is going to do the things Someone Else did? Remember, we can't depend on Someone Else anymore.

Dates & Places Used:

909

TOPIC: Technology

Einstein Describes the Radio

You see, wire telegraph is a kind of a very, very long cat. You pull his tail in New York and his head is meowing in Los Angeles. Do you understand this? And radio operates exactly the same way: you send signals here, they receive them there. The only difference is that there is no cat.

Dates & Places Used:

910

TOPIC: Technology

Kind of Like a Printer

Friday night, I brought a typewriter home from work so I could fill in a seven-part form. My four-year-old daughter took a look and said, "What's that, Daddy?"

I answered, "A typewriter."

She asked again, "What's that?"

I scrambled to find an analogy a four-year-old could handle. "Uh, it's like a printer."

"Oh, okay," she said.

Dates & Places Used:

911

TOPIC: Teenagers

Teen Rent

Kevin, a friend of mine who lives at home, is not the neatest person in the world.

One day his mother was lecturing him. "Look at your room!" she yelled. "It's a disaster! The bed isn't made, there's a stack of papers over there, and a pile of clothes over here. I should be charging you three hundred dollars a month."

"What?" Kevin replied. "For this pigsty?"

Dates & Places Used:

912

Dying for Treatment

"Hurry!" the doctor cried to his teenage daughter. "Put my stethoscope and medicine bag in my car. I just received an emergency call from someone who says he will die if I don't come immediately."

"Oh, Dad, that call wasn't for you," the daughter saucily responded. "That was a call for me."

Dates & Places Used:

913

Bad Grades

Two teenagers were talking as they were coming out of their high school building on the way home from school. The first asked, "Would your parents be mad if you were to flunk out of school?" The second one thought for a minute and then said, "Not really. They'd just rent out my room."

Dates & Places Used:

914

They Just Don't Work That Well

A teenage fellow was working on his car and just could not get it to work. His father patted him on the back and encouraged him: "Don't let it bother you Son, your mother and I have been trying to get you to work for about seventeen years, and we have not had much luck either."

Dates & Places Used:

915

Not So Hard Times

It seems like today's teenagers will have a hard time telling children of their own what they did without.
Dates & Places Used:

916

Full-Time Father

Teddy Roosevelt once said about his sixteen-year-old daughter, "I can either be President of the United States, or I can control Alice. I cannot do both."
Dates & Places Used:

917

Getting Past the Phone

A certain teenage girl has been trying to run away from home for years, but every time she gets to the front door, the phone rings.
Dates & Places Used:

918

Capture the Moment

Recently a teenage boy was rushed to the hospital with appendicitis. Surgery had been scheduled, so it was puzzling when the boy's father asked the surgeon if there was a barber in the hospital.

"Why do you want to know?" the surgeon asked.

"I thought," replied the father, "that we might as well get his hair cut while he's under the anesthetic."
Dates & Places Used:

919

Never No News

The one function that TV news performs very well is that when there is no news we give it to you with the same emphasis as if there were.

Dates & Places Used:

920

Whistler's Mother's Television

A kindergarten tot described the painting "Whistler's Mother" as follows: "The painting shows this nice old lady who is waiting for the repairman to bring back her TV set."

Dates & Places Used:

921

Black-and-White War

A cartoon of a classroom situation appeared in the *Wall Street Journal:* A little boy has been called on by his teacher to tell about World War II.

The boy stands and asks his teacher, "Is that the one that's always in black and white?"

Dates & Places Used:

922

Temper Trouble

The problem with losing your temper is that no one else wants it either.

Dates & Places Used:

923

Source of Bad Dreams

On a Sunday morning at First United Methodist Church in Pensacola, Florida, the young woman who is the director of Christian Education was discussing dreams with the children during the Children's Time. She said, "I used to have bad dreams when I was a child, and sometimes I still have bad dreams. For example, the other night I dreamed that I blew up Preacher Henry's house." (Preacher Henry is the Senior Minister.)

One little girl's hand went up and stayed up. Finally the director called on her and said, "Do you want to say something?"

The little girl put her hand down and very clearly said, "My mamma told me if you don't have bad thoughts, you won't have bad dreams."

Dates & Places Used:

924

TOPIC: Temptations

You Can Always Run

An old southern preacher once told his congregation how to escape temptation with this advice:

"When your lookin' at your neighbor's watermelon patch, you can't keep your mouth from waterin' but you sure can run!"

Dates & Places Used:

925

TOPIC: Temptations

Problem with Gravy

Grandpa asked his grandson one day, "Jimmy, why don't you ever eat your gravy?"

Jimmy furrowed his brow and said, "Grandpa, you just never know what's going to be under it."

It's the same way with temptation. Most of the things we are tempted with are like gravy. They look good but you just never know what's going to be under it. You never know what will lead you astray.

Dates & Places Used:

926

TOPIC: Temptations

Jam of Forbidden Fruit

On a church bulletin board: "Forbidden fruit has resulted in many a jam."

Dates & Places Used:

927

TOPIC: Temptations

Temptation Kicks in Door

The trouble with opportunity is that it only knocks. Temptation kicks the door in.

Dates & Places Used:

928

TOPIC: Temptations

Fighting Temptation

Mother: "Billy, what are you doing there in the pantry?"
Billy: "Fighting temptation, Mom."

Dates & Places Used:

929

Temptation and Cowardice

There are several good protections against temptation, but the surest is cowardice.

Dates & Places Used:

930

A Look That Took

Eyes that see, and eyes that want,
Eyes are they temptations taunt.

Job vowed he would not look,
But David saw and then he took.

Dates & Places Used:

931

Thou Shalt Pick Up Thy Toys

Mother and her two small boys were having a serious discussion about stealing and why it was wrong. Mother asked the boys why they thought stealing was wrong. Five-year-old Luke said that stealing was against God's laws. He had learned about the Ten Commandments in Sunday school.

Mother asked the boys if they knew any other of the Ten Commandments. Luke remembered two others: "You shall not murder," and "Honor your father and mother." But they could not think of any others. After some time of thinking, Patrick piped up, "I know one: 'Pick up your toys!"

Dates & Places Used:

TOPIC: Thanksgiving

Even When It's Painful

As two men were walking through a field one day, they spotted an enraged bull. Instantly, they darted toward the nearest fence. The storming bull followed in hot pursuit, and it was soon apparent they would not make it. Terrified, the one shouted to the other:

"Put up a prayer, John. We're in for it!"

John answered, "I can't. I've never made a public prayer in my life."

"But you must!" implored his companion. "The bull is catching up to us."

"All right," panted John, "I'll say the only prayer I know, the one my father used to repeat at the table: 'O Lord, for what we are about to receive, make us truly thankful.'"

This fictitious story suggests a valuable truth. No matter how severe the trial, Christians should give thanks in everything.

Dates & Places Used:

TOPIC: Thanksgiving

Always Thankful

A woman was always able to find something for which she was thankful. One morning there was a terrible snowstorm, but she still showed up in time for work, and she was thankful. Her supervisor was surprised to see her, and was equally surprised to hear that she was thankful to make it to work in such a storm.

When asked why she was so thankful, she said that she was thankful that she lived so close to work. Her supervisor still did not understand how she could even walk on the icy sidewalks with the blowing winds. She said that she was so thankful that she was able to crawl to work on her hands and knees. Her supervisor was astounded, and asked what was so wonderful about crawling to work on her hands and knees. The woman smiled and said, "During the blizzard in the early morning light, no one was able to see me!"

Dates & Places Used:

934

TOPIC: Threats

Talent Threat

The exasperated piano teacher told her unruly student, "If you don't behave yourself, I'll tell your parents you have talent!"
Dates & Places Used:

935

TOPIC: Time

Speed-Thinking Needed

What's the point in taking speed-reading courses if they don't teach you how to speed-think?
Dates & Places Used:

936

TOPIC: Time

All Night Not As Long

A little boy woke up at his grandparents' house after a particularly sound sleep. He jumped out of bed and ran into the kitchen to see his grandparents. As he entered the kitchen, he exclaimed, "It doesn't take as long to sleep all night at your house as it does at my house!"
Dates & Places Used:

937

TOPIC: Time

Delayed Turtle Actions

A family of turtles—Father Turtle, Mother Turtle, and Junior Turtle—went on a picnic. They did not move very fast, so it took them three years to get to the picnic grounds. They got all the food unpacked from the picnic basket and suddenly realized that they had left the ketchup at home. Mother Turtle asked Junior Turtle if he would run home and get the ketchup. Junior Turtle did not want to do it; he was afraid that his dad and mom would start eating without him. His dad and mom promised that they would not begin their picnic until Junior returned from home with the ketchup.

Father Turtle and Mother Turtle waited for Junior Turtle. They waited for years. Five years passed and no sign of Junior. They waited some more. Nine years passed, and they could wait no longer. They had to eat something. Each one took a bite.

As soon as Father Turtle and Mother Turtle took their first bite, Junior Turtle appeared from behind a bush and screamed, "I knew you would start eating without me . . . I'm not going!"

Dates & Places Used:

938

TOPIC: Time

Time to Worry

A man once said, "I've got so many troubles that if anything bad happens today it will be two weeks before I can worry about it."

Dates & Places Used:

939

TOPIC: Time

Pig Time

A man from the city was driving through the country and saw a curious sight. Along the side of the road was a farmer holding a pig in a cornfield, feeding the pig ears of corn that were still on the cornstalk. The man from the city pulled to the side of the road and walked over to the farmer.

"I don't know if you realize it, but it's going to take a long time for you to fatten up that pig."

The farmer answered, "I don't know if you realize it, but this pig doesn't have that much to do anyway."

Dates & Places Used:

TOPIC: Time

Telling Time

An Air Force lieutenant with a terrible cough went to see a doctor. "This cough is serious," diagnosed the doctor. "Do you smoke?"

"No," answered the lieutenant, "I gave smoking up."

The physician was not convinced. "When did you give it up?"

The lieutenant's response was immediate: "Nineteen fifty-nine."

"That long ago?" questioned the surprised doctor, "I don't think that is possible."

"What's the big deal," asked the annoyed lieutenant as he looked at his watch. "It's only twenty-one sixteen now."

Dates & Places Used:

TOPIC: Tithing

The Treasurer and Tithing

A church in Kansas needed to replace its treasurer. The deacons asked one of their members, the manager of the local grain elevator, to take the job.

"I'll do it on two conditions," he responded.

"What are they?"

"I'll take the job only if no reports are required for one year, and only if no one asks me any questions for a year."

The man was trusted, respected, honest, and well-known. Though the deacons gulped once or twice, they agreed. They all did business with him since he managed the only grain elevator for miles around.

At the end of the year the treasurer gave his report to the congregation: The debt of the church building had been paid in full. The salaries of all the staff were increased substantially. Several new buses had been purchased and paid for. All missions commitments had been met. There were no outstanding bills, and there was a surplus of several thousand dollars.

The shocked congregation asked the inevitable question: "How could this be?"

"It's simple," the treasurer replied. "Most of you bring your grain to my elevator. As you did business with me during the year, I withheld ten percent on your behalf and gave it to the church in your name. You never missed it."
Dates & Places Used:

942 TOPIC: Traditions

Not So Good Old Days

At one time "Good Old Days" were referred to as "These Trying Times."
Dates & Places Used:

943 TOPIC: Traditions

How Many Magi?

A story is told of a pastor and a scripture scholar who find themselves sitting together on an airplane. The pastor immediately complains to the scholar: "You know, sir, there are some Scripture scholars these days who are saying we don't know how many Magi there were.

The scholar quickly says, "I am not one of them."

Relieved, the pastor says, "Am I glad to hear that."

But the scholar quickly adds: "That's right, there were six magi."

"Six?" shouted the surprised pastor. "How do you figure six magi?"

"Well," replied the scripture scholar, "in the reliquary at Cologne there are the heads of three wise men, and in the reliquary at Milan there are the heads of three wise men. Three plus three equal six."
Dates & Places Used:

TOPIC: Traditions

Proper Mode
of Communion

Too Much Static from the Lips

I heard a story recently, supposedly true, about the new pastor at the Methodist? Episcopal? Lutheran? church. After the first worship service, the pastor heard rumblings that he had not done Communion the right way. Puzzled at this, he studied his worship books, but came away with the conviction that he had used the proper order. He next asked an officer of the church. The officer told him, "Yes," he had done it the "wrong way."

"What am I doing wrong?" he asked.

"Well," replied the man, "the previous pastor [who had been at this church for many years] always touched the radiator before serving the cup. You don't touch the radiator."

Only half enlightened, the pastor called his predecessor, who said, "Yes, I touched the radiator before serving the cup. I did it to get rid of static electricity. The members were complaining of sparks on their lips."

Dates & Places Used:

TOPIC: Traditions

No Joy Allowed

A young Dutch pastor confronted a serious situation on a Sunday morning. A severe storm had hit during the night, and his church was located some distance outside the village. There was no way, it seemed, to get to the church for Sunday worship. But then an idea came to him. He could get to the church if he put on his ice skates and went by way of the canal which ran in front of his church.

When he began to think seriously about his plan, however, he concluded that it might not be such a good idea. The people of his church were fine folk, but they were also very strict about Sabbath observance. Skating was simply not to be done on the

Sabbath. The young pastor thought about the matter and then made up his mind. It was important that worship be conducted, he would therefore run the risk.

So he put on his skates and made his way without difficulty to the church. Just inside the door the official board waited for him; no smiles welcomed him. They were obviously disturbed that their pastor had so clearly violated what they felt to be proper behavior on the Sabbath day. But if they were displeased, they were also uncomfortable. They were very fond of the young pastor, and they really didn't want to cause any rupture in their relationship. After considerable discussion, one of them asked the pastor a question. "Did you enjoy the skating?" he asked.

"No," said the pastor, "I didn't enjoy it."

A sigh of relief went up from the group. It was all right. Since there had been no joy in the incident, it was acceptable to the church people!

Dates & Places Used:

946

TOPIC: Trials

End of the Line

You know you're in trouble when you realize that the light at the end of the tunnel is an oncoming train . . .

Dates & Places Used:

947

TOPIC: Trinity

God, the Father, Is the Tallest One

Talking to my children about God and the Trinity I asked them a trick question. "Of the Father, Son, and Holy Spirit, which of them is God?"

Natalie, my four-year-old girl, answered, "The tallest one."

Dates & Places Used:

948

TOPIC: Troubles

Bad Investments

One guy tried to diversify just before the stock market crashed. He invested in paper towels and revolving doors. He said he got wiped out before he could get turned around.
Dates & Places Used:

949

TOPIC: Truth

Truth Is Tough

Truth is tough. It will not break, like a bubble, at a touch. Nay, you may kick it about all day, and it will be round and full at evening.
Dates & Places Used:

950

TOPIC: Truth

Bombastic Bible

Ye shall know the truth, and the truth shall make you mad.
Aldous Huxley

Dates & Places Used:

951

TOPIC: Truth

The Truth Will Make You Miserable

The truth will set you free, but first it will make you miserable.
Dates & Places Used:

952

Only Feet She Has

One proud grandmother in our church told me of a touching encounter with her five-year-old granddaughter. Noticing something wrong about the little girl's feet, the grandmother corrected gently, "Honey, you've got your shoes on the wrong feet."

The child looked down and then sadly stated, "But, Grandma, these are the only feet I've got!"

Dates & Places Used:

953

Want to Be Five

During his children's sermon, the pastor was speaking to the children about the need for unity within the church. The pastor looked at the children and emphasized, "God wants us to be one!"

One of the youngest children who was four years of age immediately protested, "I've already been one; I want to be five."

Dates & Places Used:

954

Vacation Spot

A vacation spot is where they charge you enough to make up for the rest of the year you're not there.

Dates & Places Used:

955

Flute Flattened

The parable is told of a reed flute, which was passed down from the time of Moses. Crudely made, the instrument nevertheless produced wonderful music which inspired thousands over the years. Then, the priests of the temple decided such an heirloom should be decorated with fine gold to reflect the majesty of its music. But after the gold was applied, the flute produced only flat, metallic notes.

Dates & Places Used:

956

TOPIC: Values

The Marriage Prize

A dad said to his girl's boyfriend, "The man who marries my daughter will get a prize."

"Okay," said the boy, "but let me see the prize first."

Dates & Places Used:

957

TOPIC: Values

Why Take It with You?

Determined to "take it all with him" when he died, a very wealthy man prayed until finally the Lord gave in to his prayer request. There was one condition: He could only bring one suitcase of his wealth with him. Therefore the rich man filled his suitcase with gold bullion.

The day came when God called him home. St. Peter greeted him at the gate and told him he could come in, but his suitcase would have to be left. "That's okay because I have an agreement with God to allow me one suitcase in heaven."

"That's very unusual," replied St. Peter. "Would you allow me to take a look inside?"

The man opened the suitcase to reveal the shining gold bullion ingots. St. Peter was amazed and asked, "Why in the world would you bring pavement to heaven?"

Dates & Places Used:

958

No Glow

The world has a lot of glitter, but it doesn't have the glow.
Dates & Places Used:

959

God's Fuss over Prunes

A little boy refused to eat his prunes, so his mother told the lad that God was angry with him and sent him to bed.

Soon after the boy went to his room a violent thunderstorm broke out. The flashes of lightning and the sounds of thunder were so intense that the mother looked into her son's room to see if he was alright. When she opened the door, she saw her son standing by the window and mumbling, "My goodness, such a fuss to make over a few prunes."
Dates & Places Used:

960

Standing in the Need of Praise

Our four-year-old daughter Jenny was in the backseat having a good old time singing to herself. Here's the song I heard: "It's not my brother, not my sister, but it's me, oh Lord, standing in the need of *praise*."

Certainly, we all need to know God's affirmation and, from time to time, we all stand in the need of *praise*.
Dates & Places Used:

961

TOPIC: Victory

Missing a Loser

One night at a basketball banquet the president of a junior college was congratulating the coach and the team profusely. The beaming coach asked the president, "Would you still like me as much if we didn't win?"

"I'd like you as much," the president replied. "I'd just miss having you around."

Dates & Places Used:

962

TOPIC: Virtue

Samples of Virtue

No one will ever know of your honesty and sincerity unless you give out some samples.

Dates & Places Used:

963

TOPIC: Vision

A Confident Look

Show me a man with his head held high, and I'll show you a man who can't get used to his bifocals.

Dates & Places Used:

964

TOPIC: Vision

Direction

A waitress was once asked how she managed to carry all those dishes of food through the crowd without spilling any.

She replied, "I look where I'm going and not at the food!"

Dates & Places Used:

965

God's Name in Spain

Our first grader, Ben, came home from public school with the following story. He said that classmate Bobby had been using God's name the wrong way. He said his teacher finally told Bobby, "Do not use God's name in Spain."

Dates & Places Used:

966

Fewer Insults

The chairman of the deacon board approached the new pastor: "Now, Pastor, we only pay our pastors fifty dollars a week around here."

"Why, that's an insult!" responded the pastor.

The deacon agreed: "Yes, but we only pay every other week. That way you aren't insulted as often."

Dates & Places Used:

967

Bombs and Bake Sales

It will be a great day when our schools get all the money they need and the Air Force has to hold a bake sale to buy a bomber.

Dates & Places Used:

968

Rust in Peace

The best toast for the weapons of war is: "May they rust in peace!"

Dates & Places Used:

969

TOPIC: Wealth

He Left Everything

A very wealthy man died. Shortly thereafter a neighbor asked, "How much did he leave?"

A wise woman replied, "Everything!"

Dates & Places Used:

970

TOPIC: Wealth

Protected Riches

Lyndon Johnson, speaking in the early 1960s, reflected the American spirit of greed when he said, "Don't forget, there are two hundred million of us in a world of three billion. They want what we've got—and we're not going to give it to them."

Dates & Places Used:

971

TOPIC: Weddings

I Will Too

At the wedding of my friend's daughter, the minister asked Randy, the nervous young groom, "Will you take Dianne to be your lawfully wedded wife?" This was met by a long silence. Finally the minister prompted the groom by saying, "I will."

Randy quickly replied, "I will too."

Dates & Places Used:

972

TOPIC: Weddings

Marriage Trade-Ins

The four-year-old daughter of a used car salesman, attending her first church wedding, watched as the bride walked to the altar on the arm of an elderly gray-haired man. She stared in amazement after the ceremony ended and the bride walked back with her groom.

"Mother," the girl whispered rather loudly, "is that how weddings are? You trade off an old man for a nice, new model?"

Dates & Places Used:

973

There Goes the Best Man

We all have our favorite stories of wedding catastrophes. One of my favorites is the very first wedding I performed. We were halfway through the ceremony, and I was amazed that all had gone without any problem at all.

And then it happened. We were all solemnly listening to the organ play the Lord's Prayer. I figured I would close my eyes and look extra spiritual. I do think it gave a nice appearance with the exception of the thud. While closing my eyes, I felt like I was losing my balance. When I heard the thud, I was horrified with the thought, "Oh no, I've fallen over!"

I opened my eyes and was relieved to find that I was still standing. The best man had fallen backward off of the stage and had landed like a board on the floor. While the groomsmen rushed to pick him up, I regained my composure, vowing I would never close my eyes in a wedding ceremony again.

Dates & Places Used:

974

Spur-of-the-Moment Weddings

The phone rang on Tuesday morning. The call was from a young woman who didn't identify herself. She simply stated that she wanted to be married on Friday of that week. This was to be for her, the sixth time she had been married. Not wanting to sound rude, I said that I did not do "spur-of-the-moment wed-dings." I told her I like to counsel with the couple before the wedding.

She sounded somewhat irritated by my response. After a pause, she continued, "Well, I'll find someone else to perform the ceremony, but I want you to know something: I believe you are wrong about 'spur-of-the-moment weddings.' Some of my BEST marriages have been 'spur-of-the-moment.'"

I just had to laugh!

Dates & Places Used:

975 TOPIC: Weddings

The Hiring Party

Dad was watching television after supper. Mom was doing dishes while another load of clothes were in the washing machine. The children were in the den looking at pictures from the family album. The older brother pointed to the wedding pic-tures and confidently instructed his younger sister, "This was the party they had when Dad hired Mom."

Dates & Places Used:

976 TOPIC: Willingness

He Won't Take the Ball

It seems that a fellow named Calhoun was the favorite ball-carrier of the local fans, but on this particular day the quarter-back was not giving him the ball.

As the game wore on with the home team behind, the fans grew increasingly impatient. The next time the home team got the ball the fans began to chant, "Give the ball to Calhoun, give the ball to Calhoun."

On the second play the quarterback dropped back to pass and was smothered for an eight-yard loss. It was third down and eighteen and the chant "Give the ball to Calhoun" was so loud that the team could not hear the quarterback in the huddle.

Finally the frustrated quarterback walked out of the huddle and motioned for silence from the crowd. He then cupped his hands to his mouth and shouted to the stands, "Calhoun doesn't want the ball!"

Dates & Places Used:

977
TOPIC: Winning

A Sure Way to Win

Anyone can win ... unless there happens to be a second entry.

Dates & Places Used:

978
TOPIC: Wisdom

Anatomy of Communication

"God gave us two ears but only one mouth. Some people say that's because he wanted us to spend twice as much time listening as talking. Others claim it's because he knew listening was twice as hard as talking!"

Dates & Places Used:

979
TOPIC: Wisdom

Grains of Wisdom

A wise woman puts a grain of sugar into everything she says to a man and takes a grain of salt with everything he says to her.

Dates & Places Used:

980

Wise and Otherwise

A few people are wise; most are otherwise.
Dates & Places Used:

981

TOPIC: Wisdom

People Beginning to Talk

One afternoon when Casey Stengel was managing the Mets, his starting southpaw showed signs of fatigue. As one pitch after another missed the strike zone, the crowd groaned, then hissed, then booed.

Finally, when the catcalls became deafening, Casey went out to the mound to replace the left-hander. "But, Casey," the hurler pleaded, "I want to pitch myself out of this hole. Why take me out now?"

"Well, in case you haven't noticed," Stengel said, "people are beginning to talk."
Dates & Places Used:

982

TOPIC: Wisdom

The Value of Debate

It is better to debate a question without settling it than to settle a question without debating it.
Dates & Places Used:

983

TOPIC: Wisdom

Mouth Shut Wisdom

Wisdom is the ability to keep your mouth shut while your mind continues to talk to itself.
Dates & Places Used:

984

TOPIC: Wisdom

Newton's Seventh Law

A bird in the hand is safer than a bird overhead.
Dates & Places Used:

985

TOPIC: Wisdom

When the Boss Tells a Joke

When the boss tells a joke and you laugh, it doesn't prove that
you have a sense of humor; it proves that you have sense.
Dates & Places Used:

986

TOPIC: Wisdom

Speak Up and Sit Down

Courage is what it takes to stand up and speak. Also what it
takes to sit down and listen.
Dates & Places Used:

987

TOPIC: Wisdom

Wit and Wisdom

Wisdom is a shield that protects;
Wit is a sword that attacks.
Dates & Places Used:

988

TOPIC: Women

The Right Stuffing

A small child came home from Sunday school and told his mother: "The teacher told us how God made the first man and the first woman. He made man first, but the man was very lonely with no one to talk to, so God put the man to sleep, and while he was asleep, God took out his brains and made a woman out of them."

Dates & Places Used:

989

TOPIC: Work

Saved by Dad

"When I was your age," the millionaire bragged to his son, "I carried water for a gang of bricklayers."

The son thoughtfully said, "I'm mighty proud of you, Father. If it hadn't been for your great determination, I might have had to do something like that myself."

Dates & Places Used:

990

TOPIC: Work

No Job for a Lady

A motorist noticed a woman standing beside her car, looking helplessly at a flat tire. He stopped and began removing the tire.

"Oh, thank you," said the woman, "I don't know a blessed thing about changing tires."

"You don't have to, ma'am," said the motorist. "It's no job for a lady."

After the tire was changed the woman put her finger to her lips and said, "Please put the jack down easily. My husband's taking a nap in the backseat!"

Dates & Places Used:

991

Tie All My Life

A surprised mother found her four-year-old son crying as he was tying his shoes. "Why are you crying?" she asked.

"I have to tie my shoes," he sobbed.

"But you just learned how. It isn't that hard, is it?"

"But I'm gonna have to do it the rest of my life!"

Dates & Places Used:

992

When Work Speaks

When your work speaks for itself, don't interrupt!

Dates & Places Used:

993

At Your Age

A father was scolding his teenage son for being lazy. "You ought to be ashamed," he said. "When Lincoln was your age, he was busy building rail fences. You won't even do your homework."

"Sure," said the boy, "and when Lincoln was your age, he was president of the United States."

Dates & Places Used:

994

Blister Workers

Too many people are like blisters ... they don't show up until the work is all done.

Dates & Places Used:

995

Visit the Cemetery

A businessman, harassed and discouraged from overwork, took his problem to a psychiatrist who promptly told him to do less work. "Furthermore," prescribed the doctor, "I want you to spend an hour each week in the cemetery."

"What on earth do you want me to do that for? What should I do in the cemetery?"

"Not much. Take it easy and look around. Get acquainted with some of the men already in there and remember that they didn't finish their work either. Nobody does, you know."

Dates & Places Used:

996

Miller Time

When Abraham Lincoln was a young man he took a sack of grain to be ground at the mill. The owner had the reputation for being the slowest and laziest miller in Illinois. After watching him for a while, Lincoln said, "You know, I think I could eat that grain as fast as you are grinding it."

"But how long could you keep it up?" the miller replied ungraciously.

"Until I starve to death," the future president retorted.

Dates & Places Used:

997

Confusing Complaints

This news clip appeared in the papers after an electricity blackout: "During the power failure many people complained of having gotten stuck for hours on escalators."

Dates & Places Used:

TOPIC: Work

Human Pretzel Work

I heard it said, "Put your nose to the grindstone, put your shoulder to the wheel, your hands to the plow, and feet to the feat. Put your money where your mouth is, your tail to the task, and never a question ask."

But I want to know just how effectively a human pretzel can work?

Dates & Places Used:

TOPIC: Worry

Unseen Symptoms

A woman was so certain that she had an incurable liver condition that she went to the doctor to find out about it.

The doctor assured her she was all right. "You wouldn't know if you had this condition, because it causes no discomfort of any kind."

"Oh, my goodness," gasped the lady. "Those are my symptoms exactly."

Dates & Places Used:

TOPIC: Worship

God Talks

Tom was a member of the Stewardship Board of our church. He had gone into the alcove which holds the organ pipes to check on the humidifier. While he was there, hidden from the sanctuary behind the screen which covers the pipes, some of the younger children came bursting into the sanctuary.

As they ran down the aisle, Tom shouted out, "Stop running!"

There was a moment of stunned silence, and then came the query, "Who's there?"

Tom couldn't resist. "God," he replied. "Don't run in my house."

The children walked out of the sanctuary and at least one of them, now an adult, still remembers that lesson about the need for reverence for God's sanctuary.

Dates & Places Used:

1001

TOPIC: Worth

When There Is Nothing to Do

The real worth of a person is determined by what that person does when there is nothing to do.

Dates & Places Used:

Index of Subtopics

Each illustration number is cross-referenced from two
to five times. Numbers indicate entry number, not page.

Calculations: 14
Campaigns: 701
Camping: 612
Care: 387
Careers: 478
Cars: 60
Catalogs: 71
Catholics: 192
Causes: 408
Caution: 2, 762, 792, 964
Celebrations: 140, 485
Census: 632
Ceremonies: 973
Certainty: 275, 288
Chance: 885
Chances: 871
Change: 15, 18, 89, 104,
    231, 237, 277, 325,
    412, 434, 446, 461,
    533, 572, 576, 66,
    755, 843, 878, 910,
    942, 972
Character: 263, 324,
    420, 745, 849, 962
Charismatics: 124
Charity: 181
Cheap: 396
Cheating: 196
Childishness: 569
Children: 5, 31, 44, 64,
    67, 71, 85, 105, 131,
    132, 136, 137, 138,
    141, 142, 143, 153,
    173, 177, 210, 223,
    227, 260, 261, 262,
    263, 265, 283, 309,
    314, 337, 338, 339,
    340, 341, 343, 358,
    380, 384, 390, 392,
    425, 435, 442, 457,
    485, 514, 529, 531,
    535, 542, 561, 603,
    610, 613, 615, 616,
    619, 621, 623, 624,
    625, 626, 654, 656,
    658, 659, 660, 661,
    672, 692, 708, 721,
    723, 727, 729, 734,
    751, 774, 798, 813,
    825, 925, 928, 931,
    934, 936, 947, 952

Chivalry: 990
Choice: 357, 422, 547,
    811, 930
Chores: 789, 975
Christian Education:
    694
Christianity: 953
Christmas: 77, 210, 383,
    459, 793, 796, 798,
    835, 943
Church Growth: 277
Church: 1, 223, 243,
    267, 305, 308, 705,
    771, 819, 826, 907,
    966, 1000
Circumstances: 754
Civilization: 818
Cleaning: 17, 911
Cleanliness: 67
Clergy: 670
Cliches: 241
Climate: 373
Coincidence: 578
College: 707
Comfort: 635
Commandments: 637,
    638
Commitment: 256, 364,
    365, 545, 553, 554,
    586, 971
Common Sense: 997
Communication: 2, 46,
    76, 86, 106, 184, 189,
    202, 218, 257, 265,
    362, 398, 475, 476,
    527, 543, 546, 562,
    571, 608, 649, 667,
    672, 718, 732, 774,
    939, 952, 956, 978
Communion: 277, 282
Communism: 633
Community: 953
Companions: 208, 674
Company: 484
Comparison: 206, 253,
    413, 479, 522, 563,
    610, 625, 648, 749,
    809, 882
Compassion: 51, 428,
    491, 492, 493, 524,
    565, 669, 769, 854

Competition: 178, 395,
    977
Complacency: 146
Complaints: 103, 202,
    221, 332
Compliments: 68, 717
Compromise: 101, 636,
    699, 872
Compulsion: 401
Computers: 371, 910
Conceit: 741
Conception: 75
Condemnation: 950
Confession: 729, 815
Confidence: 275, 483,
    509, 570, 805, 811
Conflict: 46, 186, 280,
    353, 355, 651, 855
Conformity: 98
Congregations: 587
Conscience: 901
Consequences: 235, 311,
    316, 374, 438, 490,
    495, 499, 714, 839,
    926, 959
Consideration: 219, 405,
    691, 725, 761
Consistency: 95, 128,
    185, 436, 453, 564,
    787, 945
Consumers: 830
Contentment: 378, 414,
    426, 588, 635
Contracts: 504
Contradictions: 253
Control: 556, 652, 855,
    881
Convenience: 438
Conversation: 362, 398,
    498, 808
Conversion: 66
Conviction: 409, 733,
    951
Convictions: 188, 622,
    699, 919
Cooking: 127, 620
Cooperation: 48, 126,
    158, 737, 905, 906,
    907, 976
Corrections: 304
Counseling: 974

Counselors: 219, 564
Courage: 5, 333, 630, 846, 986
Courtesy: 436, 725
Courting: 230
Courts: 486, 489
Courtship: 169, 544, 547, 847
Cowards: 929
Creation: 116, 449, 584
Creativity: 3, 264
Creator: 216
Credibility: 284
Creditors: 349
Crime: 609, 657
Criticism: 12, 179, 224, 238, 318, 469, 496, 533, 591, 698, 812, 987
Crosses: 147, 840
Crucifixion: 840
Cruelty: 784
Culture: 592, 818
Cures: 160, 417
Curiosity: 291, 764
Customers: 830
Customs: 227
Cynicism: 487

Danger: 381, 468
Dating: 155, 534, 544, 547, 550, 645, 912
Death: 21, 47, 53, 151, 180, 249, 271, 300, 371, 372, 423, 428, 474, 520, 522, 529, 557, 689, 780, 805, 825, 841, 867, 969
Debate: 982
Debts: 270, 349, 600, 897, 901
Decay: 15
Deceit: 470, 746, 990
Deceitfulness: 606
Deception: 27, 43, 117, 155, 196, 198, 199, 254, 316, 367, 440, 454, 504, 517, 518, 697, 746, 791
Decisions: 28, 98, 285, 452, 629, 778, 971
Decline: 446

Decorations: 134
Dedications: 82
Deductions: 870
Defeat: 946
Deficiencies: 220
Definitions: 244, 510
Deity: 459
Delays: 937
Denial: 27, 408, 815
Denominations: 64
Dependence: 49, 51, 207
Descriptions: 909
Design: 216, 462, 685
Desire: 414, 930
Destruction: 461
Details: 247, 676
Determination: 203, 628, 680
Diaries: 380
Diets: 16, 67, 133, 469, 493
Differences: 124, 918, 936
Difficulty: 615
Dinner: 728
Direction: 172, 386, 682, 722
Directions: 377, 585
Disappointment: 531
Disasters: 837
Discipleship: 63, 145, 346, 406
Discipline: 108, 109, 113, 141, 173, 340, 640, 659, 776, 804, 806, 884
Discounts: 726
Discoveries: 457
Discretion: 200, 441, 541, 979
Discussion: 455
Disobedience: 623
Disputes: 503, 651
Division: 819
Divorce: 557, 558, 784, 974
Doctors: 174, 259, 416, 417, 471, 912, 999
Doctrine: 768
Dogs: 65
Dominance: 652

Doubt: 393, 886
Dreams: 383, 923
Drinking: 30, 82, 477, 629
Drivers: 32, 90, 315, 499, 754, 787, 799
Driving: 278, 870
Drunkenness: 30, 279
Duty: 312

Earnings: 350
Easter: 779, 780
Eating: 493, 538
Ecclesiology: 907
Economy: 269, 338, 509, 597, 793
Edification: 495
Education: 55, 110, 154, 205, 321, 323, 327, 381, 692, 707, 764, 799, 802, 803, 869, 903, 904, 921, 967
Effectiveness: 998
Efficiency: 20, 159
Effort: 506
Eggs: 339
Ego: 275, 744, 808
Elections: 701, 704
Elvis: 283
Embarrassment: 314, 832, 973
Emotions: 519, 617, 811
Employees: 301, 310, 482
Employers: 876
Employment: 301
Encouragement: 535, 715, 846, 914
Endurance: 825
Enemies: 208, 366, 785
Energy: 24, 680
Engagement: 171, 847
Enthusiasm: 733, 824, 996
Epitaphs: 502
Errors: 170, 275
Eternity: 357, 422, 423, 566, 709, 969
Ethics: 101, 521
Eulogy: 180
Evaluation: 240

Perseverance: 203
Persistence: 330, 444,
    653, 803, 880, 888,
    892
Personalities: 573
Perspective: 8, 23, 34,
    44, 70, 76, 78, 161,
    228, 240, 251, 339,
    450, 458, 476, 478,
    534, 590, 603, 619,
    644, 769, 936, 964
Persuasion: 295, 510,
    792
Pessimism: 193, 634,
    977
Pessimists: 589
Pests: 40, 853
Pets: 40, 65, 84, 348, 682,
    706
Pettiness: 866
Pew: 1
Philosophy: 521, 549
Phones: 718, 795, 851,
    917
Physics: 984
Planning: 736
Plans: 104
Play: 343
Pledges: 874
Plumbers: 269
Poem: 281
Police: 499
Politeness: 436, 538
Politicians: 81, 273, 295,
    704
Politics: 81, 187, 295,
    698, 700, 701, 702,
    707, 739, 899
Popularity: 385, 748
Population: 632
Positive: 650
Positivity: 646
Possessions: 567
Poverty: 181, 633, 915,
    970
Power: 26, 191, 307, 358,
    389, 511, 569, 855,
    860, 876
Practicality: 328, 799
Practice: 248, 397, 453,
    578, 750, 884

Pragmatism: 750
Praise: 68, 403, 421, 933
Prayer: 54, 390, 623,
    774, 851, 873, 883,
    884
Preachers: 693, 731,
    820, 827
Preaching: 164, 201,
    820, 821, 824, 827
Predictions: 373, 848,
    870
Preferences: 19, 918
Pregnancy: 614
Prejudice: 293, 810
Preparation: 741, 889
Presidents: 513, 916
Pressure: 246, 629
Presumption: 247, 886
Prices: 37, 183, 463, 52
Pride: 4, 102, 207, 273,
    275, 288, 406, 449,
    450, 483, 501, 526,
    579, 677, 716, 717,
    763, 808, 817, 863,
    890, 893, 895, 896
Priests: 89, 192
Priorities: 130, 152, 350,
    394, 474, 540, 552,
    600, 604, 740, 828,
    850, 854, 867, 887,
    917, 920, 960, 961,
    967, 995
Probability: 889
Problems: 193, 289, 394,
    427, 434, 661, 696,
    853, 856, 857, 858,
    982
Procrastination: 151
Procreation: 708
Profanity: 642
Programs: 402
Progress: 942
Promises: 156, 695, 697
Promptness: 686
Proposals: 171, 548
Protestants: 90
Providence: 32, 213,
    307, 375, 388, 719,
    720
Psychiatrists: 70
Psychology: 108

Publicity: 738
Punishment: 259, 640,
    806, 959
Puns: 205, 223, 257, 463,
    466, 490, 611, 948
Purity: 872
Purpose: 7, 48, 146, 182,
    248, 353, 402, 462,
    508, 521, 530, 685,
    829, 993, 995

Qualifications: 527, 877
Questions: 35, 226, 291,
    392, 626, 734
Quitting: 332, 679, 940

Radio: 909
Readiness: 889
Reading: 935
Reality: 242, 949
Reasons: 313, 466, 631
Rebellion: 261, 585, 917
Receiving: 137, 138
Recitals: 596
Recycling: 369
Refunds: 794, 902
Regard: 545
Regret: 238, 809
Reinforcement: 903
Rejection: 483, 981
Relationships: 368, 553,
    554, 738, 849
Relaxation: 995
Relevance: 86, 475
Religion: 147, 241, 357
Rent: 911
Repentance: 409, 817,
    843
Repetition: 639
Reports: 631
Reproduction: 448
Reputation: 180, 745
Requests: 548
Rescue: 622
Resolution: 186
Respect: 204, 342, 467,
    513, 577, 772, 1000
Responses: 35, 62, 214,
    274, 332, 672, 742,
    767, 791, 795, 981
Responsibility: 114, 237,
    299, 447, 654, 656,
    661, 829, 908

Alphabetical Index of Titles

Several titles have been abbreviated for convenience.
Numbers indicate entry number, not page number.

360

Numerical Index of Titles

371

List of Sources

Brackets contain date of use in Saratoga Press publications:
[PEJan96] indicates *Parables, Etc.*, January 1996
[SFAug95] indicates *The Pastor's Story File*, August 1995

#1: Dr. Joe Harding [SFFeb92]

#2: Submitted by Bruce Rowlison [PEJun93]

#3: Submitted by Mark Toback [PEJun95]

#4: No source available [PEJun95]

#5: Submitted by Billy D. Strayhorn [SFApr94]

#6: Ben Franklin, submitted by Ron Yates [PEOct92]

#7: Submitted by Wayne W. Eisenbrenner [PEFeb95]

#8: Submitted by Jay Martin [SFJan93]

#9: Submitted by Bill Flanders [PEFeb92]

#10: No source available [PEJun94]

#11: S. H. Britt, submitted by Bruce Rowlison [PEMay93]

#12: Submitted by Dicky Love [PEApr95]

#13: No source available [PEOct95]

#14: Ruth Naylor, submitted by C. Richard Stone [PEJul95]

#15: Anonymous [PEApr95]

#16: Submitted by Robert J. Strand [PEMay96]

#17: Submitted by Calvin Habig [PEAug94]

#18: Edgar M. Burns, submitted by Mac Fulcher [PEMar94]

#19: Submitted by George W. McNeese [PEDec95]

#20: Submitted by Bruce Rowlison [PENov92]

#21: Submitted by Richard Cox [SFAug93]

#22: Submitted by Gene Sikkink [PEOct92]

#23: Submitted by Lucy Anderson [PEOct92]

#24: Submitted by Rose Hodgin [PEMay92]

#25: Sydney Steele, *Rotarian*, submitted by Bruce Rowlison [SFJan93]

#26: Jimmy Townsend, submitted by Bill Flanders [SFAug93]

#27: Submitted by Gene Sikkink [PEFeb94]

#28: Anonymous [SFMay92]

#29: No source available [PEAug94]

#30: No source available [PEOct94]

#31: No source available [SFJun93]

#32: Paul Noxon [PEAug96]

#33: Michael McGriff, M.D. [SFAug93]

#34: Michael Hodgin [SFApr92]

#35: No source available [SFJun94]

#36: No source available [SFMar96]

#37: Submitted by Charles Krieg [PESep92]

#38: Submitted by John H. Hampsch [PEJun92]

#39: Submitted by Carl Ericson [PEOct93]

#40: Submitted by Mike Jackson [PEApr96]

#41: No source available [PEMar96]

#42: Submitted by Steve Morrison [PEMar96]

#43: Submitted by William L. McDonald [PEOct95]

#44: From *Sunshine Magazine*, May 1973 [PEAug96]

#45: No source available [PEMar95]

#46: No source available [PEFeb96]

#47: Submitted by John Fitts [PEDec92]

#48: Submitted by Wayne Rouse [PEJan95]

#49: No source available [SFJan95]

#50: Anonymous, submitted by Martin R. Bartel [PEFeb95]

#51: Michael Hodgin [SFFeb93]

#52: William Schreyer, chairman of Merrill Lynch, submitted by Dr. William L. McDonald [SFMar94]

#53: Submitted by David E. Okerstrom [PEFeb96]

#54: Submitted by David E. Okerstrom [PEJul95]

#55: No source available [SFAug93]

#56: Billy D. Strayhorn [SFAug94]

#57: Billy D. Strayhorn [SFJul92]

#58: Submitted by Danny Cabaniss [SFFeb93]

#59: No source available [PEFeb94]

#60: Submitted by Alan C. Thompson [SFAug93]

#61: No source available [PEApr93]

#62: Submitted by Milton Weisshaar [SFJun96]

#63: Submitted by Mark Toback [PEJun95]

#64: Submitted by Billy D. Strayhorn [PEJan96]

#65: Submitted by Wayne Rouse [PEOct95]

#66: Submitted by Ken Langley [PEJan94]

#67: Submitted by Don Maddox [PESep95]

#68: Brian Crane, "Pickles" comic strip [PEJun95]

#69: Sam Jarrett, submitted by C. Richard Stone [PEApr95]

#70: Submitted by Allan Thompson [PEJan92]

#71: Leon Hill [SFJul92]

#72: No source available [PEOct94]

#73: No source available [PEApr95]

#74: Submitted by Stephen Deutsch [PEDec93]

#75: Submitted by Jim Pearring [SFOct95]

#76: Submitted by C. Richard Stone [PEAug94]

#77: No source available [SFDec93]

#78: Submitted by Mike Jackson [SFApr96]

#79: Submitted by Billy D. Strayhorn [PEJul96]

#80: Submitted by Michael Hodgin [SFMay96]

#81: Submitted by C. Richard Stone [PEMar96]

#82: Submitted by David E. Okerstrom [PEApr95]

#83: Submitted by Don Maddox [PENov95]

#84: Submitted by Micheal Kelley [PEJul96]

#85: Submitted by Earl T. Wheatley Jr. [PEMay95]

#86: Submitted by Michael Hodgin [PEJan95]

#87: No source available [PEJul93]

#88: Submitted by Micheal Kelley [PEMay96]

#89: Submitted by Rabbi Samuel M. Silver [PEDec92]

#90: Submitted by Robert J. Strand [PEOct96]

#91: No source available [SFAug93]

#92: Joan Vernon, submitted by Mac Fulcher [SFFeb94]

#93: Adapted from "Snafu" by Bruce Beattie, December 11, 1992 [PEJun93]

#94: No source available [SFFeb94]

#95: Submitted by Dicky Love [PEJun96]

#96: W. Clement Stone, submitted by Jay Martin [PEJul95]

#97: Submitted by Donald O. Maddox [PEJan92]

#98: Stuart Briscoe, from *Genesis*, submitted by Dave Rushton [SFSep95]

#99: Adapted from *Acts*, by Donald Grey Barnhouse, submitted by Paul A. Noxon [PEMay95]

#100: Submitted by Bill Flanders [SFApr92]

#101: No source available [PEJun94]

#102: Judith S. Martin, submitted by Dr. William T. McConnell [SFOct95]

#103: Submitted by Mary Spitzer [SFJan93]

#104: Submitted by John Looney [PEMar96]

#105: Submitted by Charles F. Krieg [PEJul96]

#106: Submitted by James Boyd [PEJan92]

#107: Submitted by Charles F. Krieg [SFJun96]

#108: No source available [PEJun93]

#109: No source available [SFMay93]

#110: No source available [SFAug92]

#111: From "Dennis the Menace" by Hank Ketchum, October 28, 1991 [PEJun93]

#112: Submitted by Bruce Rowlison [PEJun93]

#113: Submitted by Billy D. Strayhorn [PESep95]

#114: Submitted by C. Richard Stone [PENov93]

#115: Submitted by Billy D. Strayhorn [SFJun93]

#116: From "The Ryatts" by Jack Elrod, September 26, 1991 [SFJun93]

#117: Submitted by Billy D. Strayhorn [PEDec94]

#118: Susan Forman, "Teaching K–8," October 1991 [PEJul93]

#119: No source available [PEApr94]

#120: No source available [SFAug94]

#121: No source available [PEFeb94]

#122: No source available [PEFeb96]

#123: No source available [SFJun95]

#124: Submitted by Jay Martin [PEApr93]

#125: From *Sunshine Magazine*, July 1973 [SFMay95]

#126: No source available [PEDec93]

#127: Gene Brown, submitted by Nick Boeke [SFApr92]

#128: Submitted by Bill Flanders [PEFeb92]

#129: Submitted by Fred Lowery [SFDec93]

#130: Richard E. Blanchard, submitted by John M. Keolling [SFDec92]

#131: Submitted by Billy D. Strayhorn [PEDec94]

#132: Submitted by Billy D. Strayhorn [SFDec95]

#133: No source available [SFDec93]

#134: No source available [SFDec93]

#135: Submitted by Wayne W. Eisbrenner [SFDec93]

#136: No source available [SFDec93]

#137: Michael Hodgin [PEDec93]

#138: Michael Hodgin [PEDec93]

#139: Submitted by Fred Lowery [SFDec93]

#140: Submitted by Jay Martin [SFJun93]

#141: Submitted by Robert L. Sheldon [PEDec91]

#142: Submitted by Billy D. Strayhorn [SFDec95]

#143: Submitted by Billy D. Strayhorn [SFDec94]

#144: Submitted by Micheal Kelley [PESep95]

#145: Submitted by Mark Toback [PEJun95]

#146: Submitted by John Fitts [SFJun94]

#147: Submitted by Robert J. Strand [PEJan95]

#148: No source available [SFAug94]

#149: Anonymous, submitted by Jay Martin [PEMay96]

#150: By John Ed Matheson [PEMar94]

#151: Submitted by Carolyn M. Kendrick [SFJun92]

#152: No source available [SFSep95]

#153: Submitted by Teresa Yates [PEFeb96]

#154: Submitted by John H. Hampsch [PEJun92]

#155: Submitted by Calvin Habig [SFJul94]

#156: No source available [PEMay93]

#157: No source available [PEAug92]

#158: No source available [PEJul93]

#159: John F. Kennedy, submitted by Bruce A. Rowlisøn [PEMar93]

#160: Submitted by Calvin Habig [PEAug94]

#161: No source available [PEJan93]

#162: Submitted by Steve Morrison [SFJan96]

#163: No source available [SFAug93]

#164: Submitted by Jeff Taylor [PEOct94]

#165: Submitted by Bruce Rowlison [PEOct95]

#166: Submitted by Wayne W. Eisbrenner [SFNov94]

#167: Submitted by Don Maddox [PESep95]

#168: Suzanne Attebery, submitted by Dicky Love [SFJun95]

#169: Submitted by John Fitts [PEJun92]

#170: No source available [PENov94]

#171: From wire reports, submitted by Brant D. Baker [SFAug95]

#172: Submitted by Alan C. Thompson [PEDec91]

#173: Submitted by Bill Boyer [PEDec91]

#174: Anonymous, submitted by James R. Oliver [SFAug93]

#175: Submitted by Grant Darling [PEFeb94]

#176: Submitted by C. Richard Stone [PEJul93]

#177: Submitted by Jay Martin [PEJan96]

#178: Submitted by Calvin Habig [PEJul95]

#179: Submitted by Mark Toback [PEJun95]

#180: Submitted by Jim Mathewson [SFSep92]

#181: No source available, submitted by Robert J. Strand [SFMar94]

#182: Submitted by Steve Morrison [SFSep93]

#183: Submitted by John H. Hampsch [PEJun92]

#184: Submitted by Jay Martin [SFAug93]

#185: Submitted by Robert J. Strand [PEMay96]

#186: Submitted by John H. Hampsch [PEJun92]

#187: Haley Barbour, Bush-Quayle Advisor, on ABC's *Nightline* on August 7, 1992 [PESep92]

#188: No source available [PEApr95]

#189: From *PC Computing,* September, 1992, submitted by Jay Martin [PEJul93]

#190: No source available [PEOct96]

#191: Randall Tobias, *In Today Walks Tomorrow*, submitted by Mark Shepard [PEJul93]

#192: Submitted by Brant D. Baker [PEAug95]

#193: Submitted by Robert J. Strand [PEMay96]

#194: No source available [SFSep92]

#195: Submitted by Robert J. Strand [PEMay96]

#196: No source available [PEOct94]

#197: No source available [PENov96]

#198: Michael Hodgin [PEFeb96]

#199: Submitted by Micheal Kelley [SFJul96]

#200: Mortimer B. Zuckerman, editor-in-chief, *U.S. News & World Report* [PEMay94]

#201: Dr. Richard Dobbins in *The Pastor's Confidential,* November-December 1992 [SFFeb93]

#202: Bill Flanders [PEFeb92]

#203: No source available [PEMar95]

#204: Submitted by John H. Hampsch [PEJun92]

#205: Submitted by Nick Boeke [SFApr92]

#206: No source available [SFMay93]

#207: Submitted by Wayne Rouse [PEOct92]

#208: Submitted by Lester M. Weeks [PEMay94]

#209: Adopted from *Bits & Pieces,* March 2, 1995, published by Economics Press, Fairfield, NJ submitted by John Looney [PEAug95]

#210: Submitted by Peter K. Perry [SFDec94]

#211: Submitted by Kenneth L. Dodge [PENov95]

#212: No source available [SFApr94]

#213: Submitted by Dicky Love [SFJul96]

#214: Submitted by Micheal Kelley [SFMay96]

#215: No source available [SFAug93]

#216: Submitted by George W. McNeese [SFNov94]

#217: Submitted by Robert Strand [PEJun92]

#218: Doc Palmas [PENov91]

#219: No source available [PENov93]

#220: Submitted by Timothy J. Helm [PENov94]

#221: Submitted by Calvin Habig [PEDec94]

#222: Submitted by David Rushton [PENov96]

#223: Submitted by Calvin Habig [PEMay94]

#224: Submitted by Dennis Kamper [PEJul92]

#225: Submitted by Carolyn M. Kendrick [PENov91]

#226: Submitted by John H. Hampsch [PEMay92]

#227: Submitted by Steve Morrison [PEJan96]

#228: Submitted by Jerry Hickson [PEJan92]

#229: Arturo Toscanini, submitted by Nick Boeke [SFFeb92]

#230: Submitted by Robert J. Strand [SFMay96]

#231: Submitted by John Fitts [PEOct93]

#232: No source available [PEMar96]

#233: No source available [SFJun95]

#234: No source available [SFJan94]

#235: Submitted by Rick Sams [PEJan94]

#236: Submitted by Doris S. Bray [SFJun96]

#237: No source available [SFJan92]

#238: Submitted by J. Danny Doss [SFJun96]

#239: Submitted by Robert J. Strand [PEMay96]

#240: George Eliot, novelist, submitted by Dr. William L. McDonald [SFAug94]

#241: Submitted by Dicky Love [SFJun95]

#242: Arch Napier in *The Wall Street Journal*, submitted by C. Richard Stone [PEMay95]

#243: Submitted by Galen E. Skinner [PEDec92]

#244: Submitted by John H. Hampsch [PEMay92]

#245: Submitted by John C. Fitts [SFDec92]

#246: Anonymous, submitted by James R. Oliver [PEMay94]

#247: No source available, submitted by Byron Neufeld [PEMar92]

#248: Submitted by Malcom McPhail [PEApr92]

#249: Submitted by John Seville [PEApr92]

#250: No source available [SFAug94]

#251: Submitted by Jay Martin [PEOct96]

#252: An old camp poem, submitted by Lester M. Weeks [PENov95]

#253: From Lea Groth-Wilson [PEJul94]

#254: Will Rogers [PEJul94]

#255: Brian Bowling, submitted by Dicky Love [PEMay95]

#256: No source available [SFOct93]

#257: No source available [SFAug93]

#258: Submitted by Robert Jarboe [PEMay93]

#259: Submitted by Charles F. Krieg [SFJun96]

#260: Ann Landers, September 15, 1989 [PEJun93]

#261: No source available [SFJun93]

#262: Submitted by Nick Boeke [PEDec93]

#263: No source available [PESep95]

#264: Submitted by C. Richard Stone [PEMay95]

#265: Submitted by Don Maddox [PEJan92]

#266: Submitted by Calvin Habig [PEAug95]

#267: Submitted by Billy D. Strayhorn [SFJun92]

#268: Submitted by Jeff Taylor [SFMay95]

#269: Submitted by Bruce A. Rowlison [PEMar93]

#270: Anonymous, submitted by James R. Oliver [PENov93]

#271: Submitted by Robert Jarboe [PENov92]

#272: Submitted by John H. Hampsch [PEJun92]

#273: Submitted by Mac Fulcher [PEOct93]

#274: No source available [SFApr94]

#275: Submitted by John Looney [PEJul95]

#276: Submitted by Kenneth Langley [SFJun96]

#277: Submitted by an anonymous worship committee member [PEMar92]

#278: Submitted by George W. McNeese [PEMar96]

#279: Ann Landers [PEJul96]

#280: No source available [PENov91]

#281: Paul Noxon [SFAug92]

#282: Submitted by J. D. Brown [SFApr96]

#283: Submitted by Doug Sabin [PEDec94]

#284: Submitted by Bruce Rowlison [PEJul93]

#285: George Bernard Shaw, submitted by Robert J. Strand [PEMay93]

#286: Submitted by Calvin Habig [SFJun95]

#287: Henry R. Luce, founder of *Time*, submitted by Robert J. Strand [PEMay93]

#288: Submitted by Diane Sickler [SFJul96]

#289: Submitted by John H. Hampsch [PEJun92]

#290: Submitted by Robert S. Jarboe [PEJun93]

#291: Submitted by Jay Martin [SFAug92]

#292: Submitted by Nick Boeke [SFAug92]

#293: Martin H. Fischer, submitted by Diane Sickler [SFJul96]

#294: No source available [PEApr95]

#295: Submitted by Dicky Love [PESep96]

#296: From the Internet, submitted by John Looney [PEOct96]

#297: Cher, submitted by Jay Martin [SFApr92]

#298: No source available [SFJan94]

#299: No source available [SFAug93]

#300: Submitted by Ronald J. Hipwell [SFJan93]

#301: Coach Vince Lombardi [PEJan94]

#302: Submitted by David Rushton [PESep96]

#303: From *Coffee Break*, Vol. 5, No. 9, September 1991, p. 1, submitted by Richard H. Cox [PEJul93]

#304: Submitted by Steve Morrison [SFJan96]

#305: Submitted by Carolyn M. Kendrick [SFJun92]

#306: No source available, submitted by Wayne Rouse [PEJun93]

#307: Corrie Ten Boom, submitted by Byron Neufeld [SFApr93]

#308: No source available [SFMay95]

#309: Submitted by Bruce Rowlison [SFJun93]

#310: Anonymous, submitted by James R. Oliver [SFAug93]

#311: Submitted by Bruce Rowlison [PEMay93]

#312: Laurie Patton, submitted by Keith Knauf [PEMar92]

#313: Ben Franklin [SFJul93]

#314: Submitted by Melynie Tooley [SFApr92]

#315: Submitted by Jeff Taylor [SFJan95]

#316: Submitted by Bruce Rowlison [PEJul95]

#317: Submitted by Robert Jarboe [PEJul93]

#318: Submitted by Bruce Rowlison [PEMay93]

#319: Submitted by Micheal Kelley [PEJan96]

#320: No source available [SFJul95]

#321: Mark Twain [SFJan96]

#322: Submitted by Jan Hodgin-Hartlove [PEJul93]

#323: No source available [PEDec93]

#324: Aldous Huxley, British author, submitted by Richard H. Cox [SFJul94]

#325: Earl Wilson, submitted by Dicky Love [SFOct95]

#326: Submitted by Diane Sickler [SFJul96]

#327: Will Rogers, submitted by Diane Sickler [SFJul96]

#328: Paul A. Samuelson, submitted by Robert J. Strand [PESep93]

#329: C. Richard Stone [PEFeb95]

#330: No source available [SFMay94]

#331: No source available [PEOct93]

#332: Submitted by C. Richard Stone [PEOct92]

#333: T. Boone Pickens Jr. [SFJul93]

#334: From *Lexington Herald-Leader*, March 10, 1993, p. C2, submitted by Billy D. Strayhorn [SFSep95]

#335: No source available [SFSep93]

#336: Submitted by Calvin Habig [SFJul94]

#337: No source available [PEJun93]

#338: Submitted by Richard Price [SFJun93]

#339: SFJun93

#340: No source available [PEJun93]

#341: Submitted by Nick Boeke [SFNov92]

#342: Submitted by Milton Weisshaar [SFMay96]

#343: Submitted by Don E. McKenzie [PEOct93]

#344: Submitted by Jay Martin [PEJun92]

#345: Submitted by Chris Thore [PEDec93]

#346: Submitted by Robert J. Strand [PEMay96]

#347: Gloria Steinem in *MS.* [SFMay96]

#348: Submitted by Calvin Habig [PEApr96]

#349: No source available, submitted by Edie Charlesworth [PEApr92]

#350: Submitted by John H. Hampsch [PEJun92]

#351: No source available [SFJul96]

#352: No source available [PEOct96]

#353: No source available [SFApr94]

#354: No source available [PEJun94]

#355: Submitted by Mary Spitzer [SFApr93]

#356: Dwight L. Moody, submitted by Dicky Love [PEApr92]

#357: No source available [SFFeb94]

#358: Submitted by John Fitts [PEMar94]

#359: Submitted by Gene Sikkink [SFFeb96]

#360: Submitted by Gene Sikkink [SFJan93]

#361: No source available [PEMay96]

#362: W. Cunningham, submitted by Steve Morrison [SFFeb96]

#363: No source available [PENov93]

#364: No source available [SFFeb96]

#365: No source available [SFFeb96]

#366: G. K. Chesterton, submitted by John Fitts [PESep92]

#367: Submitted by Calvin Habig [SFFeb96]

#368: No source available [SFJun94]

#369: Anonymous, submitted by James R. Oliver [SFJun94]

#370: Judy Ruths, submitted by her pastor, Ray Pichette [PEFeb93]

#371: Submitted by Brant D. Baker [PEAug95]

#372: Reported as true by Mr. Mayo of the local funeral home, submitted by Earl Wheatley, Jr. [PEMay94]

#373: No source available [PEJul94]

#374: M. Scott Peck [PEAug95]

#375: Jimmy Jones, jockey, submitted by Calvin Habig [PEAug95]

#376: No source available [PEFeb93]

#377: Submitted by Billy D. Strayhorn [PESep94]

#378: No source available [SFJan94]

#379: Submitted by Steve Morrison [PENov93]

#380: No source available [SFDec95]

#381: No source available [SFDec95]

#382: Submitted by Mike Jackson [SFFeb96]

#383: Submitted by Bill Flanders [SFDec92]

#384: No source available [PEJun93]

#385: Submitted by Bruce A. Rowlison [PEMar93]

#386: Submitted by Wayne W. Eisbrenner [PEApr93]

#387: Submitted by Doug Sabin [PEJul96]

#388: Martin Luther [SFJun94]

#389: Arthur Schlesinger Jr., historian [SFJul92]

#390: John Buchan, submitted by David E. Okerstrom [PEMay95]

#391: Submitted by Dicky Love [SFSEP96]

#392: Submitted by George Maronge Jr. [PENov95]

#393: Submitted by Milton Weisshaar [SFNov95]

#394: Submitted by George W. McNeese [SFSep94]

#395: Submitted by an anonymous golfer [PEMar92]

#396: No source available [PEJun92]

#397: Submitted by Bruce Rowlison [PEJan93]

#398: Submitted by Bill Flanders [PEFeb92]

#399: Submitted by Bruce A. Rowlison [PEMar93]

#400: Submitted by John H. Hampsch [PEJun92]

#401: Submitted by Lester M. Weeks [PEMay94]

#402: Submitted by Steve Hodgin [PESep93]

#403: Submitted by Bruce Rowlison [SFNov92]

#404: From "Peanuts," submitted by Kit Buschman [PEApr93]

#405: Anonymous, submitted by Wayne Rouse [PEJul94]

#406: Submitted by Mark Toback [PEJun95]

#407: William H. Walton, submitted by Dicky Love [PEJul95]

#408: Sean Donovan, submitted by Dicky Love [SFAug95]

#409: A true story submitted by Rich Thomson [PENov94]

#410: Submitted by Jay Martin [SFAug93]

#411: Coach Vince Lombardi [PEOct96]

#412: Submitted by Bruce Rowlison [PEMay93]

#413: Submitted by Paul Wakefield [PEMar95]

#414: No source available [PENov93]

#415: Albert Schweitzer, submitted by Jay Martin [SFJan93]

#416: Submitted by John H. Hampsch [PEJun92]

#417: From a Dutch proverb [PEFeb92]

#418: Henry Boye, *The American Legion Magazine,* submitted by Dicky Love [SFJan96]

#419: Submitted by Norma Franke [PEApr93]

#420: Seen on a church sign in Tampa, Florida, submitted by Dan Stephens [PEMar95]

#421: Submitted by Micheal Kelley [SFJan96]

#422: Submitted by Calvin Habig [PEApr96]

#423: Submitted by Micheal Kelley [PEApr96]

#424: Submitted by Roy Roberts [PEAug95]

#425: A true story from Moe and Jackie Fagan, submitted by Jay Martin [PESep95]

#426: Submitted by David E. Okerstrom [PEJul95]

#427: No source available [SFJan93]

#428: Anonymous, submitted by James R. Oliver [SFJan93]

#429: Submitted by John H. Hampsch [PEJun92]

#430: A true story from Terry L. Irish [PEMay94]

#431: Submitted by Micheal Kelley [SFSep95]

#432: Submitted by Bill Flanders [PEFeb92]

#433: No source available [PEApr95]

#434: Clarence Darrow [PEMar96]

#435: No source available [SFNov94]

#436: Submitted by Eugene Barron [PEJan95]

#437: Submitted by Doug Sabin [SFJun94]

#438: Tom Sims, submitted by Dicky Love [PEDec95]

#439: From the *New York Times* [PEJul93]

#440: Submitted by C. Richard Stone [SFJul96]

#441: Submitted by J. D. Brown [SFMay96]

#442: From "Dennis the Menace," by Hank Ketchum, January 11, 1992 [SFJun95]

#443: Submitted by Jay Martin [SFJan93]

#444: Submitted by Micheal Kelley [PEApr96]

#445: Submitted by David Rushton [PEMay93]

#446: Garrison Keillor [PEJun94]

#447: Swahili proverb, submitted by Dicky Love [PEOct93]

#448: Submitted by Milton Weisshaar [PEJun95]

#449: Martin Luther, submitted by Dennis Kamper [PEJul92]

#450: No source available [PEMay96]

#451: Submitted by Jay Martin [SFFeb95]

#452: Submitted by Micheal Kelley [SFSep95]

#453: Anonymous, submitted by Robert J. Strand [PEAug92]

#454: Joe Barnett, submitted by James Johnston [PEMay92]

#455: No source available [SFAug93]

#456: Submitted by J. D. Brown [PEDec95]

#457: No source available [PEFeb96]

#458: Submitted by Steve Hodgin [SFMay95]

#459: Submitted by Eugene Barron [SFDec94]

#460: Submitted by Stuart M. Pederson [SFDec95]

#461: Submitted by John H. Hampsch [PEJun92]

#462: Submitted by George W. McNeese [SFJun95]

#463: Submitted by John H. Hampsch [PEJun92]

#464: Submitted by Robert J. Strand [SFMay96]

#465: Submitted by Nick Boeke [PEMay94]

#466: Submitted by Jeff Taylor [PEJul95]

#467: Submitted by Peter K. Perry [SFMay95]

#468: Cordell Hull [SFAug94]

#469: Submitted by Doug Sabin [PEJan93]

#470: Submitted by Don Maddox [PEOct96]

#471: Submitted by Bruce Rowlison [PEOct95]

#472: Submitted by Billy D. Strayhorn [SFJul96]

#473: Submitted by John H. Hampsch [PEJun92]

#474: Submitted by John H. Hampsch [PEJun92]

#475: No source available [PEApr95]

#476: Submitted by Calvin Habig [PEFeb96]

#477: Louis Valbracht, submitted by Gene Sikkink [PEJul95]

#478: Submitted by Lester M. Weeks [PEAug92]

#479: As quoted by Ben Holden, submitted by Ron Yates [PEJun93]

#480: Submitted by Dr. Roger E. Kleinheksel [PEMar93]

#481: Leo Aikman, submitted by Steve Morrison [SFNov94]

#482: Anonymous, submitted by James R. Oliver [SFJun94]

#483: No source available [PEDec95]

#484: No source available [SFNov92]

#485: Submitted by William L. McDonald [SFOct95]

#486: Submitted by Robert J. Strand [PEMay96]

#487: Robert Frost, submitted by Malcolm MacPhail [PEJan93]

#488: No source available [SFAug93]

#489: No source available [SFJun94]

#490: Submitted by John H. Hampsch [PEJun92]

#491: Brennan Manning, submitted by Robert J. Strand [SFMar94]

#492: No source available [SFMar94]

#493: Brian Harbour, submitted by George W. McNeese [SFAug95]

#494: Submitted by James Johnston [PEJul92]

#495: Submitted by James Johnston [PEJul92]

#496: No source available [SFMar94]

#497: Oliver Wendell Holmes Sr., submitted by Steve Morrison [PEJan96]

#498: No source available [PESep96]

#499: Submitted by Robert S. Jarboe [SFMar93]

#500: No source available [SFAug93]

#501: No source available [SFAug93]

#502: Submitted by Ken Langley [PENov95]

#503: Submitted by Ken Langley [PENov95]

#504: No source available [PEOct93]

#505: Submitted by Jay Martin [PEJul95]

#506: Submitted by Steven Hodgin [SFJun94]

#507: No source available [PEMar94]

#508: Submitted by Richard J. Frazer [PEApr94]

#509: No source available [PEMar92]

#510: Dwight D. Eisenhower [SFMay92]

#511: Plato [SFJul94]

#512: William C. Shereos, submitted by Wayne Rouse [PEFeb93]

#513: As told by Hillary Clinton on February 20, 1995, on CBS morning news program [PEApr95]

#514: No source available [PEFeb96]

#515: No source available [PEMar94]

#516: Ben Holden, submitted by Ron Yates [PEJul93]

#517: Adapted [PENov93]

#518: Submitted by Micheal Kelley [SFJan96]

#519: Submitted by Gene Sikkink [PEMar94]

#520: Submitted by J. D. Brown [PEJul95]

#521: From "Calvin and Hobbes," March 3, 1992 [PEAug95]

#522: No source available [PEJun96]

#523: Larry Lorenzoni, submitted by C. Richard Stone [PEFeb95]

#524: Dietrich Bonhoeffer, submitted by Calvin Habig [SFSep94]

#525: Submitted by C. Richard Stone [SFDec94]

#526: No source available [SFAug93]

#527: Submitted by William F. Stehr [PESep92]

#528: Phillip Gibbs [SFJun95]

#529: Submitted by Dr. William L. McDonald [PENov95]

#530: Submitted by Calvin Habig [PEApr96]

#531: From "Born Loser," by Chip Sansom, July 19, 1991,

submitted by Billy D. Strayhorn [PEJun93]

#532: Submitted by David Rushton from Pastor's Conference Notes, 1990 [PEApr94]

#533: Submitted by William T. McConnell III [SFFeb94]

#534: Nietzsche [SFFeb92]

#535: No source available [PEMar96]

#536: No source available [SFNov92]

#537: No source available [SFSep95]

#538: From *Omni Magazine*, June 1985, submitted by Rich Bersett [PENov95]

#539: Steve Moore, "In the Bleachers," January 20, 1993 [PEMar93]

#540: Richard J. Schwieterman, submitted by Dicky Love [SFMar93]

#541: No source available [SFAug94]

#542: No source available [PEDec93]

#543: From *Chicago Tribune Magazine*, October 3, 1993, submitted by David Rushton [SFMay96]

#544: Submitted by David Rushton [SFMay96]

#545: Submitted by Milton Weisshaar [SFMay96]

#546: Submitted by Jim Pearring [SFMay96]

#547: Robert Schuman, submitted by Milton Weisshaar [SFMay96]

#548: No source available [PEDec93]

#549: Socrates, submitted by Dicky Love [SFApr92]

#550: From H. A. Ironside, *Joshua, Nehemiah, Ezra and Esther*, p. 111 [PEJun93]

#551: Berl Williams, submitted by Nick Boeke [SFMay92]

#552: Submitted by Jim Pearring [PEAug95]

#553: Submitted by Billy D. Strayhorn [SFApr92]

#554: No source available [PEJun96]

#555: G. K. Chesterton [SFApr92]

#556: Submitted by Jim Pearring [PEJan96]

#557: Submitted by Milton Weisshaar [SFJan96]

#558: Submitted by Jim Pearring [SFFeb96]

#559: From *The Wit and Wisdom of George Bernard Shaw*, submitted by Dr. William T. McConnell [PEDec95]

#560: Erica Jong, submitted by Jim Pearring [SFNov94]

#561: Submitted by Mary Spitzer [PEJan95]

#562: No source available [SFAug94]

#563: Submitted by Susan Jellett [SFFeb95]

#564: Submitted by Doug Sabin [PEJul95]

#565: Submitted by Micheal Kelley [PESep96]

#566: Submitted by David Deselm [PEMar95]

#567: Submitted by Jay Martin [SFJan93]

#568: Former Beatle Paul McCartney on the notion of selling out [SFJun95]

#569: Submitted by Bruce Rowlison [PENov92]

#570: Submitted by Malcolm MacPhail [PEJan93]

#571: G. K. Chesterton [PEMay96]

#572: No source available, submitted by Jay Martin [PEMay96]

#573: Submitted by Sam Holden, *The Rotarian*, submitted by Bruce Rowlison [SFFeb93]

#574: Submitted by Billy D. Strayhorn [SFAug92]

#575: Submitted by Nick Boeke [PEAug92]

#576: George W. McNeese [PENov94]

#577: Submitted by Bruce Rowlison [PESep93]

#578: No source available [SFJan95]

#579: Submitted by Micheal Kelley [PEApr96]

#580: Submitted by Wayne Rouse [PEApr93]

#581: Submitted by Martin R. Bartel [PEMay95]

#582: Submitted by Bruce A. Rowlison [PEMar93]

#583: Woody Allen, submitted by John H. Hampsch [PEJun92]

#584: Submitted by Steven Morrison [PEApr94]

#585: Submitted by Jeff Taylor [SFMay95]

#586: Submitted by John H. Hampsch [PEJun92]

#587: No source available [SFAug92]

#588: Submitted by John Looney [PEJul95]

#589: No source available [PEOct96]

#590: No source available [PEOct96]

#591: From a letter written to Dr. James Dobson, Focus on the Family, submitted by Jay Martin [PEJun93]

#592: No source available [PEMay94]

#593: Submitted by John H. Hampsch [PEJun92]

#594: Submitted by Billy D. Strayhorn [PESep95]

#595: Submitted by Steve Morrison [PEJan95]

#596: No source available [SFJan94]

#597: No source available [SFJun95]

#598: Submitted by Steve Morrison [SFJun95]

#599: No source available [SFJun95]

#600: Submitted by Mary Spitzer [PEFeb93]

#601: Submitted by Bruce A. Rowlison [PEMar93]

#602: Submitted by Bruce Rowlison [PEMay93]

#603: No source available [PEOct94]

#604: Clement of Alexandria [SFJan94]

#605: Submitted by Robert J. Strand [PEMay96]

#606: Paul L. Walker, adapted from Courage for Crisis Living, submitted by Wayne Rouse [PEJul93]

#607: Submitted by Robert J. Strand [PEMay96]

#608: Submitted by Don E. McKenzie [SFOct92]

#609: Submitted by Dennis Kamper [PEJul92]

#610: Submitted by Alan C. Thompson [SFAug93]

#611: Michael Hodgin [SFMay95]

#612: Submitted by Billy D. Strayhorn [SFMay95]

#613: Submitted by Fred Lowery [PEMay94]

#614: Submitted by Gene Sikkink [PEMay94]

#615: Submitted by Micheal Kelley [PEMay96]

#616: From Margaret Maneschmidt, submitted by Steve Hodgin [SFMay93]

#617: Michael Hodgin [SFMay95]

#618: Submitted by David Goerzen [SFMay93]

#619: Jim Luttrell, *The Courier-Journal* (Louisville, Ky.), March 31, 1992, p. D2, submitted by R. Wayne Hollaway [SFMay93]

#620: No source available [SFMay93]

#621: Helen True, submitted by Steve Hodgin [SFMay93]

#622: From an Atlanta newspaper, December 1994, submitted by Rose Hodgin [PEJul95]

#623: Submitted by Wayne W. Eisbrenner [SFMay93]

#624: Submitted by Wayne W. Eisbrenner [SFMay93]

#625: Adapted from Reminisce, September-October 1992, submitted by Valeria Little [SFMay93]

#626: No source available [SFMay93]

#627: Submitted by Charles F. Krieg [PESep96]

#628: Submitted by George Maronge Jr. [PEFeb93]

#629: Submitted by Jay Martin [SFNov92]

#630: Anonymous, submitted by Dicky Love [PEJul95]

#631: Anonymous, submitted by Dicky Love [PESep96]

#632: No source available [SFMay93]

#633: Submitted by Calvin Habig [PEMay94]

#634: Submitted by Robert J. Strand [PEMay96]

#635: Submitted by Jan Hartlove [PEApr95]

#636: Winston Churchill, as quoted by Newt Gingrich on June 11, 1995 [SFJul95]

#637: Submitted by Wayne Rouse [PEJun92]

#638: Adapted from Jack Seberry, The Christian Reader, May 1994, p. 70, submitted by George W. McNeese [SFFeb95]

#639: Submitted by Mike High [PESep95]

#640: Submitted by Charles F. Krieg [SFJun96]

#641: Submitted by Robert J. Strand [PEMay96]

#642: Adapted from speech by Sylvia Harvey, submitted by Herb Shaffer [PEJun95]

#643: Carolyn Wells, submitted by Dicky Love [PEMay95]

#644: Submitted by Steve Morrison [PEMar94]

#645: Submitted by Robert J. Strand [SFMay96]

#646: Submitted by Don E. McKenzie [PEJul92]

#647: Quoted by John W. Gardner, On Leadership, p. 196, submitted by Dicky Love [SFJun93]

#648: No source available [PEApr95]

#649: Quoted from a printed sermon by Dr. Charles Bugg, submitted by George W. McNeese [PEDec91]

#650: W. A. Criswell [PEFeb94]

#651: From Rotarian Magazine, April 1994, submitted by John Looney [PENov95]

#652: Submitted by Milton Weisshaar [PEJan96]

#653: Submitted by Fred Lowery [SFMay94]

#654: Submitted by Billy D. Strayhorn [SFMay94]

#655: No source available [PEOct96]

#656: Submitted by Calvin Habig [SFMay96]

#657: Submitted by Robert J. Strand [SFMay96]

#658: Adapted from a quip by Frank A. Clark [PENov91]

#659: Mell Lazarus, submitted by Jim Pearring [SFJun94]

#660: Submitted by Bruce Rowlison [PEJun93]

#661: No source available [SFJun93]

#662: Michael Hodgin [PEAug93]

#663: William Penn [PEAug93]

#664: Submitted by Michael Jackson [PEMay94]

#665: Howard Hendricks, submitted by David Deselm [PEMay94]

#666: Submitted by Don Maddox [PEMar95]

#667: No source available [PEJan94]

#668: Submitted by Keith H. Knauf [PEMay95]

#669: No source available
[SFMay92]

#670: Edward Jeffrey, as quoted in
the June 21, 1964, issue of
New York Times [PEAug95]

#671: No source available
[SFMar93]

#672: No source available
[PEOct95]

#673: No source available
[PEApr93]

#674: Submitted by Steve
Morrison [SFJun94]

#675: Alfie Kohn, *Boston Globe,*
submitted by Dr. William T.
McConnell [SFOct95]

#676: Anonymous, submitted by
Robert Strand [PEJan93]

#677: Adapted from a submission
by Calvin Habig [PEMar96]

#678: Submitted by Robert J.
Strand [SFJul96]

#679: Milton V. Burge, *Arizona
Highways,* June 1992, p. 52,
submitted by R. Wayne
Hollaway [PEFeb93]

#680: Submitted by John Looney
[PEFeb94]

#681: Submitted by Bill Flanders
[PEFeb92]

#682: Lori Kitchens, submitted by
C. Richard Stone [SFJun93]

#683: No source available
[SFAug93]

#684: Haddon Robinson,
submitted by Steve Hodgin
[SFNov92]

#685: Submitted by Milton
Weisshaar [PEJul92]

#686: Otto Whittaker, submitted
by Dicky Love [SFJan96]

#687: Submitted by David
Tysinger [PEFeb93]

#688: Submitted by Jan Hartlove
[PENov96]

#689: Dustin Hoffman in a
televised interview with Bob
Costas on March 9, 1995
[PEFeb96]

#690: Submitted by Malcolm
MacPhail [PEJan93]

#691: No source available
[SFNov92]

#692: No source available
[SFMay93]

#693: Submitted by Norma Franke
[SFJun95]

#694: No source available
[SFFeb94]

#695: Submitted by Robert J.
Strand [PEOct96]

#696: Groucho Marx, submitted
by William L. McDonald
[SFJun94]

#697: Nikita Khrushchev,
submitted by Chris Newport
[PENov95]

#698: Submitted by Bruce
Rowlison [PEMay93]

#699: H. L. Mencken, submitted
by Chris Newport
[PENov95]

#700: Harold Macmillan,
submitted by Chris Newport
[PENov95]

#701: Oscar Ameringer, submitted
by Chris Newport
[PENov95]

#702: Lily Tomlin, submitted by
Chris Newport [PENov95]

#703: Harry S. Truman [PENov93]

#704: Fletcher Knebel, *Register &
Tribune Syndicate,*
submitted by Robert Strand
[PEDec92]

#705: Anonymous, submitted by
Gene Sikkink [PENov96]

#706: Robert Louis Stevenson,
submitted by C. Richard
Stone [PEAug96]

#707: No source available
[SFAug93]

#708: No source available
[SFJan94]

#709: Submitted by Bill Johnston
[SFJun95]

#710: Submitted by Steve
Morrison [SFJun95]

#711: Submitted by George
Maronge Jr. [SFAug95]

#712: Submitted by Bruce
Rowlison [PESep93]

#713: No source available [SFFeb94]

#714: No source available [PEJul92]

#715: Madge M. Mullin [SFAug93]

#716: Will Rogers [SFAug93]

#717: Mark Twain, to the Society of American Authors on November 15, 1900 [SFNov95]

#718: A true story by Kent Russell, submitted by Kim Wilson [PENov94]

#719: Source unknown, submitted by Wayne Rouse [PEApr93]

#720: Submitted by Daniel R. Koehler [PEJun94]

#721: Submitted by Valeria Little [PEApr93]

#722: Submitted by Mark D. Stucky [SFJun93]

#723: Submitted by Dave Baldridge [SFJun93]

#724: Submitted by Billy D. Strayhorn [PENov92]

#725: Submitted by Wayne Rouse [PEJul93]

#726: Submitted by John H. Hampsch [PEJun92]

#727: SFJun93

#728: Submitted by Jay Martin [SFJun93]

#729: Hank Ketchum, "Dennis the Menace," July 18, 1991, submitted by Billy D. Strayhorn [PEJun93]

#730: Submitted by Stephen Deutsch [SFNov94]

#731: Submitted by Micheal Kelley [PEJul96]

#732: Submitted by John Looney [PEJun92]

#733: Submitted by Micheal Kelley [SFSep95]

#734: Submitted by Fred Lowery [PEDec93]

#735: Submitted by Jan Hartlove [PEMay95]

#736: Chinese Proverb [PEFeb96]

#737: No source available [PESep94]

#738: Harry Truman, submitted by Dicky Love [SFMay92]

#739: Adlai Stevenson, submitted by Chris Newport [PENov95]

#740: Kent Hughes [SFAug94]

#741: Submitted by Wayne Rouse [PEApr93]

#742: Submitted by Bill Flanders [SFAug93]

#743: Submitted by John H. Hampsch [PEJun92]

#744: Submitted by David Lusk [SFMay92]

#745: Submitted by Robert Strand [PEAug92]

#746: Submitted by Don E. McKenzie [PEFeb92]

#747: Submitted by Bill Flanders [PEFeb92]

#748: Submitted by Bill Flanders [PEFeb92]

#749: Steve Brown, submitted by Wayne Rouse [PEJul93]

#750: Otto von Bismarck, submitted by Dicky Love [PEDec95]

#751: Submitted by Charles F. Krieg [PEJul96]

#752: Louis B. Lundborg, submitted by J. D. Brown [PEAug95]

#753: Ernest Campbell, submitted by Dicky Love [PEJul93]

#754: Submitted by Steve Morrison [PEFeb95]

#755: Charles Haddon Spurgeon, submitted by Dicky Love [PEJun96]

#756: No source available [PEMar95]

#757: From *The Wit and Wisdom of Mae West*, edited by Joseph Weintraub, Putnam [SFJan96]

#758: Submitted by Lester M. Weeks [PEMay94]

#759: Submitted by C. Richard Stone [PENov91]

#760: Submitted by Carolyn M. Kendrick [SFFeb92]

#761: From a speech by Earnie Deavenport, chairman and CEO of Eastman Chemical, submitted by Dr. William L. McDonald [SFMar94]

#762: No source available [PEMay96]

#763: No source available [PEJul93]

#764: Chinese Proverb [PEDec93]

#765: H. L. Menken [PEMar96]

#766: Submitted by Bill Flanders [PEFeb92]

#767: Paul Powell, submitted by Jim Pearring [PEJun94]

#768: Submitted by Eugene Barron [SFAug93]

#769: No source available [SFSep95]

#770: Submitted by Micheal Kelley [SFMay96]

#771: No source available [SFSep94]

#772: Submitted by Robert Jarboe [PEJun93]

#773: Submitted by Billy D. Strayhorn [SFJul96]

#774: Submitted by Dale Wolf [SFJan93]

#775: Submitted by William L. McDonald [PEOct95]

#776: Abigail Van Buren, submitted by Steve Morrison [SFMay95]

#777: From *Fence Posts,* submitted by Dan Stephens [SFMar95]

#778: No source available [PEJan94]

#779: Submitted by Micheal Kelley [SFApr96]

#780: Submitted by Mark Heiss [SFApr96]

#781: Submitted by James C. Wideman [PENov91]

#782: No source available [SFAug93]

#783: Submitted by Jay Martin [SFJan93]

#784: No source available [PEFeb96]

#785: Submitted by Dennis Kamper [PEJul92]

#786: No source available [SFJul94]

#787: Submitted by J. D. Brown [PEJan96]

#788: Submitted by Billy D. Strayhorn [PEAug92]

#789: No source available [SFMay95]

#790: No source available [PENov95]

#791: Submitted by Kenneth Langley [SFJun96]

#792: Submitted by Jay Martin [SFJan93]

#793: No source available [SFDec93]

#794: No source available [PEJan92]

#795: Submitted by Bruce Rowlison [PEFeb93]

#796: Submitted by Tom Sikes [SFDec92]

#797: No source available [SFJul93]

#798: No source available [SFDec93]

#799: No source available [PESep93]

#800: Submitted by John Seville [SFAug92]

#801: Submitted by J. Danny Doss [SFJul96]

#802: Submitted by Robert J. Strand [PEMar96]

#803: Submitted by Milton Weisshaar [SFJun96]

#804: A true story submitted by Michelle Hodgin [PENov94]

#805: Submitted by Dennis Fountain [PENov93]

#806: Submitted by Robert Strand [PEFeb93]

#807: Submitted by Mary Spitzer [PEJun95]

#808: Submitted by Jay Martin [PEJul95]

#809: Woody Allen [PEJan94]

#810: From *Prime Time,* submitted by Carl Ericson [PEJan94]

#811: Eleanor Roosevelt [PEOct92]

#812: Steve Schoepf, submitted by Wayne Rouse [SFFeb93]

#813: No source available [SFMay93]

#814: Bill Leary, *Los Angeles Times Syndicate* [SFAug93]

#815: H. L. Mencken, quoted by Bill Husted in "Glitterati," the *Rocky Mountain News,* December 6, 1992, p. 3-M [SFFeb93]

#816: Submitted by John H. Hampsch [PEJun92]

#817: Martin Luther, submitted by Steve Morrison [PEJun94]

#818: No source available [PEApr92]

#819: Submitted by Vance Havner [SFJun92]

#820: Submitted by Micheal Kelley [PEJul96]

#821: No source available [PEJan93]

#822: Submitted by C. Richard Stone [PEJul92]

#823: Submitted by Dave Fernlund [PEJun95]

#824: Submitted by J. D. Brown [PEJul95]

#825: Submitted by Dennis Kamper [SFSep92]

#826: Submitted by Robert J. Strand [PEOct96]

#827: Submitted by Robert J. Strand [PEOct96]

#828: Submitted by Gene Sikkink [PENov92]

#829: Submitted by Steve Morrison [SFMar94]

#830: Submitted by Robert J. Strand [PEMay93]

#831: Pearl Scully in *The Saturday Evening Post,* submitted by C. Richard Stone [SFMay95]

#832: Submitted by Diane M. Sickler [PEJan96]

#833: No source available [PEAug96]

#834: Submitted by Earl Wheatley [PESep92]

#835: From *Sunshine Magazine,* December 1989, p. 28 [SFDec93]

#836: No source available [SFSep92]

#837: Michael Hodgin [PEDec92]

#838: No source available [SFJan96]

#839: No source available [PEApr92]

#840: No source available [PENov96]

#841: No source available [PEOct96]

#842: No source available [PEJun96]

#843: Submitted by Jay Martin [SFSep93]

#844: No source available [SFMar96]

#845: No source available [SFFeb94]

#846: No source available [SFApr94]

#847: Submitted by Norma Franke [SFApr92]

#848: Submitted by Bill Flanders [PEMay92]

#849: No source available [SFAug95]

#850: Gene Brown, *News-Times,* Danberry, Conn., submitted by C. Richard Stone [PEAug92]

#851: Submitted by Sue Kennedy [PEDec91]

#852: No source available [SFOct93]

#853: Helen Castle, *National Enquirer* [PEApr95]

#854: From *INK, Inc.,* submitted by George W. McNeese [SFSep94]

#855: Jim Reed, "The Way I Heer'd It," The Ozarks Mountaineer, May and June 1985, submitted by Steve Hodgin [PEAug95]

#856: No source available [PEAug94]

397

#857: No source available
[PESep94]

#858: No source available
[PEJun94]

#859: Submitted by Billy D.
Strayhorn [SFJul96]

#860: Submitted by John Looney
[SFJan96]

#861: Submitted by John H.
Hampsch [PEJun92]

#862: No source available
[SFAug93]

#863: Submitted by C. Richard
Stone [SFJan96]

#864: Submitted by Dicky Love
[PEOct95]

#865: Submitted by Bill Flanders
[PEFeb92]

#866: No source available
[SFJul94]

#867: Submitted by Micheal
Kelley [PEDec95]

#868: Submitted by Steve
Morrison [PESep93]

#869: Submitted by Diane Sickler
[SFJul96]

#870: Submitted by Malcolm
MacPhail [PEJan93]

#871: No source available
[PEOct96]

#872: Submitted by Alan C.
Thompson [PEAug93]

#873: Submitted by Robert Strand
[PEJan95]

#874: Submitted by Kenneth
Dodge [PENov94]

#875: Denis Waitley, *Seeds of
Greatness,* submitted by
Rich Bersett [PEDec95]

#876: Submitted by Norma Franke
[SFAug95]

#877: Submitted by Calvin Habig
[PEJul95]

#878: A true story submitted by
Michael Hodgin [PENov94]

#879: No source available
[PENov96]

#880: Michael Hodgin [PEDec94]

#881: Jean Kerr, submitted by
Dicky Love [PEMay95]

#882: Anonymous, submitted by
Dicky Love [PENov95]

#883: Submitted by Bruce
Rowlison [SFAug92]

#884: Submitted by C. Richard
Stone [PEJun92]

#885: No source available
[PESep93]

#886: Bertrand Russell, submitted
by C. Richard Stone
[PEMay96]

#887: No source available
[PEJan94]

#888: Ray Kroc, submitted by
John Looney [PEFeb94]

#889: Louis Pasteur, submitted by
Lester M. Weeks [PEAug92]

#890: Submitted by George W.
McNeese [PEApr95]

#891: George Burns, submitted by
Dicky Love [PEOct93]

#892: Submitted by Bill Flanders
[PEMar93]

#893: Submitted by Dicky Love
[SFJul96]

#894: Anonymous, submitted by
James R. Oliver [PEJan93]

#895: Submitted by Jay Martin
[SFJan93]

#896: Submitted by Bill Flanders
[PEFeb92]

#897: Mortimer Caplin, I.R.S.
Commissioner [SFJul95]

#898: No source available
[PENov96]

#899: George Bernard Shaw,
submitted by Chris Newport
[PENov95]

#900: Submitted by Bruce
Rowlison [PE May93]

#901: Submitted by Nick Boeke
[SFJan94]

#902: F. J. Raymond, submitted by
Nick Boeke [SFJan94]

#903: Submitted by Nick Boeke
[SFAug92]

#904: Henrietta Mears, submitted
by Dicky Love [SFAug92]

#905: Submitted by John H.
Hampsch [PEJun92]

#906: Submitted by Dicky Love [PEApr95]
#907: Michael Hodgin [SFMar96]
#908: Submitted by Jay Martin [SFMay92]
#909: Albert Einstein [PEAug96]
#910: Submitted by Jay Martin [PEApr93]
#911: Charlotte Barkett, submitted by Dicky Love [SFMay95]
#912: Submitted by Bruce Rowlison [PEMar93]
#913: No source available [PESep94]
#914: No source available [PEJun93]
#915: Submitted by Bruce Rowlison [PEMay93]
#916: Submitted by Nick Boeke [PEOct92]
#917: Submitted by Nick Boeke [SFJun93]
#918: No source available, submitted by Gene Sikkink [PEJun93]
#919: David Brinkley, submitted by C. Richard Stone [PEMar96]
#920: Submitted by Diane M. Sickler [SFMay96]
#921: Adapted from the *Wall Street Journal* [PEJun95]
#922: No source available [PEMar93]
#923: Submitted by Henry E. Roberts [PEAug96]
#924: Submitted by Mary Spitzer [PEJan95]
#925: Billy D. Strayhorn [PESep94]
#926: John Sierzant, *Catholic Digest*, October 1987 [PEJul93]
#927: No source available, submitted by C. Richard Stone [PENov91]
#928: Submitted by John H. Hampsch [PEJun92]
#929: Mark Twain [SFAug93]
#930: Paul Noxon [PEApr92]
#931: Submitted by Doris S. Bray [SFMay96]

#932: Clarence E. Macartney, submitted by Wayne Rouse [PENov93]
#933: Submitted by Dr. James Wideman [SFNov94]
#934: Submitted by Billy D. Strayhorn [SFMar94]
#935: No source available [SFAug94]
#936: No source available [SFJan96]
#937: Submitted by Stephen Deutsch [SFJan96]
#938: Submitted by Dennis Kamper [PEJul92]
#939: No source available [SFAug93]
#940: Submitted by Jim Pearring [PEJan94]
#941: As told by Marvin Rickard, submitted by Daniel R. Koehler [SFMar96]
#942: No source available [PEJul93]
#943: Submitted by Charles Krieg [SFDEC96]
#944: Submitted by Allan L. Sturtevant [PEJan93]
#945: No source available [PESep94]
#946: No source available [PEDec91]
#947: Submitted by Nick Boeke [SFJun93]
#948: Submitted by Fred Lowery [PEAug95]
#949: Oliver Wendell Holmes,Sr., submitted by Dicky Love [PEFeb96]
#950: Submitted by C. Richard Stone [SFMar96]
#951: Submitted by Nick Boeke [SFAug92]
#952: Submitted by Rick Sams [PEDec93]
#953: Submitted by Billy D. Strayhorn [PESep96]
#954: Anonymous, submitted by James R. Oliver [PEJul93]
#955: No source available [SFJan94]

#956: Submitted by Mary Spitzer [PEMay93]

#957: Submitted by Robert J. Strand [PEMay96]

#958: Bill Frye [SFJan94]

#959: No source available [PEFeb96]

#960: Submitted by Dave Baldrige [PEFeb92]

#961: Submitted by Nick Boeke [PEFeb92]

#962: Source unknown, submitted by Lucy Anderson [PEFeb96]

#963: Submitted by David Goerzen [SFJul93]

#964: Submitted by Jay Martin [PEMay92]

#965: Submitted by Dave Baldrige [PEFeb92]

#966: Submitted by Earl Wheatley [PESep92]

#967: From a statement seen on a sweatshirt, submitted by Don Maddox [PEApr93]

#968: Submitted by Robert Strand [PEJan93]

#969: No source available [SFJan94]

#970: Submitted by Calvin Habig [SFJun95]

#971: Mary E. Pieper, submitted by C. Richard Stone [SFMay95]

#972: No source available [SFMay96]

#973: Michael Hodgin [SFApr92]

#974: Submitted by J. Danny Doss [SFMay96]

#975: No source available [SFAug93]

#976: From *Christian Communications Laboratory*, copyright 1982, p. 39 [SFAug93]

#977: George Ade, humorist, submitted by Robert J. Strand [PEMay93]

#978: Submitted by John Seville [SFSep94]

#979: Submitted by Lester M. Weeks [PEMay94]

#980: No source available [SFAug93]

#981: No source available [SFAug94]

#982: Joseph Joubert, French essayist, submitted by Richard Cox [SFAug94]

#983: No source available [PEApr94]

#984: No source available [SFJul93]

#985: Submitted by Gene Sikkink [PEJun93]

#986: Submitted by Mary Spitzer [SFJul93]

#987: No source available [PEJul94]

#988: Submitted by Bruce Rowlison [PEMay93]

#989: No source available, submitted by Gene Sikkink [PENov91]

#990: Submitted by Steve Hodgin [PESep93]

#991: Submitted by Steve Morrison [SFJan96]

#992: Anonymous, submitted by Rich Bersett [SFJan96]

#993: Submitted by Nick Boeke [PEFeb92]

#994: Submitted by Robert J. Strand [PEMay96]

#995: Submitted by Jay Martin [PEApr92]

#996: Peter Hay, submitted by Robert J. Strand [SFMar96]

#997: Submitted by Calvin Habig [PEDec94]

#998: Submitted by Steve Hodgin [PESep93]

#999: Submitted by Carl Ericson [PEJan92]

#1000: Submitted by J. Stuart Wells [PEJul92]

#1001: No source available [SFNov92]